Antifeminism *in the* Academy

Antifeminism in the Academy

Edited by

VèVè Clark
Shirley Nelson Garner
Margaret Higonnet
and Ketu H. Katrak

Routledge
New York / London

Published in 1996 by
Routledge
29 West 35th Street
New York, NY 10001

Published in Great Britain by
Routledge
11 New Fetter Lane
London EC4P 4EE

Copyright © 1996 by Routledge

The copyrights for individual essays are held by the corresponding contributors.

Printed in the United States of America on acid-free paper.

Library of Congress Cataloging-in-Publication Data
Antifeminism in the academy / VèVè Clark ... [et al.], editors.
    p. cm.
    Includes bibliographical references (p.) and index.
    ISBN 0-415-91070-6 (hc). — ISBN 0-415-91071-4 (pbk.)
    1. Feminism and education—United States. 2. Sex discrimination in higher education—United States. 3. Sexism in education—United States. I. Clark, VèVè A.
    LC197.A58 1995
    370.19'345—dc20   95-32371

Contents

For all of the women who shared their stories with us

Introduction

Feminists perceive inequalities between men and women in their treatment, prospects, education, opportunities for employment, roles in the family.... Feminists write and speak about these inequalities, seek to explain them, and work to remove them. Anyone, then, who opposes any of these activities—speaking or writing about women's situation, exposing inequalities, seeking to change and improve the lives of women—is by definition anti-feminist.
>   ——Cynthia D. Kinnard, *Antifeminism in American Thought*

In regards to pedagogical practices we must intervene to alter the existing pedagogical structure and to teach students *how to listen, how to hear one another.*
>   ——bell hooks, *Teaching to Transgress*

Feminist educators in the 1990s throughout the industrialized world face similar problems and issues. Despite national differences, they share a concern about the future of education for women in societies marked by the resurgence of right-wing ideology and the conservative control of the state.
>   ——Kathleen Weiler, in Arnot and Weiler, eds.,
>   *Feminism and Social Justice in Education*

Intellectual harassment is the most recent version of antifeminist behavior erupting methodically in the academy and in U.S. society generally. Unlike well-defined and widely reported misconduct aimed at a lone woman—misogyny and sexual harassment—this particular phenomenon of assault is broader and collective, representing new extensions of the backlash intended to ridicule feminist activisms and overturn achievements made since the 1970s. There are, of course, analogues that exist in international settings, as several recent studies demonstrate.[1] For every step forward to include women in the sites of opportunity and leadership in the United States, citizens beholden to the *"stasis" quo*—from Congress to college campuses—seek to halt the progress that feminist scholarship has imprinted on our intellectual legacy. This contemporary antifeminism takes particular forms and is rooted in previous waves of negativity towards feminism in U.S. history. Resistances to assaults on feminism—as in this volume—are part of the struggles of the Women's Movement today.

Throughout U.S. history, resisting women and men have fought back against, talked back to, and overturned the privileges unduly accorded to Fathers founding themselves as the story of us all. In the introduction to her comprehensive, annotated bibliography, Cynthia Kinnard reminds us that antifeminism has been with us since 1798 (xi–xvii). As she points out, "Antifeminism implies, indeed requires, feminism. It does not exist in a vacuum, as does misogyny" (xi). Acknowledging the obvious anachronism of applying the terms feminism and antifeminism to social conflicts occurring before 1900, Kinnard recognizes, nonetheless, a pattern of behavior useful for contemporary readers to discern: when demands for women's rights enter into published discourse, antifeminists take notice and respond with scorn.[2] As we demonstrate here, in *Antifeminism in the Academy*, antagonisms toward feminist intellectual advance exist across gender lines. In the "changing same" of U.S. conservatism from the eighteenth century until today, increasing numbers of women and born-again feminists have joined the ranks of legislators who intend to discontinue affirmative action, eliminate programs that promote women's health, and repress free speech by attacking intellectual debate that smacks of "political correctness." Since much of the staying power of previous feminist dissent resides now in universities, colleges, women's centers, and caucuses throughout this nation and the world, it is not at all surprising to find the intellectual harassment that is emerging in the academy directed at tenured and untenured feminists across the generations. *Antifeminism in the Academy* is our call, in poet Audre Lorde's words, to break "the tyrannies of silence" (3); it stands as our collective analysis, inviting ongoing response.

This volume of essays identifies various forms of antifeminist harassment: the use of vilification and distortion or even violence to repress certain areas of research and forms of inquiry. Our intention was to name the problem, gather documentation, and examine antifeminist intellectual harassment in three related areas: the history of feminist activisms; campus politics; academic sites of power. These three venues frame the story contained in this collection. Most of the scholars represented here were associated between

1988 and 1994 with the Committee on the Status of Women in the Profession (CSWP) of the Modern Language Association.

History of the Project

In October 1988, on a crisp fall day, the Modern Language Association's Commission (called Committee since 1991) on the Status of Women in the Profession met in New York City at MLA Headquarters on Astor Place. As part of our charge, we began discussing issues facing academic women, issues raised both by our own experiences and by those of our female colleagues working in different geographic and institutional locations all over the United States and Canada. In that rather daunting, airless room, dominated by a huge, wooden conference table, we started sharing ideas for future collaborative projects. This volume grew out of those discussions and emerged from a story shared with us by one of the commissioners at that meeting: a feminist scholar faced an intellectual battery for her presentation of ideas in public. What seemed to be an individual, isolated incident had striking resonances with other stories we heard; overlays of *ad feminam* racism and violence were evident. In the extremely supportive atmosphere created by cochairs Moira Ferguson and Diana Velez, the incident was taken seriously, and we started a wide-ranging exploration of what, after many years of work, we now call antifeminist harassment—a new form of mistreatment that is related to, though different from, sexual harassment. When we launched this project, we were also motivated by broad concern in the MLA membership about the proposed Helms and Fowler Amendments restricting freedom of speech in the National Endowments of the Humanities and Arts.

From the outset, the 1988–1989 commissioners—Mary Carpenter, Moira Ferguson, Ketu Katrak, Mary Lydon, Biddy Martin, Valerie Miner, Celeste Schenck, Valerie Smith, Diana Velez—maintained a spirit of feminist collaboration. Some of us continued to remain actively involved with the project even after completing the three-year terms for which we had been nominated to the CSWP. Each year, from 1988, new members also joined the project in various roles as writers (Sara Lennox, Elaine Ginsberg), editors (VèVè Clark, Shirley Nelson Garner, Margaret Higonnet), and advisors. We would like to thank all CSWP members for their intellectual support during the years over which this project has unfolded. For solidarity with our efforts, we are particularly indebted to Electa Arenal, Françoise Lionnet, Mary Lydon, Elizabeth Ordóñez, Celeste Schenck, and Valerie Smith.

Since the birth of the project in October 1988, the process of consolidating this volume has been instructive. Initially, we published a short piece describing our new project in the Spring 1989 *MLA Newsletter*. We gathered further testimony about intellectual harassment by sending out a letter to members of the MLA's Women's Division and the Women's Caucus. We wish to thank all those who found courage and time to narrate their individual stories of harassment. In December 1989, at the MLA Convention in Washington, D.C., the CSWP sponsored an "Open Hearing," cochaired by Moira Ferguson and Ketu Katrak, to present the working parameters of what we then called "intellectual harassment" and to obtain responses from women in the academic language profession, one of the largest professional associations in the United States. We were overwhelmed to find a packed room at this 8:30 A.M. session, and to hear women eager to speak into the microphone. They told their stories, differently and yet with uncannily similar evocations of incidents in which, for example, people act anonymously against women and feminist scholars or deface their offices or belongings. Ferguson and Katrak presented the working parameters of intellectual harassment as

> the demeaning or devaluing of feminist work and of feminists in terms of their academic progress and their professional lives. It also includes threatening or intimidating behavior in intellectual situations such as classrooms, public presentations, job interviews, conferences. Such behavior is expressed in ridicule, heckling, political baiting, homophobia, racist, ethnic slurs and physical threats.

As we heard women talking from their personal locations in terms of race, class, sexuality, nationality, however differently situated within their academic institutions, we were convinced of the multilayered dimensions of an antifeminism that takes both overt and covert forms. CSWP continued its work on this project in December 1990, when Mary Carpenter organized a session on "sexagism," her word for the intersection of "sexism" and "ageism"; a year later, in 1991, we prepared a public forum and related workshops on censorship and antifeminist harassment. As our work progressed, it required us to bring together the many contributors who had collaborated over these years, so we held a coordinating meeting in Cambridge, Massachusetts in June 1992.

In the interim, before publication of this book, the kinds of painful disclosures that we documented were dismissed repeatedly as mere "whining" on the part of women. Activists from a variety of persuasions and backgrounds, working to foster change and combat discrimination, have been accused of imposing "political correctness." In the fighting words of journalist Richard Bernstein, feminists engage in "a generalized killjoy ideology of faultfinding and professed victimization" (Bernstein, 214). The process and product of this volume, then, was conceived dually, through mutual feminist support, and "in defense of ourselves."[3]

Antifeminist Intellectual Harassment

We open the volume with Annette Kolodny's provocative essay, "Paying the Price of Antifeminist Intellectual Harassment," in which she outlines the parameters of what might appear to be random occurrences of antifeminist behavior by examining three career episodes. These testimonies, drawn from several public and private sources, "reveal a chilling commonality," as the reader will no doubt detect. During a CSWP-sponsored panel chaired by Sarah Webster Goodwin and in which Dale Bauer also participated, Kolodny provided a working description of the phenomenon at the MLA 1991 Convention in San Francisco:

> Antifeminist intellectual harassment, a serious threat to academic freedom, occurs when (1) any policy, action, statement, and/or behavior has the effect of discouraging or preventing women's freedom of lawful action, freedom of thought, and freedom of expression; (2) *or* when any policy, action, statement, and/or behavior creates an environment in which the appropriate application of feminist theories or methodologies to research, scholarship, and teaching is devalued, discouraged, or altogether thwarted; (3) *or* when any policy, action, statement, and/or behavior creates an environment in which research, scholarship, and teaching pertaining to women, gender, or gender inequities are devalued, discouraged, or altogether thwarted. (9)

Anyone wishing to evaluate the presence or absence of antifeminist intellectual harassment within the academy might organize, as Kolodny suggests, a series of campus-wide conferences under the general rubric of academic freedom. Focusing solely on present threats is not enough, given the broad generational differences existing at any university, college, or school, and the varying degrees of knowledge about women's studies and feminism across the disciplines. Participants must examine as well the historical terrain of activisms and counterresponses out of which 1970s feminism emerged in the United States.

Following such a proposal for further investigation, Part One of *Antifeminism in the Academy* reads backwards into the 1950s activist movements and forwards well into the multicultural 1990s. In their essay, "Feminism and Antifeminism: From Civil Rights to Culture Wars," Moira Ferguson, Ketu H. Katrak, and Valerie Miner (three former members of the CSWP) reconstruct the roads we have traversed from feminist activism in the 1960s to backlash and forgetfulness throughout the seventies and eighties, moving ever closer to outright hostility in 1994 and 1995. Ferguson, Katrak, and Miner have recovered histories of resistance in which many of us participated at the time. From the balkanized positions of identity or single-issue politics, we were thrust into struggle against the power of patriarchy to control citizens because of their ethnicity, gender, or sexual orientation. Clearly, these contributors are writing for the present and the next generations who were not there in the streets when demonstrators were attacked by vicious dogs and their handlers, who know little firsthand of the mighty power fire hoses and tear gas have to incapacitate a body, to stifle legally sanctioned dissent. Ferguson, Katrak, and Miner take the reader through the persistent trials-by-fire into the seemingly less threatening areas of academic discourse. They show us that, despite the gains promoted by a host of activists in the 1960s and 1970s, a formidable backlash has assumed center stage in 1990s media representations—targeting the academy in particular—promoted by right-wing ideologues and their sympathizers, from Allan Bloom and Dinesh D'Souza to the histrionic antifeminist Camille Paglia. In response to such writers, the strong voice of dissent in Susan Faludi's *Backlash: The Undeclared War Against American Women* (1991) appears prominently in this essay and resurfaces as well throughout the volume. As we hear the clamor of the culture wars, the next section takes us into another volatile discursive landscape—academic freedom, free speech, student resistance to feminism, anti-lesbian bias, and age discrimination—that might well be described as uncivil wars on college campuses.

Multiple Jeopardy on College Campuses

Whose free speech is it anyway? For how long must we tolerate distorted interpretations of an eighteenth-century principle of free speech that has little bearing on the perverted actions of our contemporaries? Hate groups proliferate, hate talk shows garner favorable ratings, hate speech has become acceptable on the airwaves and the Internet. Overall, the tendency to sanction violent confrontations "in your face" works to destroy our abilities to listen to and hear one another—a basic tenet of democratic dialogue which writer bell hooks recalls to mind in several of her publications, especially in *Teaching to Transgress* (1994).[4] Failing to engage, refusing to learn beyond the proverbial picket fences, leads inevitably to collective paranoia as the millenium wanes. There is something extraordinary about the fears of change that we are now facing. Why do we need citizen militias across this country to defend us, when it is clear that the only people who will be protected by them look and act as they do? Largely white and male, leftovers from world and regional wars waged outside this country, these "wanna-bes" are basically "wanna-wins" who have been dismissed from the front or elite military lines. As a group of disaffected white-supremacists, they have persistently failed to analyze the shifts in economic privilege promoted by the Reagan and Bush administrations that left too many of their socioeconomic class unemployed, while their bosses made off like bandits. Depending upon their status and literacy, some do recognize the political causes of their economic predicament. However, the prevailing message that we hear from *angry white males*—an insidious and newly invented moniker—would "beam" women and ethnic groups back to the age of Eisenhower in the 1950s. In this Disneyland or "Father Knows Best" fantasy, white males were supposedly kings of their domains, wives and the occasional maid their servants. Large numbers of those same women had left the kitchen to support the Second World War effort; afterwards, once the men had returned, women were expected to stay home on the range. As the essays in Part One demonstrate, the 1950s were an age of inequity, hardly the age of innocence that a multicultural populace needs now to revisit.

In the 1990s, those supporting and promoting antifeminist harassment invoke in their favor several constitutional guarantees, including the rights to bear arms and to engage in free speech. As law professor Patricia Williams implies in "Talking about Race, Talking about Gender, Talking about How We Talk," free speech is a misnomer for a right that was not accorded equally to Native Americans, African Americans, or women when the Constitution was originally signed. Reflecting on the provinces of free speech, Williams writes:

> There is no place where this particular battle has been more visible than in universities; there is no fiercer entrenchment than the lines drawn around the perceived property of culture. It is a battle marred by the persistence of prejudice: as women are still trying to overcome presumptions that they really *like* getting fondled in the back office, blacks are trying to overcome presumptions that they really *deserve* to be on the bottom of the heap. It is a battle marred by ignorance and denial. (72)

In an effort to reconstruct the arts/responsibility of engaging in civilized conversation, Williams moves our discussions from the wider society to classrooms and campuses, where one would expect informed dialogue to remain a prerequisite.

In the following three essays, by Dale Bauer with Katherine Rhoades, Greta Gaard, and Mary Wilson Carpenter, we find testimony about the multiple jeopardies suffered by feminists because of student resistance, anti-lesbian biases, and a combination of sexism and age discrimination which Carpenter calls *sexagism*. Drawing on a variety of documents, including student end-of-term evaluations, statistics, and personal narratives, Bauer, Gaard, and Carpenter demonstrate that all is not well in the feminist classroom, despite tremendous advances over the past twenty-five years. [5]

When calls to dialogue failed miserably in the 1990s, we witnessed hostile, public confrontations that erupted in Crown Heights, in the Los Angeles insurrections, in Anita Hill's testimony before the Senate, and most tragically in Oklahoma City. Where do we learn a different method, perhaps a more creative means of representing and hearing ideas and ideologies that seem foreign to us? Anna Deavere Smith has shown in print, on stage, in classrooms across the country that through careful collection of oral histories documenting the discordant views of events—in Crown Heights and L.A.—one can begin to hear the other sides. Her one-woman shows, *Fires in the Mirror* and TWILIGHT *Los Angeles, 1992*, although not concerned with harassment *per se*, are fine examples of how feminists continue to transform the academy and its environs.

Changing Systems of Knowledge: Feminist Resistance in the Academy

Women in the academy who came to political consciousness during the past three decades of second-wave feminism are increasingly assuming administrative and leadership positions in universities and on editorial boards. Even in these high-status arenas just above the glass ceilings, they have found that antifeminism persists. In one of the concluding essays, Elaine Ginsberg and Sara Lennox uncover the disturbing details of "Antifeminism in Scholarship and Publishing," where one might not expect such practices to be maintained. Their careful research delves into those institutional areas of scholarship that sociologist G. William Domhoff has called *power structure research*. [6] The piece by Ginsberg and Lennox describes conservative organizations, such as the National Association of Scholars, and their funding agents, such as the Olin Foundation, which support the research of antifeminists.

Shirley Nelson Garner, in "Transforming Antifeminist Culture in the Academy," deftly shows us how to handle harassment issues and insensitivity among our colleagues by invoking the reasoned strategies of a seasoned administrator. Beyond the personal approach to resolving gender conflicts, Garner walks the reader through various campus resources established to "improve the climate for women" at the University of Minnesota and other institutions. Among the most important of these initiatives fought for and won by powerful women faculty members is the Minnesota Plan II (1988). Like so many other affirmative action and faculty development plans across the nation, these efforts will endure as long as concerned faculty resist their erosion.

This final Part examines the world of publishing and the university itself as sites of power. These are systems of knowledge production that we academics have invested all of our lives in—from K through 12, bachelor's to doctoral degrees, and on the tenure trail. To criticize these institutions seems somehow sacrilegious, but examine critically and transform them we must, when the inequities of treatment described in this volume strike us in the face.

In that ongoing process, we would like to acknowledge the work of our colleagues in education who have looked closely at the state of feminist critical pedagogy both in the United States and internationally. These recent studies include *Feminisms and Critical Pedagogy* (1992), *What Schools Can Do* (1992), *Feminism and Social Justice in Education: International Perspectives* (1993), and *The Feminist Classroom* (1994). *Antifeminism in the Academy* stands at the beginning of a series of discussions about antifeminist harassment. Further analyses and remedies need to be devoted to fields and disciplines where women's studies have not yet taken a firm hold, including business schools, religious studies, military history, and congressional studies, to name the more obvious. The price we pay now for ignoring antifeminist harassment will surely inflate if we keep silent.

Acknowledgments

We wish to acknowledge the support of the University of Minnesota Graduate School for a grant-in-aid award that allowed Shannon Olson, Shirley Garner's research assistant, to devote part of her time to this project. The editors wish to thank both Ms. Olson and Laureen Larson, secretary in the English Department at the University of Minnesota, for their invaluable assistance in preparing the manuscript. Finally, we are grateful to William Germano and his staff for their advice and encouragement through every stage of this project.

Notes

1. See the U.S.-located works by Madeleine Arnot and Kathleen Weiler, Carmen Luke and Jennifer Gore, Chandra Talpade Mohanty, *et al.*, and the European-located Mona Ozouf in the Works Cited and Consulted.

2. In the introduction to her annotated bibliography, Kinnard has located documentation of "feminist" activism and "antifeminism" well before the Women's Rights Convention of 1848. She cites Judith Sargent Murray's essay on the equality of the sexes (1790), Mary Wollstonecraft's *Vindication of the Rights of Woman* (1792), and William Godwin's *Memoir of the Author of A Vindication of the Rights of Woman* (1798) as forerunners in the first-wave feminist debates.

3. The phrase "in defense of ourselves" refers to the massive support of Professor Anita Hill following the Senate hearings on the nomination of Clarence Thomas to the Supreme Court. African American women in academia organized a grassroots protest against Ms. Hill's treatment and dismissal in the public arena and the failure of legislators to take sexual harassment and misogyny seriously. Dissent was expressed by activists across gender, color, and class lines in a series of ads which appeared in prominent newspapers. For the broader contexts of this confrontation, see Jane Mayer and Jill Abramson.

4. The reference to hooks is taken from a dialogue with Ron Scapp, a white male comrade and friend of hers, in the chapter "Building a Teaching Community," in hooks, 150.

5. For a comprehensive study of six institutions that have promoted feminist critical pedagogy, see Frances A. Maher and Mary Kay Thompson Tetreault.

6. Domhoff's publications in this area are widely known. See for example, *The Bohemian Grove and Other Retreats, Power Structure Research, Who Rules America Now?*, and *The Power Elite and the State* .

Works Cited and Consulted

Alcoff, Linda and Elizabeth Potter, eds. *Feminist Epistemologies.* New York and London: Routledge, 1993.

Arnot, Madeleine and Kathleen Weiler, eds. *Feminism and Social Justice in Education: International Perspectives.* London and Washington, DC: The Falmer Press, 1993.

Bernstein, Richard. *Dictatorship of Virtue: Multiculturalism and the Battle for America's Future.* New York: Alfred A. Knopf, 1994.

Brimelow, Peter. *Alien Nation: Common Sense About America's Immigration Disaster.* New York: Random House, 1995.

Committee on the Status of Women in the Profession. "Commission on the Status of Women." *MLA Newsletter* 21, 1 (1989): 2 pars.

Domhoff, G. William. *The Bohemian Grove and Other Retreats.* New York: Harper and Row, 1974.

————. *The Power Elite and the State*. New York: A. de Gruyter, 1990.

————. *Power Structure Research*. Beverly Hills, CA: Sage Publications, 1980.

————. *Who Rules America Now? A View for the '80s*. Englewood Cliffs, NJ: Prentice-Hall, 1983.

Faludi, Susan. *Backlash: The Undeclared War Against American Women*. New York: Crown, 1991.

hooks, bell. *Teaching to Transgress: Education as the Practice of Freedom*. New York and London: Routledge, 1994.

Kinnard, Cynthia D., compiler. *Antifeminism in American Thought: An Annotated Bibliography*. Boston: G.K. Hall, 1986.

Lorde, Audre. *The Cancer Journals*. San Francisco: Aunt Lute Press, 1980.

Luke, Carmen and Jennifer Gore, eds. *Feminisms and Critical Pedagogy*. New York and London: Routledge, 1992.

Maher, Frances A. and Mary Kay Thompson Tetreault. *The Feminist Classroom*. New York: Basic Books, 1994.

Mayer, Jane and Jill Abramson. *Strange Justice: The Selling of Clarence Thomas*. Boston and New York: Houghton Mifflin, 1994.

Mohanty, Chandra Talpade, Ann Russo, and Lourdes Torres, eds. *Third World Women and the Politics of Feminism*. Bloomington and Indianapolis: Indiana University Press, 1991.

Ozouf, Mona. *Les mots des femmes: essai sur la singularité française*. Paris: Fayard, 1995.

Reardon, Kathleen Kelley. *They Don't Get It, Do They? Communication in the Workplace—Closing the Gap Between Women and Men*. Boston: Little, Brown and Company, 1995.

Smith, Anna Deavere. *Fires in the Mirror: Crown Heights, Brooklyn and Other Identities*. New York: Anchor, 1993.

————. *TWILIGHT, Los Angeles, 1992*. New York: Anchor, 1994.

Weiler, Kathleen and Candace Mitchell, eds. *What Schools Can Do: Critical Pedagogy and Practice*. Albany: State University of New York Press, 1992.

I

Antifeminist Intellectual Harassment

1

Paying the Price of Antifeminist Intellectual Harassment

Annette Kolodny

Ginger Rogers did everything that Fred Astaire did, but she had to do it backward in high heels.
——Ann Richards, Governor of Texas[1]

Many of us have modulated our voices out of fear. I have. I am ashamed of it.
——Beth Kalikoff, Ph.D. in English[2]

I

On June 11, 1993, Jane Schaberg, a professor of religious studies at the University of Detroit–Mercy, was awakened after midnight by the sound of fire engines hurtling through the neighborhood. She hardly expected them to stop at her house. Seeing the flames through her bedroom window, however, she realized that her 1987 Toyota Tercel, parked out front, was on fire. A rag had been stuffed in the gas tank and then ignited. The police report listed the motive as "revenge."[3] But to Schaberg it was simply what the *Chronicle of Higher Education* characterized as "the latest salvo in a nasty battle raging over her scholarship" (Wilson, A7).

In 1987, the scholar and former nun published *The Illegitimacy of Jesus*, a historical and literary critique that examined internal evidence that the writers of the Gospels were handing on a tradition in which Jesus was not miraculously conceived but, rather, illegitimately conceived, perhaps as the result of the rape of Mary. By crediting divine love as intervening in the fate of Mary and her child, with God relieving Mary's humiliation through His special relationship with her son, Schaberg offered a theology of God's caring

3

for the socially outcast—and thus endangered—mother and child. Understandably, Schaberg's thesis was controversial, and not just in Catholic circles. Schaberg received hate mail and threatening phone calls, and she became a target of public attack by Detroit's Archbishop. Most troubling to Schaberg in all this was her home institution's lack of a forceful stand and its refusal to support unequivocally the value of serious scholarship, whatever its findings. In response to rumors of alumni threatening to cancel their contributions, the school's administration began distancing itself from her and her work, both through public statements and internal silence, according to Schaberg.[4] "I didn't know the university was going to cave in like this," she told the *Chronicle of Higher Education.* And although she still had a job at the Jesuit school, she acknowledged that her "will is a bit broken" (Wilson, A7). In fact, Schaberg has now stepped down as head of religious studies because of what she experienced as Detroit Mercy's continuing lack of support.

While the torching of her automobile is surely an extreme response to a scholar's findings, unfortunately it represents only one event in the escalating campaign of intimidation directed at feminist teachers and researchers in a variety of fields all across the country. Stories are legion about right-wing organizations moving onto campuses in order to finance publications whose sole purpose is to attack (and, they hope, shut down) a women's studies program.[5] In such an atmosphere, faculty look the other way when colleagues openly discourage students from taking courses in women's studies on the grounds that these courses are inevitably anti-male. Many schools harbor senior faculty who refuse to sit on qualifying examinations or to serve on dissertation committees where the candidate employs feminist approaches. Deans and department chairs still quietly reassure recruitment committees that once they have hired one woman, they need seek no further, thus reducing affirmative action to the revolving door of tokenism. At some schools, faculty teaching gay or lesbian subject matter are forced to include a statement on all course descriptions and syllabi warning students about "sexually explicit material," while equivalently explicit (or even violent) content in courses treating only heterosexual authors requires no similar warning.[6] And in a typically incongruous situation, at Scripps College, "a women's college dedicated to the education of women," professor of English and well-published feminist critic, Gayle Greene, has seen her "course in feminist theory [repeatedly] ... refused credit as 'the senior seminar,'" while a supposedly "real theory" course "taught by a white male" *was* given senior seminar status.[7]

Should anyone suppose that the resistance to feminist scholars and their work is grounded in reasonable concerns for academic excellence, the public statements of those who oppose such work prove otherwise. The "self-proclaimed conservative watchdog," Peter Shaw, for example, served on the National Council on the Humanities, the twenty-seven-member advisory board to the National Endowment for the Humanities, during Lynne Cheney's tenure as chair of the endowment.[8] Reflecting on his own predilections in the awarding of NEH grants, Shaw told the *Chronicle of Higher Education* that "what I truly believe is that second-rate traditionalist scholarship is ultimately more valuable to the country than first-rate feminist works" (Burd, A25).

Not surprisingly, this cumulative resistance has surfaced at the very moment that a graying professoriate of mostly white, Christian males looks toward retirement. Between 1995 and 2010, according to Department of Education projections, over 300,000 faculty are expected to retire, leaving vacancies in all fields and disciplines across higher education. At the same time, according to a recent Modern Language Association survey, women have been making "dramatic gains at the Ph.D. level," almost doubling "their share of the doctorates granted in English and increas[ing] their representation among foreign language degree recipients by just over half."[9] As a result, especially in the humanities disciplines, the 1990s is certain to be the last decade in which tenured white males over fifty control what gets published and who gets tenured.

The transition, however, is proving extremely difficult because, as a rule, academics are not comfortable with rapid change. But these changes have taken hold within a single generation, and are massive in both their intellectual *and* their social implications. For, beyond challenging the orthodoxies of their chosen disciplines, the increasing numbers of women faculty also demanded that the academy scrutinize its daily behaviors and customary procedures. Once commonplace in hallway conversations and over faculty club luncheons, exchanges of sexual banter, sexist humor, ethnic jokes, and racial slurs were no longer without consequences. Sexual overtures to students or demands for sexual favors from untenured colleagues could now result in a sexual harassment charge. And whole departments splintered over outdated promotion and tenure procedures that gave them no way to evaluate the junior colleague who had designed a traveling museum exhibition or studied the works of a long-forgotten woman author.

If resistance to the magnitude of change was predictable, the fierceness and tenacity with which some groups and individuals have chosen to express that reflex was not. For almost a decade, Dr. Bernice Resnick Sandler, former Senior Associate at the Center for Women Policy Studies, has reported that, at some colleges, posters announcing any lecture or course with a feminist theme are routinely destroyed or vandalized.[10] In one instance in the spring of 1988, the chair of the Women's Law Association at Harvard put up a poster publicizing a weekly luncheon series in which the topic was "The 'F' Word: To Be or Not To Be a Feminist." Within hours, according to Sandler, the words "a feminist" were crossed out, and the new title was "The 'F' Word: To Be or Not To Be Fucked" (Sandler, 7).

On other campuses, any negative reviews or published critical comments pertaining to the work of feminist faculty are duplicated and mailed out anonymously. At a small New England college recently, a feminist professor in the French department took great pleasure from the fact that her critical theory book had received laudatory reviews in the major professional journals. Thus, it was with some surprise that she and her students arrived on campus one day to discover a poster-sized blowup of the only negative review to have appeared, prominent in the department's hallway display case, safely locked behind glass. The nastiest sentences in the review were highlighted in red. It was three weeks before the key to the display case could be located and the poster removed. In the meantime, she heard from students that some of her colleagues were reciting portions of the negative review to their classes or making fun of her work based on the distorted readings of this particular reviewer. When she shared her anger with feminist faculty in other departments, the French professor discovered that the feminist critics in the English Department (both male and female) had long been the subjects of obscene verses circulated almost monthly by unknown persons. And her colleagues in the School of Nursing told of needing to take extra security precautions for their labs whenever their grants supported research on women's health issues.

Given this kind of anecdotal evidence, it is hardly surprising that national reports from every source regularly document "that the experiences of women on campus are substantially different from those of men" (Sandler, 1). Nor do we wonder that "a study of graduate students at the University of Michigan revealed that women are more likely to consider the university as alienating and less likely to describe it as accepting than are men."[11] National studies notwithstanding, few administrators in higher education have measured the full scope of the problem or examined their own responses as a possible contributory factor. It is difficult to command a provost's undivided attention or to invoke institutional responsibility, after all, in the face of seemingly unrelated and random events, however disturbing. Those who do not want the larger problem accurately named and understood, moreover, actively encourage this perception that each event is isolated, *sui generis*, and without aim or method connected to anything else. But the real problem may be just here, in the institutional habit of uncritically accepting "problems" as *only* discrete events, rather than probing for larger patterns.

The appeal from a feminist assistant professor denied promotion and tenure because her research area was unfamiliar to her department colleagues, for instance, rarely is viewed by the provost as having any connection to the vandalizing of posters announcing a women's studies speakers' series. At best, a dean or provost will acknowledge that there is a "climate problem" on campus. But this may only compound the situation by further masking the fact that women's—and especially feminist—intellectual activities are being repeatedly attacked and hobbled. Accordingly, unaware that others on campus may be enduring different forms of the same malice, the targets of such harassment too often perceive themselves as alone and isolated. Without an adequate support network, they tend to internalize the harassment as a legitimate value judgment on their capabilities. At the best, these individuals reach out to family, friends, and sympathetic colleagues for help and guidance; and though their self-confidence remains deeply shaken, they develop coping mechanisms to see them through. At the worst, the vulnerable untenured assistant professor shies away from the activity that brings with it so much pain and struggle, even putting aside her most cherished research project.

For their part, faculty and students outraged at the attacks on feminist faculty and feminist activities are forced to respond on an ad hoc basis to each specific event. Some organize a letter campaign on behalf of the outstanding feminist scholar who has been denied tenure, while others file a complaint with the campus police to protest the repeated destruction of posters advertising the women's studies speakers' series. Unquestionably necessary and helpful, such ad hoc activities lead only to piecemeal solutions (if at all), and they never identify the larger problem of which these events are a part.

II

At the 1991 meeting of the Modern Language Association, that organization's Commission on the Status of Women sponsored a forum and associated workshops on the topic, "Antifeminist Harassment in the Academy." Within this complex topic, the commission encouraged participants to recognize "antifeminist *intellectual* harassment" as a specific and independent category. While the conveners of these sessions fully recognized that different modes of harassment often overlap and reinforce one another, their stress on the word "intellectual" was intended to distinguish certain kinds of events from more commonly understood forms of harassment, including sexual harassment, emotional battering, and physical threats.

As the speaker asked to address antifeminist *intellectual* harassment, I suggested that whatever form this kind of harassment takes—vandalizing posters or the threat of physical violence—its object is always to foreclose further feminist inquiry and, more generally, to shut down women's access to unfettered intellectual activity in any field or discipline. Publicly humiliating a colleague by anonymously circulating scurrilous verses about her or torching a scholar's parked car, in other words, are means—punishing means, to be sure—but means to the further end of intellectual silencing. And intellectual silencing, I insisted, was anathema to every definition of the academic freedom that our colleges and universities claim to protect.

Thus, at the heart of my remarks was an appeal for the preservation of the principle of academic freedom undiminished by bias, prejudice, or discomfort with difference. What makes this principle so difficult to grasp, however, is the fact that until its practice is historically situated, or until its practice takes meaning within a specific context, academic freedom remains only a vague, rather amorphous, abstraction. Retaining *The Catcher in the Rye* on a freshman English reading list, for example, enacts (and thereby defines) the concept of academic freedom only when a school or teacher enunciates the reasoning behind rejecting some local call to ban the novel. But while most teachers of literature nowadays would be quick to defend J.D. Salinger's work under the flag of academic freedom, the same probably is not the case for Rita Mae Brown's *Rubyfruit Jungle*, with its exuberant and unapologetic lesbian narrator. This is because the teaching, research, and scholarly practices that, to date, have been traditionally protected by the concept of academic freedom—that is, the practices that make the concept recognizable and constitute its meaning—have largely been practices forged without the participation of women (especially feminists), African Americans, Asian Americans, Native Americans, Latinos and Latinas, (open) lesbians and gays, or the disabled. (Indeed, this is true of almost all the practices of the academy.) Having enjoyed no role in defining the concept of academic freedom, these groups are understood to be protected by it only insofar as their products and activities *conform to the accepted products and activities of the past.* As a result, when these groups interrogate inherited paradigms and try to introduce new creative or intellectual directions, the very unfamiliarity of their efforts renders those efforts vulnerable to charges of narrow partisanship or political contrivance. But, in truth, these new areas of interest—feminist inquiry, ethnic studies, queer studies, or the emerging field of disability studies—are no more nor less narrow, political, or partisan than earlier categories of research and analysis. And, to their credit, they have the potential to revitalize moribund corners of the more established (and ossified) disciplines. The challenge ahead, I suggested in 1991, was to reconstitute the meaning of academic freedom yet once more by enrolling our colleagues in scenarios that declared these new areas of research and scholarship *to matter.* For feminist scholars, the process could not begin soon enough.

If we are to preserve our few hard-won spaces for women's research, scholarship, and innovative pedagogy—and create more adequate spaces for the future—I urged that it was essential to develop a workable definition of the term *antifeminist intellectual harassment* so that, as it is named, it also can be readily recognized and effectively contained. Building on the groundbreaking work of the commission, I then offered the following tentative definition as at least a place to start:

> Antifeminist intellectual harassment, a serious threat to academic freedom, occurs when (1) any policy, action, statement, and/or behavior has the effect of discouraging or preventing women's freedom of lawful action, freedom of thought, and freedom of expression; (2) *or* when any policy, action, statement, and/or behavior creates an environment in which the appropriate application of feminist theories or methodologies to research, scholarship, and teaching is devalued, discouraged, or altogether thwarted; (3) *or* when any policy, action, statement, and/or behavior creates an environment in which research, scholarship, and teaching pertaining to women, gender, or gender inequities are devalued, discouraged, or altogether thwarted.

Implicit in this definition is the understanding that the harmful policies or behaviors may be enacted by women as well as by men, and that men—as well as women—may also be the targets of such harassment. No less important, this definition does not require that the agent of the harassment—whether a person or a university policy—be burdened with the guilt of intentionality (*intention* being difficult to prove even in the best-documented circumstances). Instead, following the legal precedents established under Title VII of the 1964 Civil Rights Act, this definition concentrates on effects and consequences.

Under this definition, promotion and tenure procedures that worked well two decades ago may now be deemed technically harassing if those procedures provide no mechanism for evaluating newer forms of scholarship and research productivity (interdisciplinary women's studies research, for example, or the computer program instead of a book) in which many feminist and minority faculty are now engaged. Obviously, the procedures were not originally designed to devalue these kinds of scholarly productions; the procedures were simply designed before such productions become possible. Even so, unless a department or college takes responsibility for periodically revising and rethinking its promotion and tenure procedures, that inaction will have the *effect* of devaluing the work of many newer scholars, feminist and minority faculty prominent among them. The *consequence* will be a campus environment hostile to excellence in a wide variety of areas, and hostile, too, to those innovative women faculty who dare push beyond the encrusted conventions of their disciplines.

III

After offering this definition at the 1991 Modern Language Association meeting, I was approached over the ensuing days and weeks by a number of women who shared their own stories of antifeminist intellectual harassment. What these women kept emphasizing was that, despite its apparent randomness and the seeming lack of connection between incidents, this form of harassment is nonetheless extremely costly to the woman who is targeted and increasingly pervasive in its cumulative effects across the profession. From that generosity of response, I have culled three very different career episodes—episodes which might not at first appear to have anything in common. But if my definition of antifeminist intellectual harassment is applied, the episodes reveal a chilling commonality.

In reconstructing the stories for this essay, I have altered some details in order to protect the privacy of individuals. Because the graduate student is now an untenured assistant professor, her field of study as well as her graduate school affiliation are extensively disguised. The story of Dr. Jean Jew has been pieced together from public sources, including articles in *Newsweek* and the *Chronicle of Higher Education*. The longest and most detailed story, that of an administrator, is a composite: two remarkably similar experiences have been combined as one. My five years as Dean of the Faculty of

Humanities at the University of Arizona unquestionably made me particularly sympathetic to these narratives, but nothing from those years as dean figures into the history of "Susan Smith." I have written about my own experiences elsewhere.[12]

1. An advanced graduate student going through her first round of job interviews at a Modern Language Association meeting, Diana Franklin (not her real name) repeatedly found herself in the same uncomfortable situation. In several interviews, one or more of the faculty present challenged her to defend the theories of the well-known, African American, feminist critic who served as her dissertation director. In more than one interview, reported Franklin, she was not given any opportunity to discuss her own research or teaching interests. Instead, the conversation was dominated by individuals who objected to a particularly controversial article that her dissertation director had published recently in a prominent journal. During this grilling, the other members of the interview committee sat silent.

The reception she encountered in these interviews, however, jarred sharply with the assumptions of some of her colleagues in the corridors. There, ominous rumors circulated about the lack of jobs and the oversupply of applicants. But Diana would be exempt from such worries, commented a number of the young, white men waiting with her in little clusters outside hotel suites. "You've got it made," they asserted. "Everyone's looking for women and minorities—you don't even have to publish. I don't stand a chance as a white male—no matter how much I've done already."

2. As reported in the *Chronicle of Higher Education*,[13] Dr. Jean Jew, an associate professor at the University of Iowa medical school, was awarded tenure in the anatomy department in 1979. Despite the award of tenure, Dr. Jew continued to experience harassing behaviors from some of her departmental colleagues, behaviors that had begun in 1973. She repeatedly filed formal requests with administrators to have the matter resolved, but no action was taken until 1984. That year a university committee specifically appointed to investigate her complaints found that she *had* been harassed. The faculty committee's findings notwithstanding, the university still took no action. Finally, in 1985, Dr. Jew sued the University of Iowa for failing to respond promptly to her cries for help. Her suit charged that faculty members in her department—especially one individual—spread false rumors that she had engaged in a sexual relationship with a former department chair and received preferential treatment from him in exchange. According to her attorney's brief, these rumors created a hostile work environment for Dr. Jew

11

that resulted in the curtailment of her research activities and the subsequent denial of her promotion to full professor.

As the trial progressed, it became clear that Dr. Jew had been harassed not only by the colleague intent on spreading false rumors about the supposed relationship with a former department chair. According to *Newsweek*:

> others in the department joked about her ethnic background. Jew is an American of Chinese descent. Explicit sex-based graffiti about her appeared on the walls of the department's men's room when she was being evaluated for promotion. In 1979, another professor, apparently drunk, yelled at her as she walked down a hallway in the department, calling her a "slut," a "bitch," and a "whore."[14]

Despite such damaging testimony, as the *Chronicle of Higher Education* wryly observed, "her case dragged on and ... the university fought her every step of the way" (Blum, A15), resisting court intervention in promotion and tenure as a matter of principle, and claiming to defend the First-Amendment rights of the colleague who had slandered her. For the university, in other words, this had become a case about protecting freedom of speech—even if that speech was sexist, racist, or slanderous—rather than protecting an accomplished faculty woman from sexual harassment. When, finally, in October 1990, the court ruled in her favor, and Jean Jew had reason to hope that her ordeal might be over, the university announced its intention to appeal. The Board of Regents had released a statement reiterating that the case raised First-Amendment issues, and the board thereby contested the clear implication of the judge's ruling that the university did indeed have a "responsibility to police its professors' activities and speech" (Blum, A16). Five years after filing suit, Dr. Jew's situation still remained unresolved.

3. A nationally prominent feminist critic in the field of British Modernism was hired away from one school, where she chaired the English Department, in order to assume the Deanship of the College of Fine Arts and Letters at a small, private, Midwestern university famous for its championship basketball teams. As such, Susan Smith (not her real name) was the first woman ever to be appointed as an academic dean at her new institution (the Dean of Students being the only other high-ranking female administrator on campus), and she was the first Dean of Fine Arts and Letters to enjoy national visibility, based on her scholarship and her extensive publications on feminist critical theory. When she was hired, in fact, the president told her he had chosen her *because* of that record. He hoped her scholarly reputation would attract high-caliber faculty and thus upgrade certain departments within Fine Arts and Letters, and he hoped that her feminist commitments might energize what he viewed as only sluggish progress toward improving the school's record in tenuring and retaining women and minority faculty. Indeed, the president strongly implied that Susan Smith was to take his comments as a mandate—which she did.

Moving swiftly while employing a widely consultative style, Dean Smith asked the school's affirmative action office to work with a variety of faculty committees, department heads, support staff, and students in order to develop a three-year faculty recruitment plan in Fine Arts and Letters that would result in increased numbers of women faculty and faculty from other underrepresented groups. She asked an elected faculty governance council to review promotion and tenure procedures for any inadvertent biases against women or minority candidates. And she modestly increased financial support for a fledgling women's studies program, including assigning them two tenure-track faculty lines on which to recruit. Although a few faculty, and even some department heads, were vocal in their complaints that the new dean was "moving too fast" or practicing "social engineering," the majority of staff and faculty remained supportive and cooperative.

After several months in which she concentrated on getting to know faculty in the sixteen departments and five programs within Fine Arts and Letters, Dean Smith came to realize that her positions on certain issues were being distorted and erroneously represented to faculty by some of the department heads who had been most vocal in their opposition to her. After redoubling her efforts to reach out to these men, however, Dean Smith had to admit to herself that two would never be team players and one simply could not abide a woman in authority. Because all administrators at this institution serve on annual contracts at the pleasure of their supervisor; and because she had seen her male colleague deans routinely remove department heads and appoint new ones in their place, she requested the resignation of two department heads at the end of her first year. Preferring to accept resignations rather than summarily inform them of the nonrenewal of their administrative contracts, Smith talked with each man at length and, in exchange for his resignation, she offered a package that included a semester's paid research leave, a period of reduced teaching assignments, and a small research budget—to ease the transition out of administration and back to full-time faculty status. Once the terms had been agreed to by both parties, the dean announced her acceptance of both men's resignations, and praised their years of administrative service. Her fellow deans (still all male) commented on her generosity but boasted that when they saw the need to remove a department head they just "threw the bum out on his ass," without face-saving resignations or transitional packages. Even so, in her second year, Smith repeated the same scenario with three more department heads. With that, and with the appointment of less authoritarian administrators in their place—two white women and one African-American male among them—the dean felt she now had a congenial working team.

But three of the former department heads went to the student newspaper and accused Smith of forcing them out in favor of "less-qualified" women and minorities. No mention was made of the transition packages they had accepted or, in one instance, of the vote of no confidence in the head taken by his faculty only months before. Instead, the dean was labeled as "unskilled in administration," "a tenured radical hostile to men," "temperamental," and "too controversial." And for the first two years of her administration, Smith saw herself caricatured in a recurring cartoon in the campus and local papers: dressed in shorts and a T-shirt with the Fine Arts and Letters logo, she was pictured on a basketball court, dribbling the heads of two or more of her former administrators.

When the department heads' charges and the cartoons were picked up by several national education publications, as well as by the right-wing press, a woman who had always prided herself on a low-key, nonconfrontational style encountered an unfamiliar portrait of herself as "abrasive" and "controversial." Rarely did these stories mention the policy implications of her actions or compare her treatment of department heads with treatment meted out by male deans at the same institution. And, of course, no one interviewed the president to inquire about—nor did the president volunteer—the implied mandate under which the dean had been hired. Still, confident that the majority of the faculty remained comfortable with their new role in recommending affirmative action recruitment priorities, and assured, further, by the elected faculty governance council that their members all saw the wisdom of reviewing tenure and promotion procedures, the dean shied away from reporters and continued to work with students, staff, and faculty to implement recommended changes. She did not defend herself to the press, nor did any senior university administrator call her to account.

Toward the end of a relatively quiet third year, therefore, it came as a shock when the president requested Smith's immediate resignation. Her tenure as dean had become too "volatile" and too "publicly controversial" to be effective, he explained. Dean Smith resigned in May, making no statement to the press, and took a long summer vacation, after which she resumed full-time duties as a professor in the English Department. In July, the Vice President for Academic Affairs named a new dean, one of the department heads whom Susan Smith had asked to tender his resignation.

IV

While it is easy to condemn these events as deplorable, it is likewise easy to dismiss them as isolated and unrelated. For the women who lived through them, however, these stories represent only tiny strands teased out of even larger tapestries of harassment and intimidation with which they contend daily.

Consider the graduate student—smart, attractive, articulate. But by the time Diana Franklin attended the Modern Language Association meeting, she had already spent five years stifling her rage and turning away from colleagues' hints that her two graduate-school fellowships had been awarded on the basis of her color or her gender, rather than her straight-A record and her two published articles in refereed journals. As a teaching assistant in freshman English, moreover, she had received no counseling from faculty or course supervisors on how to handle a returning older, white, male student who repeatedly disrupted the class, challenging her authority on both gender and racial grounds. And now, at her first Modern Language Association meeting, added to the hostility of some of the job interviewers and the disturbing assumptions of some of her fellow job-seekers, Franklin also encountered the misguided goodwill of one of her most supportive teachers. A bit tipsy from the evening's cocktail party, this kindly older professor put one arm around her shoulder and, in an avuncular fashion, confided that he had helpfully de-emphasized her "feminist side" in his letters of recommendation by commenting at length on her charming personality and the "delicious fudge brownies" she baked for the department's yearly spring picnic.

Or consider Dr. Jean Jew's career history. Given the scarcity of women in most fields of medicine and science, Jean Jew called upon heroic reserves of determination just to get through the grueling semesters at Tulane University medical school. Then, for most of her years as a faculty member at the University of Iowa medical school, she was forced to live daily with rumors and their aftermath. Not only was she the object of open sexual speculation among her colleagues; in addition, the gossip drove off potential research partners, as colleagues shied away from joining her or inviting her to participate in large collaborative projects. This, in turn, diminished her capacity to attract substantial research grants and pursue her work. And without grants, she could not support graduate student research assistants and advisees, thus limiting her opportunity to train the next generation in her particular area of neuroscience.

Susan Smith was older and, she thought, toughened by experience. But her brief years as dean also took place within a larger pattern of challenge and struggle. She had completed her Ph.D. at a prestigious Ivy League university that, in those days, never awarded fellowships or teaching assistantships to women and, in fact, discouraged women from going beyond the master's degree. Her husband, like so many bewildered men of his generation, had never understood her desire for an independent career and, on the very day that Smith successfully defended her dissertation, he announced that he was filing for divorce.

A single mother with a small child, she at first had difficulty locating a tenure-track position and, when she did find one, she spent years earning half the salary of her male colleagues while routinely being assigned heavier course loads. Working around the clock at two full-time jobs—being a parent *and* an academic—she managed to publish a series of influential books and articles, and was finally elected chair of her department. In that capacity, she had worked with the faculty to update promotion and tenure documents, and to revise graduate and undergraduate course offerings to reflect the latest scholarship in the field, and she had quickly recruited a number of outstanding women and minority faculty. With support from the dean, she had also analyzed faculty salaries, and made adjustments where past inequities based on gender were still in evidence. Her well-known successes in these areas contributed to making her a desirable candidate for a deanship.

But, as the first female academic dean at her new institution, Smith found it almost impossible to break into the camaraderie that marked the long-term relationships between most of the male deans. As a single woman, she was often overlooked for their "married couples only" dinner parties. And never did any of the other deans invite her for lunch, dinner, coffee, or a drink—as they regularly did with one another. When she began inviting them to lunch, one at a time, her fellow deans each reciprocated—once. After that, it always took *her* initiative to get any of them to meet her for coffee or lunch (the only invitations they would accept, as two made explicit), in order to discuss concerns of mutual interest in an informal setting. When she sat with her fellow academic deans at the president's monthly Academic Policies Council, she heard them habitually interrupt or speak over her even while she was still talking—something they rarely did to one another. And whenever she introduced issues pertaining to women or minorities, or when she asked that some pending budget reallocation be analyzed for its impact on women or minority students, she would later be told—by one or another of the deans who had been friendlier to her—that she should be wary of developing a reputation as a "one issue administrator."

My point here is simple: the stories that women choose to tell about the difficulties encountered, because of their sex, in their professional lives have force and resonance *because* those stories are not experienced in isolation. Each incident was part of a larger matrix which again and again assaulted the integrity and self-esteem of the woman, challenging her capacity to perform her job (or research) effectively, undermining her ability to develop any sustained sense of professional competence, and draining her creative energies in the endless need to invent stratagems of self-protection. Moreover, for the purposes of the present essay, the individual anecdotes reveal yet another set of connections. When measured by my earlier definition of antifeminist intellectual harassment, each numbered anecdote illustrates the reach and depth of that harassment, as well as the price we pay for it as an academic community. That price is perhaps most accurately totalled if we reverse the order of the anecdotes, beginning with the woman we might have expected to represent meaningful influence and authority.

The short-lived tenure of the feminist Dean of Fine Arts and Letters illustrates the pitfalls of bringing a lone woman into a highly visible position, asking her to correct an entire history of problems, and then offering her no support network. And it reminds us of the cynicism with which some university presidents and provosts make grand gestures of hiring feminist and minority administrators specifically to respond to a poor affirmative action record, only to back away when these individuals encounter predictable pockets of resistance in their efforts to initiate the required changes.

Because of this, Susan Smith's story also plays out all sections of my definition of antifeminist intellectual harassment. Though fully within the regulations by which this campus functioned, her summary dismissal by the president had the long-term effect of discouraging other feminist scholars there from even considering a move into administration; and it had the short-term effect of eroding the former dean's ability to speak with an influential voice on matters of discrimination, gender equity, and the need to support a developing women's studies curriculum. In addition to thus inhibiting women's freedom of action and expression, the president also effectively derailed a set of innovative policies that had already resulted in the increased hiring of women and minority faculty within the College of Fine Arts and Letters. And he shut down an environment newly receptive to cross-disciplinary research areas (including women's studies). To be sure, the president's only conscious motives may have been to placate conservative alumni threatening a withdrawal of financial support or to calm a Board of Trustees made nervous by unwanted publicity. But, in fact, both in his manner of removing Dean Smith and in his tacit approval of her replacement, the president reconstituted an earlier environment on campus in which research, scholarship, and teaching pertaining to women and gender inequities were understood to be a low priority, and perhaps even hazardous to one's professional health.

Even as Jean Jew's story raises questions about the adequacy of the University of Iowa's internal grievance procedures and the effectiveness of its affirmative action office, her story also challenges us to justify the personal toll exacted by the ongoing stress and financial burden of a lawsuit.[15] "Her pursuit of sexual harassment complaints against the university and individual administrators," noted the *Chronicle of Higher Education*, has left Dr. Jew "drained financially and emotionally," her reputation as a competent scientist shattered (Blum, A15). As a result, as with so many Title VII cases, the real benefits of Dr. Jew's perseverance will be enjoyed by women who may not even know her name. Her suit forced the University of Iowa's affirmative action office to organize training programs on sexual harassment issues and to develop specific sexual harassment policies. The *Chronicle of Higher Education* also reported that the institution was clarifying and streamlining its complaint procedures and intended to provide all employees with informational booklets on what constitutes sexual harassment (Blum, A16). However belated, such remediating steps are to be applauded—even though they do not address, nor even recognize, the pernicious *intellectual* harassment to which Dr. Jew was also subjected.

Although Jean Jew's research does not focus on women nor address questions of gender, the treatment she received at the University of Iowa's medical college—and the university's lack of response—still falls within my definition, because that treatment had the effect of curtailing her research activity. The department's rumor mill made most graduate students wary of working with Dr. Jew. For that same reason, Dr. Jew was unable easily to collaborate with colleagues on research projects. Thus, she was forced to pursue her work under burdens not faced by her male colleagues and under burdens which inevitably had a chilling effect on the progress of that work. While all of this, combined with the years of litigation, had personal consequences for Dr. Jew—inhibiting her intellectual potential and robbing her of years of professional productivity—it also had consequences for the women and minority students for whom, under other circumstances, she might have served as mentor and friend.

In the science fields and on medical school faculties, women—especially women from nontraditional backgrounds—are notoriously underrepresented. Amid all the curricular reforms and community outreach programs that have been devised to correct this situation, one strategy has been universally endorsed: bringing more women and minorities into visible faculty and research positions. But by turning Dr. Jew into an object of gossip within her department, and thus effectively isolating her, the University of Iowa undoubtedly deprived some eager graduate student of the very support she needed for survival there. Or, even worse, the treatment accorded Dr. Jew may have warned another talented young Chinese-American woman that science and medicine were simply minefields too dangerous to enter. As the only woman faculty member in the anatomy department at Iowa during most of her years there, and as one of only three women in a twenty-two-member department in 1994, Dr. Jew herself commented that "one of the reasons these sorts of problems about gender in the workplace persist is that there are so few women here to begin with" (Blum, A16).

Like Jean Jew, the graduate student at the Modern Language Association meeting had enjoyed a strong and supportive relationship with her mentor as she completed her dissertation. It was only during her first foray into the larger profession that Diana Franklin found herself intimidated and silenced. For, whether they consciously intended it or not, the behavior of the job interviewers who grilled her about the work of her feminist adviser had the effect of a covert warning: "Women who display the intellectual daring of your adviser," they seemed to be saying, "are dangerous and too controversial to be admitted to *our* department. We have no place for such women or for anyone they train." This experience, coupled with the condescending admission from one of her strongest references that he had purposefully understated her "feminist side" in his job letters for her, forced Franklin to reassess the dissertation topic she had once chosen with unalloyed enthusiasm. *Should* she de-emphasize or even altogether omit from her dissertation some of its more unsettling speculations? *Should* she, she wondered, modify her research agenda until she was safely tenured? Turning over the alternatives as she dozed on the flight back to California, Diana Franklin finally realized, with a start, that academe no longer felt to her like the haven of intellectual freedom she thought she had found.

V

When I asked a mixed group of graduate students on my home campus if they had ever heard the phrase, "antifeminist intellectual harassment," they all said no. When I asked what they thought it might mean, one young woman quickly replied, "Oh, that's easy—business as usual." No one disagreed.

When I circulated the three numbered anecdotes to friends and colleagues around the country, asking if these stories seemed like legitimate instances of antifeminist intellectual harassment, I was struck by another uniformity of response. Very few recognized my harassment category, but every correspondent was convinced that one or more of the anecdotes was based on events at her or his campus (including the story of Jean Jew, where the institution was identified).

Because such events are now both familiar and ubiquitous, each of my correspondents had ready remedies. In response to Diana Franklin's story, there were recommendations that all advanced graduate students receive formal training on handling interview situations, while faculty serving on search committees be required to attend mandatory affirmative action seminars. Jean Jew's story elicited a variety of procedural recommendations, including, for example, an ombudsperson's office with selected staff trained to deal expeditiously with charges of sexual harassment. Susan Smith's story brought the expected outcry against the suspected interference of right-wing alumni. But it also brought practical suggestions for the development of on-campus training and mentorship programs aimed at preparing women of color, white women, and all faculty from underrepresented groups for responsible roles as academic administrators. Most passionate, perhaps, were the pleas that professional and campus women's groups take responsibility for sponsoring workshops on individual survival strategies. "Someone needs to teach junior women how to reach out to senior colleagues and make them allies," one of my correspondents noted. "It's especially important for untenured women to go to conferences, sign onto e-mail, and develop a national network for themselves," wrote another.

Clearly, the three anecdotes suggested to each of my correspondents a checklist of independent activities that might prove useful on her or his own campus. And while no refusal of antifeminist intellectual harassment is ever *un*important, it may be possible to secure an even more lasting impact through a concerted effort to embed an intolerance of such harassment into all the school's pronouncements about itself. I would recommend, therefore, an additional, comprehensive approach. The object here is to educate the campus and local community to recognize antifeminist intellectual harassment, whatever its mode of expression, and to create a context in which interested parties can speak *as* and *for* the institution in condemning it. In short, change the sound of the institution's voice. This is neither as ephemeral nor as difficult as one might initially suppose.

As a singular and monolithic entity, "the institution" simply does not exist. Instead, "the institution" is merely a grammatical convenience that projects the illusion of coherence and integration. The truth is, whatever the putative institution does is really the outcome of complicated ensembles of complex relationships between and among groups and individuals. Marked by loosely bounded and overlapping areas of action and responsibility,[16] with power vacuums everywhere puncturing the appearance of hierarchy, the college or university campus is unique in its potential to be represented by a variety of (even competing) constituencies. As a result, many different groups and individuals—the president, the Board of Trustees, elected student government officers, the head of the Black Student Association, the chair of the Faculty Senate, the librarians' committee, the campus disability caucus, the Support Staff Council, organized alumni groups, and so on—all claim at different times to be speaking *for* the college, *on behalf* of the university, or *in its best interests*. And rightly so. This sense of ownership is what prompts groups and individuals to take conscious responsibility for the environment that their actions, attitudes, behaviors, and decisions are creating for themselves and others.

Once this is understood, the prospect of taking on the institution's voice in order to combat antifeminist intellectual harassment becomes less daunting. And two tasks emerge clearly: first, that harassment must be widely identified and repeatedly explained; and second, opposition to it must be projected as the *institutional* norm. That said, the vast array of governance structures coupled with the sheer variety of higher education entities in this country make it impossible to devise any universal blueprint for taking on these tasks. Interested groups at different colleges and universities will have to examine their own unique situation and explore local possibilities. As they do so, however, I would urge that they consider including some version of the following four strategies as an interrelated package, with all four—as much as possible—going forward at the same time. My experience as a dean taught me that it is always far more profitable to be overly ambitious rather than hesitatingly cautious.

1. Multiyear conference and follow-up assessments. By first employing informal internal networks—like women's studies bag lunches and e-mail— a small group can initiate an ongoing, campuswide dialogue on antifeminist intellectual harassment. Through these and other informal communications, the original group can begin to identify larger numbers of potentially interested groups and individuals. The object is to develop the widest possible coalition—such as the women's faculty association, the women's studies faculty, an appropriate student government committee, the affirmative action office, the organized librarians, and so on—so that together these groups can seek both internal and external funding for a multiyear conference. The more groups involved, of course, the greater the impact, as well as enlarging the opportunities for tapping diverse funding sources.

Wherever feasible, the conference should announce itself as an examination of antifeminist intellectual harassment and its damaging consequences for the campus community. Conference flyers and posters might include a brief definition of the term, thus helping to educate even those who do not attend—and preparing those who will. At a school where this focus cannot win wide support, organizers would be well advised to design the conference as an examination of both the history of and the present threats to the concept of academic freedom, and to position antifeminist intellectual harassment as a significant example of those threats.

Whether the conference is offered as a national or local event, it is essential to engage participation from every campus constituency—faculty, undergraduates, graduate students, librarians, support staff, and administrators. Ideally, the academic vice president, the president, the chancellor and members of the Board of Trustees will all see the wisdom of accepting invitations to appear as featured speakers or as members of panels. Publicity for these events must be carefully planned, and press coverage courted in advance.

However well attended and however comprehensive the press coverage, onetime events (even when scheduled over two or three days) have only limited usefulness—unless, that is, they are designed to initiate an ongoing process. For antifeminist intellectual harassment to continue to be recognized and rejected, it will have to be the focus of a second and very different kind of conference two years after the first. And in order to galvanize the campus into actively condemning that harassment, the first conference must set in motion a series of integrated activities that will have the effect of diminishing the opportunities for such behaviors. The second conference thereby becomes an occasion to examine the problem again and, even more important, to offer a progress report on how the campus has responded to it.

As the first conference is being planned, the program committee must ensure that the conference goes beyond merely defining the problem and pointing to its prevalence. In addition, that committee should seek out representatives from student, staff, and faculty governance groups (and unions, where appropriate), as well as members of the university's legal office, to serve on specific action-oriented sessions. These sessions might examine the institution's own policy documents to determine if they include adequate safeguards against antifeminist intellectual harassment. And these same sessions should function as occasions for encouraging designated groups and individuals to take responsibility for reviewing campus codes of conduct, faculty handbooks, and other like documents in order to determine if some new or clarifying language might be helpful.

Given the expense of mounting any kind of conference nowadays—and especially a multiyear event—several schools in a given geographic area might cooperate in joint sponsorship, thus sharing the expenses and, at the same time, increasing the audience. Or, where a school already enjoys a well-established (and funded) annual women's studies conference, that conference might be adapted as the occasion for these "special events." In that case, it will be important to attract an audience beyond those who regularly attend women's studies activities.

The school in which antifeminist intellectual harassment is a repeated problem, however, will probably not be hospitable to the multiyear conference outlined here even as a participant with several other schools in the area. Interested faculty at these institutions should turn instead to the women's caucuses and women's commissions within their disciplinary professional organizations. Either separately or together, these groups also have the capacity to find conference funding or, at the very least, to command a substantial portion of their professional organization's yearly conference program. And while such an organization-sponsored conference ordinarily would not scrutinize the policy documents of a single campus, the conference could certainly examine discipline-related policy statements at a variety of schools. And, as the feminist literary biographer, Emily Toth, has pointed out to me, a university initially wary of hosting a conference on antifeminist intellectual harassment might become far more amenable after the subject had been aired through a series of professional meetings and been rendered "topical."[17]

2. Reviewing promotion and tenure policy documents. In order to ensure that women continue to participate actively in the ongoing creation and re-creation of every discipline's knowledge base, and in order to ensure that the energizing variety of feminist approaches is fully represented, promotion and tenure policy documents must undergo careful and regular review.[18] Committees examining these documents will want to ascertain that criteria for promotion and tenure make room for work in nontraditional areas—where feminist scholarship has been particularly prominent—and acknowledge the value of cross- and interdisciplinary research and scholarship. These committees should also see to it that promotion and tenure criteria, especially in the humanities fields, allow for the evaluation of scholarly work that appears in formats other than the article, the monograph, or the book. Much important new research is now being presented through the production of documentary videos for educational television, museum exhibitions, and innovative instructional computer programs. No less important, the tenure and promotion procedural documents should declare unequivocally that the candidate's internal and external reviewers will include those knowledgeable in her field, and that her participation in a women's studies program (an African-American or an ethnic studies program, and so on) will be fully credited and evaluated.

Finally, any examination of promotion and tenure policies must include careful reading between the lines in search of covert messages suggesting that one tenured feminist is enough. This often unspoken mind-set assumes mistakenly that feminism is monolithic, adhering to some narrowly defined set of questions and methodologies. The language for containing and constraining the development of a fully polyvocal feminist dialogue in a department may be camouflaged in terminology about "programmatic needs" and "avoiding duplication." But, in fact, an English department's legitimate concern over the wisdom of hiring a second specialist in pre-Shakespearean drama when enrollments are falling should not be confused with the tenuring of both a feminist theorist in medieval studies and a feminist critic in nineteenth-century American literature, each bringing a different set of theories and methods to her classes and to the department as a whole. In this context, feminist inquiry is not by itself a field of study—as is pre-Shakespearean drama—but rather, feminist inquiry is constituted by sets of interrelated (and sometimes oppositional) theories and methods for reexamining and even renewing already-well-established subject areas. Additionally, the field of feminist theory, in all its current diversity, cuts across area and discipline boundaries to represent both a critique of and a challenge to the enterprise of theory itself. The tenuring of a feminist theorist would thus secure for a department strengths very different from those of the feminist medievalist or the feminist Americanist.

3. Bringing more women and members of underrepresented groups into higher education administration. Anyone who is unfamiliar or perceived as nontraditional within an otherwise homogenous group inevitably takes on a visibility disproportionate to that individual's actual activities within the group. She will be subjected to more intense scrutiny and quicker judgments about her performance, and her motives will be interpreted less as a function of her professional role than as an expression of her "difference" or "uniqueness." According to those who have studied the concept of *surplus visibility*, moreover, the greater the decision-making authority invested in her position, the more conspicuous that individual becomes.[19] At the same time, every student of organizational psychology knows that institutions feel "safe" to people only insofar as people see themselves—or those like them—as empowered within those institutions. In order both to diminish the debilitating consequences of surplus visibility and to enhance *everyone's* comfort within higher education, it is essential that campuses make a concerted effort to recruit members of underrepresented groups, and especially feminist-identified men and women, for all layers of administration, management, and policy-making. But that recruitment must avoid tokenism and, instead, be focused on purposefully creating a designated critical mass of change agents.

To be sure, what constitutes a critical mass will vary from campus to campus (although one third of any specifiable group is usually a minimum target). I stress the concept of critical mass because only at critical mass can mutually supportive individuals sustain one another through difficult periods while, at the same time, reaching out widely to create an ongoing atmosphere welcoming to diversity and open to all serious intellectual activity. And only a critical mass convincingly demonstrates to the larger community the role of the campus as a haven of academic freedom for many different kinds of people. The human face of these administrators, we may hope, might even help to make both feminism and diversity less threatening by building bridges of personal relationships, especially with those previously exposed only to caricature and cartoons.

This evolution beyond mere tokenism is demanded by the nation's changing demographics, of course. At the City University of New York, the nation's largest public urban university, for example, forty percent of the entering students nowadays "are black or Hispanic and trace their ancestry to the Caribbean,"[20] while slightly over half the undergraduate population nationwide is female. But the move beyond tokenism also derives from the fact that, as an affirmative action strategy, tokenism has backfired badly. Not only were individuals destroyed and careers derailed in the spotlight of surplus visibility; in addition, highly qualified white women, women of color, and others from under-represented groups witnessed the costs of these struggles, internalized the experiences as their own, and reconsidered any aspirations they once might have harbored regarding an administrative career for themselves in higher education. The result was that few women and fewer feminists believed that they had seriously been invited to any permanent place at the decision-making table. In order to avoid passing on these silent messages of inevitable failure, therefore, and in order to make it possible to move larger numbers of women and others from underrepresented groups into administrative positions, schools must develop internship programs for staff and faculty alike.

Ideally, on-campus internship and administrative mentorship programs should be open, on a competitive basis, to the entire eligible campus community. I say this because such programs face two challenges: the first challenge is to convince potential women and minority recruits that the institution is genuinely committed to change. To accomplish this will require an outlay of significant resources, usually in mentorship hours or formal training sessions, rather than large sums of money. And it will require the speedy appointment of some of the program's women and minority graduates to appropriate administrative or managerial positions. Otherwise, women and those from underrepresented groups will remain reluctant to invest themselves. The second challenge is to prepare *all* participants in an administrative training program to respond to the special stresses of bias, stereotyping, discrimination, and surplus visibility that will be encountered by some of them. To put it another way, until women and those from currently underrepresented groups are no longer anomalies in higher education administration, the on-the-job problems encountered by white women and women of color *because of who they are* can be mediated successfully only through the sympathetic interventions of colleagues who appreciate the full complexity of the situation. In other words, white males and males of color must learn how to become allies of their feminist colleagues in administration, and they must be taught appropriate responses to the particular difficulties of surplus visibility that a female president or a feminist dean will inevitably encounter. At the same time, all administrative trainees can be taught to understand and contain the scope of surplus visibility that a male from any underrepresented group will also encounter. Only in this way can administrators learn to share meaningful colleagueship across the divides of difference.

Effective administrative training programs are rarely expensive, they can be implemented relatively easily, and many schools already have them in place (albeit without always incorporating the two goals I have just cited). Additionally, schools in the same region can pool resources by establishing exchange—or "loaned administrative trainee"—programs. Many schools also take advantage of national resources, including the annual Summer Institute for Women in Higher Education Administration, held at Bryn Mawr College and sponsored by Higher Education Resource Services of Mid-America.[21]

Statewide cooperation should not be overlooked, either. Thanks to two years of modest funding from the state legislature, for example, the Florida Department of Education was able to develop the Educational Leadership Enhancement Grant Program, targeted at attracting "more women and minorities into the upper echelons of higher education administration."[22] In 1994, the first year of funding, six different leadership projects in nine schools reached "more than 60 women and minorities in Florida's public community colleges and universities." According to an article in *Women in Higher Education*, most of these projects involved "internships, mentoring and career counseling, and a series of seminars to build leadership and networking skills" ("Florida Invests," 2).

Whatever the design or scope of the program, however, every institution that has supported or participated in either on-campus or off-campus administrative training programs has learned that their continued success is determined, over time, by the institution's efforts to recruit program participants for visible managerial and administrative positions. Were the women and minority graduates of an administrative internship program repeatedly passed over for openings at the home campus or lured away to administrative posts at other schools, the home institution would not only be losing out on its best investment; it would also appear to be acting in bad faith.

4. Continuing the commitment to feminist intellectual inquiry within the academy. For all its petty turf battles and its inherently reactionary conservatism, its overheated interpersonal squabbles and public mendacities, the academy still remains the single institution in the United States that at least *claims* to protect access to unimpeded intellectual inquiry for everyone in the society and on behalf of the society as a whole. While the growing incidence of outright hostility toward feminist scholars and their research puts that claim to the test, that same hostility also challenges feminists ever more fiercely to seize our right to participate in the creation and re-creation of knowledge. Thus, in my view, the indispensable requirement for combatting antifeminist intellectual harassment is the creative, energetic, ever-expanding persistence of feminist inquiry itself. Whatever else we do, including our efforts to ward off the harassment, our scholarship, research, and teaching innovations cannot be put aside.

All by itself, academic freedom is a difficult ideal to sustain. It is an ideal, after all, that holds the potential to undermine established systems of power, to unravel the society's most cherished myths about itself, and indeed, to challenge the structures of knowledge upon which the academy once securely positioned itself. Because the best of feminist work shatters the very foundations of a full panoply of powerful cultural conventions—from class arrangements, to gender hierarchy, to men's imputed mastery over nature—resistance to it will be as powerful as the privileges and cultural beliefs being protected. But the impact of our work—the persuasiveness of our critical scrutiny, the compelling evidence produced by our research, and the disturbing questions that linger in students' minds long after our classes are over—all these contribute to changing people's beliefs and perceptions, altering forever their categories of analysis and understanding. Indeed, as most feminist scholars rather ruefully remark, the ubiquity of the harassment we now encounter is testimony to our effectiveness in bringing substantial change to the various disciplines and the educational institutions that once tried to keep us out. Feminist research and theory must inform the strategies of response to intellectual harassment, of course; but feminist research, scholarship, and teaching are themselves the most important parts of that response. Or to put it another way: the moment we abandon our research, our pursuit of better interpretations, our thoughtful reappraisal of all received truths, our epistemological insistence on asking how we know what we think we know, in that moment antifeminist intellectual harassment will have prevailed.

VI

All stories, even anecdotes, deserve endings.

As she returned from the Modern Language Association meeting to her tiny apartment in California, Diana Franklin made up her mind. She needed to have a full-time faculty position with a decent salary by the time the next school year began. Despite her fellowships and her years as a graduate teaching assistant, she had accumulated considerable debt. And her parents required financial help as they worked to put their younger children through school. The entire month of January, therefore, was given over to revising sections of her dissertation, and especially the two sample chapters she was sending out to prospective employers. Her purpose was not to censor her conclusions but, where possible, to reframe those conclusions in language that was less daring, less provocative. In several places, she also carefully deleted any hints about the kinds of feminist projects she intended to pursue in the future.

After making several campus visits, Franklin received three firm job offers, two from departments of English, and one a joint appointment with English and African American Studies. She accepted the latter, because she felt her research might be better received within an African American studies program than within a conventional English department. In fact, she continues to wonder whether the English department at her new school would have sponsored her candidacy had the search committee read her dissertation chapters in their original form. Franklin knows she is secure for the time being, she says; but she does not *feel* that way. And, she adds, as she rewrites her dissertation for book publication, she has to struggle against censoring herself at every turn.

Despite the continued harassment, and against all odds, Dr. Jean Jew tenaciously pursued her research agenda. Her circumstances compromised her opportunities for external funding, but still she succeeded in bringing in grants, thereby demonstrating not only her dedication, but also the quality of her work as judged by the larger scientific community. These successes notwithstanding, it was with profound relief that, in October 1990, five years after she filed suit in federal court and thirteen years after filing internal complaints at the University of Iowa, Jean Jew heard a judge deliver a scathing indictment of the university's failure to take "prompt, appropriate corrective action" on her behalf (Blum, A16). But her relief quickly disappeared as she heard university attorneys state their intention to appeal. At that point, groups from within the university community who were sympathetic to Dr. Jew organized in earnest, circulating copies of the judge's findings to every faculty member. The *Des Moines Register*, which had been following the case closely, "printed a full page of excerpts" from the judge's ruling, according to *Newsweek*, and ran an editorial urging the university to give up its appeal ("Diagnosis," 62). Finally, in November, after pressure from a variety of constituencies, the university dropped its plans to appeal and, as *Newsweek* put it, "paid for its laissez-faire attitude.... The university issued a humbling public apology and agreed to pay Dr. Jew $50,000 in back pay, $126,000 in damages, and $895,000 in fees and expenses to her attorney" (62). And, as the judge had ordered, she was promoted to full professor.

In response to the judge's decree that the university "take all reasonable steps to ensure a hostility-free work environment" for Dr. Jew (Blum, A16), the university's president, Hunter Rawlings III, promised to do just that, adding that "Dr. Jew deserves our apologies and our respect for her stand" ("Diagnosis," 62). For her part, Jean Jew remained skeptical. "It's so much easier to hand over money than to do what's right," she commented (62). In her view, "the hardest part of all" was still to come: actually correcting the problem (62).

After returning to faculty status in the Department of English, Susan Smith remained only two more years at the school where she had once been Dean of the College of Fine Arts and Letters. Her articles on facilitating change and renewal in higher education caught the attention of two executive search firms and a number of educators across the country. Smith's experience as a department chair and a dean, combined with strong recommendations from faculty and administrators who had worked closely with her, added to her attractiveness as a candidate for senior administrative posts. A small, private, liberal arts college in the Pacific Northwest lured her away as provost. Four years later, a similar institution in the Northeast named her as its president. Within a few years of becoming president, Smith established a solid reputation as a fund-raiser and academic leader. And she emerged as an eloquent national spokesperson for equity issues in higher education. "But I'm very, very tired," she told me, and "I don't think I can keep this up much longer. That experience as Dean of Fine Arts and Letters," she continued, "affected my health and used up all my reserves of energy. It almost broke me."

Jane Schaberg, whose torched Toyota Tercel opened this essay, miraculously remains both unbroken and undaunted. Continuing her groundbreaking studies of the New Testament, she recently used a sabbatical leave to work on a book-length analysis of Mary Magdalene traditions.

If there are lessons to be learned from these women's stories, they surely are not lessons about the triumphs of antifeminist intellectual harassment. On the contrary: in each instance, a strong, determined woman surmounted the harassment and survived, even succeeded. But there *is* a lesson to be learned, nonetheless: in each instance, the woman paid too high a price, a price that never should have been exacted in the first place. The energies of those who will be needed to lead the academy into the twenty-first century should not be so carelessly squandered.

Notes

My gratitude and admiration to the women who so generously shared their stories and allowed me to use them but preferred anonymity. My deepest appreciation to Jean Jew and Jane Schaberg for their courage and dignity, and for their kindness in reviewing a draft of these pages. My deep appreciation, also, to the friends and colleagues who read the earliest draft of this essay and responded immediately with constructive criticism and intelligent advice: Cathy Davidson, Susan Koppelman, and Emily Toth. Finally, my thanks to Lisa Gelfand for providing an epigraph and needed humor; and continuing thanks to my research assistant, Ruthe Thompson, for her care and insight.

1. Quoted in Kaufman, 162.

2. Kalikoff, "Tracking Tenure with Camera and Net," 41.

3. Robin Wilson, "A Scholar's Conclusion About Mary Stirs Ire," *Chronicle of Higher Education* 40, 7 (October 6, 1993): A7; hereafter cited in the text.

4. Jane Schaberg, "The (A) Contribution of Feminist Scholarship to Historical Jesus Research." Unpublished paper delivered to the Canadian Society of Biblical Studies 1993 Historical Jesus Seminar, The Learneds, Ottawa, June 1993. Paper provided by the author.

5. For a chilling examination of the networks of right-wing organizations currently impacting our campuses, see Ellen Messer-Davidow.

6. See Courtney Leatherman, A22.

7. Gayle Greene, "Looking at History," 17.

8. Stephen Burd, "Ready to Cry Foul: Defiant Conservative Relishes the NEH Fights to Come," *Chronicle of Higher Education* 40, 43 (June 29, 1994): A25; hereafter cited in the text.

9. Bettina J. Huber, 59–60.

10. See Bernice Resnick Sandler, 7; hereafter cited in the text.

11. "A Chilly Climate for Graduate Women," 2.

12. An overview of my own experiences as dean may be gleaned from Annette Kolodny, "Setting an Agenda for Change: Meeting the Challenges and Exploring the Opportunities in Higher Education," especially 5–15.

13. Debra E. Blum, A15–16; hereafter cited in the text.

14. "Diagnosis: Harassment," *Newsweek* 116, 22 (November 26, 1990): 62; hereafter cited in the text.

15. For the personal and emotional costs of this kind of litigation, see Annette Kolodny, "I Dreamt Again That I Was Drowning," 170–178.

16. This is also a recurrent theme in Warren Bennis's anatomy of the corporate sector in *Why Leaders Can't Lead: The Unconscious Conspiracy Continues*.

17. Private telephone conversation with Emily Toth, January 1994.

18. The rationale for such a review and one possible fruitful outcome are offered in Annette Kolodny, "Raising Standards While Lowering Anxieties: Rethinking the Promotion and Tenure Process," 16–39.

19. The best analysis of the concept of "surplus visibility" within an academic setting is Daphne Patai's "Minority Status and the Stigma of 'Surplus Visibility'," A52, to which my discussion is indebted.

20. Honan, "New Pressures on the University," 16.

21. A residential program that offers "intensive training in educational administration," the Summer Institute at Bryn Mawr is organized by HERS, Mid-America, University of Denver, Park Hill Campus, 7150 Mountview Blvd., Denver, CO 80220.

22. "Florida Invests in Women as Leaders," 2.

Works Cited and Consulted

"A Chilly Climate for Graduate Women." *About Women on Campus* 2, 4 (Fall 1993): 2.

Bennis, Warren. *Why Leaders Can't Lead: The Unconscious Conspiracy Continues.* San Francisco: Jossey-Bass, 1989.

Blum, Debra E. "Medical Professor, U. of Iowa Face Aftermath of Sexual-Harassment Case." *Chronicle of Higher Education* 37, 26 (March 13, 1991): A15–16.

Burd, Stephen. "Ready to Cry Foul: Defiant Conservative Relishes the NEH Fights to Come." *Chronicle of Higher Education* 40, 43 (June 29, 1994): A25.

"Diagnosis: Harassment." *Newsweek* 116, 22 (November 26, 1990): 62.

"Florida Invests in Women as Leaders." *Women in Higher Education* 3, 6 (June 1994): 2.

Greene, Gayle. "Looking at History." *Changing Subjects: The Making of Feminist Literary Criticism*, ed. Gayle Greene and Coppelia Kahn. New York: Routledge, 1993: 4–27.

Honan, William H. "New Pressures on the University." *New York Times,* January 9, 1994, sec. 4A: 16–18.

Huber, Bettina J. "Women in the Modern Languages, 1970–1990." *Profession 90,* ed. Phyllis Franklin. New York: Modern Language Association, 1990: 58–73.

Kalikoff, Beth. "Tracking Tenure with Camera and Net." *Iris: A Journal About Women* 30 (Winter 1993): 40–43.

Kaufman, Gloria, ed. *In Stitches: A Patchwork of Feminist Humor and Satire.* Bloomington: Indiana University Press, 1991.

Kolodny, Annette. "I Dreamt Again That I Was Drowning." *Women's Writing in Exile,* ed. Mary Lynn Broe and Angela Ingram. Chapel Hill: University of North Carolina Press, 1989: 170–178.

———. "Raising Standards While Lowering Anxieties: Rethinking the Promotion and Tenure Process." *Concerns* 23, 2 (Spring 1993): 16–39.

———. "Setting an Agenda for Change: Meeting the Challenges and Exploring the Opportunities in Higher Education." *Transformations: The New Jersey Project Journal* 4, 2 (Fall 1993): 5–30.

Leatherman, Courtney. "Dealing with Sexual Images in Iowa Classrooms." *Chronicle of Higher Education* 40, 16 (December 8, 1993): A22–A24.

Messer-Davidow, Ellen. "Manufacturing the Attack on Liberalized Higher Education." *Social Text* 36 (Fall 1993): 40–80.

Patai, Daphne. "Minority Status and the Stigma of 'Surplus Visibility'." *Chronicle of Higher Education* 38, 10 (October 30, 1991): A52.

Sandler, Bernice Resnick. *Women Faculty at Work in the Classroom, or, Why It Still Hurts To Be a Woman in Labor.* Washington, DC: Center for Women Policy Studies, 1993.

Schaberg, Jane. "The (A) Contribution of Feminist Scholarship to Historical Jesus Research." Unpublished paper delivered to the Canadian Society of Biblical Studies 1993 Historical Jesus Seminar, The Learneds, Ottawa, June 1993.

———. *The Illegitimacy of Jesus: A Feminist Theological Interpretation of the Infancy Narratives.* San Francisco: Harper and Row, 1989.

Wilson, Robin. "A Scholar's Conclusion About Mary Stirs Ire." *Chronicle of Higher Education* 40, 7 (October 6, 1993): A7.

2

Feminism and Antifeminism: From Civil Rights to Culture Wars

Moira Ferguson, Ketu H. Katrak, and Valerie Miner

Any academic discipline or social movement that speaks for women, minorities, and the disadvantaged in North American culture is perceived as threatening to a conservative mainstream. The feminist movement and women's studies were born out of the activist energies of the 1960s student movements and the struggle for civil rights. Feminism, even as an academic discipline, remains committed to social change, and continues to grapple with the integral, often complex, links between theory and practice. This activist impulse, which remains a strong undercurrent through different waves of feminisms, is scorned by conservative upholders of "objective" scholarly endeavors. One aspect of feminism's activist impulse and its alliance with other oppressed groups brings its goals into conjunction with those of ethnic and multicultural studies. The eighties and nineties have witnessed antifeminist and antiethnic attacks by adherents of a Western, canonical tradition of humanistic learning. Let us back up for a moment and contextualize these remarks.

"The sixties" has become a cliché and catchword for an era of radical change that began with civil rights and ended with the bombing of Haiphong Harbor. The explosion in print and in television viewing brought the social upheaval into U.S. households.

African Americans, Anglo women, Native Americans, and Hispanics pushed for redress of their grievances; movements variously designated as Civil Rights, Women's Liberation, Wounded Knee, and La Raza spread like wildfire. This emergence of the Civil Rights Movement, Chicana, Native American, and Asian activism and the New Left occurred almost simultaneously, with women involved in all of them. This participation would sharpen female political skills, raise self-awareness, and lead to a new phase of the Women's Movement.

Throughout the decade, the number of divorced women rose from 1,858,000 in 1960 to 3,004,000 in 1970 (Linden-Ward, ix–xxii). Women aged 55 to 64 divorced two hundred percent more than they did before 1960. Black women joined the labor force in greater numbers, more black marriages disintegrated, more black women headed households; concurrently, Daniel Moynihan created the mythology of the black matriarch.[1] Despite this collectivity of issues and demands, however, these movements advanced in fits and starts.

Five years after Rosa Parks's historical refusal to surrender her bus seat, four black students sat at a Woolworth's lunch counter in North Carolina. In Muriel Rukeyser's prophetic phrase, the world was "split open" ("The Poem as Mask," 3).

With the founding of the Student Non-Violent Coordinating Committee (SNCC) in 1960, on a basis of radical equality, Southern black students began to react to racist attitudes and policies with nonviolent tactics, such as the celebrated sit-ins and freedom rides. Everyone's opinion was considered equally in making decisions, and meetings did not end until consensus was reached. Though frustrating at times, this lack of hierarchy and structure generated a keen sense of community and idyllic democracy. Young, black women played a large part in SNCC, organizing voter registration and fighting segregation in the Southern states. Rubye Doris Smith Robinson was just one woman who held a central position in SNCC. Many young, black women, however, objected to the fact that the majority of positions of power were given to men, while women were relied upon to do the cleaning, cooking, and clerical work.

Black women, moreover, held influential positions in the churches during the Southern Civil Rights Movement, a fact that provided the backbone for the movement. Young volunteers learned to turn to these women for strength and inspiration. Fannie Lou Hamer was fifty-two years old when she got involved in politics; before that she had not known that African Americans could register to vote. She and her husband lost their jobs because they were determined to utilize that right, and she worked continuously thereafter for the Civil Rights Movement. Sara Evans comments:

> She organized citizenship schools and voter registration projects, endured brutal beatings in jail, and founded the Mississippi Freedom Democratic party to challenge the all-white political structure in that state. Young black

and white volunteers recalled the transforming power of women like Fannie Lou Hamer singing gospel hymns, organizing their communities, risking and suffering for freedom with indomitable pride and dignity. (Evans, *Born*, 271)

Other female leaders, such as Ella Baker, Septima Clark, and Dorothy Cotton, were involved in Martin Luther King, Jr.'s Southern Christian Leadership Conference (SCLC). In 1964, SNCC recruited hundreds of white student volunteers, many from the North, to participate in Freedom Summer, a mass voter registration drive in the deep South. The presence of white students drew the attention of the media as well as the government to the movement. Part of this reaction was due to hegemonic white society's protective attitudes toward young, white women. Basing their goals on an ideal of "beloved community," white and black students worked together to organize and teach in freedom schools, run libraries, canvass for voter registration, and generally raise political awareness among black communities in the South. The idea of radical equality, argued by former members of SNCC, influenced the goals of the Women's Liberation Movement.

Yet, despite SNCC's egalitarian platform and the involvement of black women in discussions of equality, tensions developed, often sexual and racial. Women frequently felt discriminated against within its ranks, with gender divisions in assignments a particular sore point later on. Black and white women did virtually all the typing and clerical work for SNCC, as well as the housework around the freedom house. But while these experiences reinforced stereotypical roles for women, other assignments—door-to-door voter registration and allied fieldwork—developed women's organizational and leadership skills.

This division of labor provoked intense discussion within the movement. At a staff retreat in November 1964, a paper entitled "Women in the Movement" was anonymously distributed. The authors, later revealed as Mary King and Casey Hayden, discussed various incidents in which women in SNCC had been discriminated against. Flora Davis calls this paper "the first blow struck for women's liberation," but the women were actually more concerned with patching up the existing movement than creating a new one (75).

By February 1965, SNCC had grown disillusioned with white membership and the disorder of the movement. (Many white students had stayed on after the summer of 1964 to become SNCC staff members.) Black members argued that SNCC should be black-dominated, black-led, and more structured. Black nationalism became a key issue, with the male-led Black Panther Party forming in 1965. Many whites in SNCC agreed that their presence was causing dissension. King and Hayden wrote a memo to other women in the movement, later published in *Liberation*, questioning sex-stereotyped roles. Many women began to question their participation in male-dominated and male-led organizations.

Such discrimination, furthermore, inspired a number of black women to become involved in the renewed struggle for women's rights that began in the late 1960s and early 1970s. They included Dorothy Height, president of the National Council of Negro Women, lawyer Pauli Murray, union leaders Aileen Hernandez and Addie Wyatt, Representative Shirley Chisholm, and Fannie Lou Hamer. Florynce Kennedy, who formed the Media Workshop in 1966, an organization that dealt with racism in the media and advertising, also participated in protests waged by the National Organization of Women against sexism in the *New York Times* and Colgate-Palmolive. She organized protests supporting H. Rap Brown in Cambridge, Maryland in 1966, becoming involved in the Black Power movement as well (Kennedy, 53–58). The links between feminism and ethnicities continued to grow. Women of different ethnic groups, inspired by feminist ideals, took stands that enabled links to be made between gender and race.

Native American women, also faced with challenges of poverty and cultural genocide, were no exception. In 1970, the annual median Native American income was $5,832, compared to a national median of $9,540 (Linden-Ward, 65–66). Ada Deer, of the Menominee tribe, for example, speaks of the years 1961 to 1973 as a "political, economic, and cultural disaster for the Menominee.... Just a few people had the power to make decisions" (Katz, 149).[2] Spiritually and culturally as well as politically based, the American Indian Movement (AIM) was born in 1968. Old traditions of female leadership reemerged, with women such as Mary Ellen Crow Dog (Brave Bird) inspired by these activities to speak her mind. (At Wounded Knee, in South Dakota, at the uprising in 1973, women like Madonnah Thunder Hawk and Gladys Bissonette appeared among the negotiators.)[3] Bissonette and Ellen Moves Camp named that movement: "Go ahead and make your stand at Wounded Knee. If you men won't do it, you can stay here and talk for all eternity and we women will do it" (Crow Dog, 80. See also 124, 189).

Many women participated at Wounded Knee, with Crow Dog recalling their response to a white volunteer nurse who ventured to criticize this "betrayal" of women: "We told her ... we had other priorities." By the seventies, Native American women had formed Women of All the Red Nations. For

African-American and Native American women, civil rights and cultural identity became priorities. Beginning in the sixties, that is, women across boundaries of race and class struggled against a patriarchal system, but within that system, white feminism still assumed certain normative privileges.

These priorities were also critical for Hispanic females, inflected with specifically feminist demands. Although many women worked in the Chicano movement along with men, activities such as the 1969 Chicano Liberation Conference, Women's Caucus, the 1971 National Chicano Conference, and the formation of Concilio Mujeres, Concilio Femenil, and the National Chicana Institute and the National Chicana Foundation also took place. In broader terms, in Martha Cotera's narrative about Chicana participation:

> It began with the Kennedy campaign in the 1960's, continued with social and economic issues in the mid-sixties, and then on to reform in the educational system in the late sixties. Further on, we moved into political participation in 1970 and to the founding of the Raza Unida Party. (*Chicana Feminist*, 17)

One major strategy of Chicanas nationally was to fill important elected positions in Texas; among them was Virginia Musquiz, one of the founders of Raza Unida in Texas and possibly the first Texas Chicana to run for a legislative seat (Cotera, *Profile*, 107–108). Other distinguished Chicanas include Jovita Gonzalez, an anthropologist and writer, and Emma Tenayuca Brooks and Manuela Solis Sager, labor leaders and activists from the area around San Antonio (Cotera, *Chicana Feminist*, 14). Student organizations were formed, such as UMAS (United Mexican American Students), which later changed its name to MECHA (Movimiento Estudiantil Chicano e de Azlan). Women also played a large part in labor organizations such as the United Farm Workers, Cesar Chavez's unique organization that concentrated on the needs of the Mexican-American workers and community. Jesse Lopez de la Cruz, who began working with Chavez in 1962, joined the United Farm Workers in 1967, and committed herself to the task of bringing women into the union. Dolores Huerta, vice president of the union and chief negotiator, began working with Chavez in 1960 (Mirandé & Enríquez, *La Chicana* 233–234). In Sacramento, she went to head a legislative program, "lobbying for benefits like old-age pensions for noncitizens, the right to register voters door to door, the right to take driver's examinations in Spanish, and disability insurance for farm workers" (Mirandé & Enríquez, *La Chicana* 233).

In the student organizations, Chicanas often commented that they felt discriminated against by men in the movement; female leadership was discouraged, and women were relegated to subordinate positions. Due to the discrepancy between what Chicanas saw as the agenda of Anglo feminism and their own agenda, however, Chicanas were not willing to attach themselves to the ethnocentric, white, Women's Movement. The women's caucus at the 1969 Chicano Youth Conference held in Denver, Colorado, emerged with this resolution: "We have come to the consensus that we do not want to be liberated." Yet within two years, the First National Chicana Conference was held in Houston, Texas.

The predominant student organization in the North during the 1960s was Students for a Democratic Society, known as SDS. Prior to the Vietnam War, much of SDS's energy was spent on a project to educate and empower the Northern poor, in much the same way as the SNCC organized indigent black people in the South. Beyond that, with the United States's increasing involvement in Vietnam, particularly after February 1965, student groups concentrated on protesting the war and the draft. Many campuses held all-night sit-ins, educating anyone who would listen about the conflict in Vietnam. Draft resistance was a major concern. On April 17, 1965, SDS organized a march in Washington protesting the Vietnam War, thus locating themselves in the forefront of the antiwar movement.

From its inception, male intellectuals had dominated Students for a Democratic Society as leaders and theorists. Unlike female participants in SNCC, SDS women felt neither welcome nor treated equally. Women undertook menial, everyday tasks in order to support the movement, but rarely spoke publicly on the organization's behalf. Additionally, the New Left's involvement in the draft resistance movement tended to downplay female activists; since women could not be drafted, men felt that they were risking less. Gradually, women's workshops began to appear at SDS conferences and conventions; many simply discussed ways in which women could support the draft resistance movement, but others dealt seriously with women's dissatisfaction and inequality in the movement. Classes for and about women began to be offered in freedom schools and universities across the country.

On another front were older, professional women reacting to the lack of legislation concerning women's issues, concerns that harkened back to the old struggle for the Equal Rights Amendment (ERA). (This struggle is still a legislative battle, not a *fait accompli*.) In December 1961, President Kennedy established the President's Commission on the Status of Women (PCSW), with Eleanor Roosevelt as chairwoman.[4] While that first commission was preparing its report for President Kennedy in 1963, the publication of *The*

Feminine Mystique by Betty Friedan identified white, middle-class, female unrest and traditional assumptions that women should be happy to forgo careers to work at home raising their children. Friedan highlighted the contradiction between the image of women, what was expected of them, and their material/psychological reality.

Commission concerns about the quality of women's lives generated more recognition of the need for a national organization. With Betty Friedan as president, the National Organization for Women (NOW) held its founding conference in Washington, D.C. on October 29 and 30, 1966. At its second annual conference in November 1967, NOW's decision to take a public stand on the ERA and abortion alienated a number of members. On the other hand, the announced agenda also attracted new members.

On the issue of class, the Women's Equity Action League (WEAL), founded in 1968 partly in response to NOW's decision to adopt such a broad agenda, wanted to concentrate more on discrimination against women in jobs and education. Many groups followed suit in forming single-issue organizations; abortion, women's health care, discriminatory law, including the fight to pass Title VII in the Civil Rights Act, were issues in the forefront.

In the academy, activism proceeded apace. Women's studies programs in colleges and universities rapidly grew. In the fall of 1969, according to Davis, there were only seventeen courses offered in this country that directly concerned women. In 1970 that number had risen to over one hundred. By 1971, almost a hundred colleges around the country offered a one-credit course or more. One door was formally opening to a fundamental change in the traditional academy that stressed interdisciplinary studies and the link between activism and scholarship.

But the split that had been developing in the white movement became undeniable by 1968 to 1969. In the summer of 1967, a group of women in Chicago's Students for a Democratic Society formed a splinter group, out of which, in 1969, New York Radical Women and the Redstockings eventually emerged (Fritz, 25–27). In the same year, 1969, an offshoot of New York Radical Women—WITCH—burned voter registration cards at the counter-inaugural demonstration. The complex background to the split partly involved controversies over homophobia and class.

Let us back up for a moment to connect the two different strands: first, the sixties offered new avenues for struggle, and inspired many lesbians to come to renewed self-definitions despite historical hostility and employment and housing discrimination. Many lesbian feminists were movement leaders. Prior to the sixties, Del Martin and Phyllis Lyon had formed the Daughters of Bilitis, publishing *The Ladder* from 1956 to 1972—"the voice of the lesbian in America" (Damon, 298). Antihomosexual laws, however, remained on the books in major cities and states, and official harassment was common (Longauex y Vasquez, 382).

According to Leah Fritz, at the beginning of the Women's Movement lesbians remained outside or closeted within it:

> In NOW and most of the early radical groups, however, lesbianism was a forbidden subject or barely tolerated as an aberration. The *right* of lesbians to exist within some groups was acknowledged, but their *need* for specific recognition and approval was ignored. To NOW, lesbians were an embarrassment; to Marxists, they were a "problem" caused by capitalism; to heterosexual radical feminists, they were invisible. (32)

Martha Shelley alludes to the difficulties when she spoke about picketing the Miss America pageant in 1968: "the most terrible epithet heaped on our straight sisters was 'lesbians'" (308). The gay-straight split became a deeply controversial issue. With her lesbian conspiracy notions, Betty Friedan fanned the flames of the debate.

Second, socialist feminists differed with radical feminists over origins: the former viewed patriarchy as stemming from the division of society into classes; radical feminists, on the other hand, stressed female autonomy. The principal enemies were denoted as capitalism and patriarchy, respectively (Deckard, 455). Thus by 1968 the radical feminist movement was taking shape; socialist feminist groups sometimes functioned autonomously, sometimes collectively within the parent "left" group.

Women's liberation and consciousness-raising groups were forming around the country (Echols, 5). Over the past three decades, cross-class and cross-race feminists have experienced both disaffection and solidarity. Ideological debates about which oppression to "privilege"—class, race, sexual preference, or gender—became urgent and ubiquitous. Myths about a collective, politically unified left and "womanhood" were finally and visibly exploding. The New Left and the Women's Liberation Movement had parted company. The baiting that ensued is now legendary.

* * *

If the 1960s in the U.S. were a decade of recognizing the contradictions between women's competence and their power, between American progressives' ideas about equality among men and their inequitable treatment of men of color and women, the sixties also provided the momentum for what is popularly known as "second-wave feminism." Questions were raised in those years. The seventies offered a time for trying out answers—in the bedroom, the kitchen, the public workplace, the community, the national political arena. Some answers were more successful than others, but just as important as proposed solutions were the female voices behind those proposals. Many Americans—male and female—began to try out a new language in which "she" was as acceptable as "he" in the third person singular, in which "Miss" and "Mrs." conflated into "Ms." and in which "girls" had become "women." In some senses, the 1970s was the "women's studies decade," with a startling growth of feminist coursework in several U.S. academic institutions, the founding of women's committees in many disciplines, and the establishment of the National Women's Studies Association. Then, because of huge strides toward equality at home, at work, and in the public consciousness, feminists and women in general became subject to a stunning backlash of negative and/or violent images of independent women conducted by the televangelists, the Catholic Church, the mass media, the Republican Party, and an increasing number of "New Right" organizations, such as the Eagle Forum spearheaded by Phyllis Schlafly.

In the early 1970s, four major sources of national momentum for feminists were the proposal for a national Equal Rights Amendment, congressional passage of Title IX of the Education Amendments of 1972, the Supreme Court decision in *Roe versus Wade*, and the aftershocks from the "Stonewall" police attack on a Greenwich Village gay bar. In establishing a woman's legal right to an abortion (within certain prescribed limits), the 1973 Supreme Court decision had the immediate impact of giving women more control over their bodies. It saved lives and changed lives. The ERA debate provided a platform for the discussion of the inequities experienced by women as workers and citizens. Congress sent the bill out to be ratified by the States in 1972, and a ten-year debate followed. Also in 1972, passage of Title IX supported the claim of U.S. women on education, and thus had resonance for the hiring of scholars in universities and the purchasing of equipment for junior high school girls' basketball teams. Stonewall was a point of no return for lesbians and gay men in the country. Six months before the beginning of the seventies, the raid on a Manhattan tavern ignited a gay and lesbian rights movement that manifested itself in public parades, self-help switchboards, legal aid centers, political lobbying, and caucuses among artists and scholars. Among the battles lesbians began to face was the confrontation of homophobia within the Women's Movement.

Although some antifeminists claim the second wave of feminism was a white, middle-class movement, in fact many of the early 1970s activists were women of color. In 1970, the North American Indian Association was founded by women from forty-three tribes. In 1971, six hundred Chicanas met at the first nationwide Chicana conference, where they passed a platform calling for legalized abortion and a resolution rebuking the Catholic Church. The Conference of Puerto Rican Women was founded in 1972. The next year the National Black Feminist Organization was founded (Hartmann, 70–71).

American courtrooms began to echo with women's voices in class action job discrimination suits and sexual harassment litigation. Meanwhile, the field of women's health was revolutionized by the publication of *Our Bodies, Ourselves* (1971), the exposure of forced sterilizations of women of color and poor women, broader distribution of contraceptives, and the establishment of women's health clinics. Karla Jay describes one of them in *Lavender Culture*:

> The health care workers explained to me in advance everything they were going to do and why. They also used simple language instead of the jargonese [that] straight, male physicians had used. And since the clinic took me seriously as a woman, they took my body seriously. The fee for this was $3 a few years ago when it opened. (61)

U.S. arts were changed with the opening of feminist and lesbian feminist galleries, theatre groups such as At The Foot of the Mountain in Minneapolis and the Westbeth Playwright's Feminist Collective in New York, and bookstores such as A Room of One's Own in Madison. The workplace was being redefined by pressure for better wages and working conditions (including maternity leave and day care). Indeed, the whole notion of paid work was being challenged by concepts such as comparable worth and salaried housework. Each of these changes resonated with others. One shift created another social disruption, and more territory was opened for question.

Books were among the most significant forces for social change, and the early 1970s revealed a revolution with the publication of Toni Cade Bambara's *The Black Women* (1970), Robin Morgan's *Sisterhood is Powerful* (1970), Eva Figes's *Patriarchal Attitudes* (1970), Shulamith Firestone's *The Dialectic of Sex* (1970), and Germaine Greer's *The Female Eunuch* (1971). The Feminist Press published its first book in 1971. *Ms.* Magazine was founded in 1972. Other channels of feminist communication included private conversation, consciousness-raising groups, rallies and demonstrations, feminist reporters gaining space in the mainstream media, and an increasingly aware female constituency on every level of the educational ladder.

With the passage of Title IX, it was safe to say women's studies was here to stay. In 1973, there were approximately 5,000 women's studies courses in the United States. By 1980, over 20,000 courses existed. By the end of the 1970s there were 350 women's studies programs around the country. Although these programs and ethnic studies programs were growing, women faculty and faculty of color still held fewer positions and positions of much lower rank than their white, male colleagues. It became clear that the project of reclaiming the academy had to take place on several fronts at once: hiring, promotion, and publication, as well as pedagogy. Women began to organize within disciplines to found committees and caucuses and to create interdisciplinary journals. The Modern Language Association's Women's Caucus first met in 1970. *Feminist Studies* was first published in 1972, and the first issue of *Signs* appeared in 1975. Feministas Unidas was founded in 1977. The National Women's Studies Association and *Sojourner: A Third World Women's Research Newsletter* were founded in 1977. In 1978, the Association of Black Women Historians was formed. Also emerging in the 1970s were women's research facilities and campus centers for outreach to community women.

The publication rate of articles on women and women's issues in journals of history, literature, education, and anthropology increased more than threefold between 1970 and 1980 (DuBois, 16). As the authors of *Feminist Scholarship: Kindling in the Groves of Academe* explain:

> The cumulative effect of the feminist critiques of the disciplines was to establish incontrovertibly the existence and varieties of male bias in traditional academic inquiry. This bias, however inadvertent, accepts and perpetuates the ideology of female inferiority. Whether the particular discipline has almost completely neglected women—as in history or philosophy—or treated them as incidental to central issues of research—as in literature or anthropology—or considered gender as an important factor for research—as in education—feminist scholars have shown that the assumption that male behavior and experience are the norm for the entire human race is common to all. So, too, do all the disciplines, whatever their other differences, provide a truncated and distorted picture of women, which reflects and justifies our society's oppressive stereotypes of what it is to be female. (36)

Academic feminist solidarity was not uncomplicated, and the feminist harmony was interrupted and stimulated by constituencies of women of color and lesbians who demanded a deeper commitment to inclusiveness. In 1974, less than one percent of the women's studies courses in the U.S. listed a focus on black women. As Gloria T. Hull and Barbara Smith write, in the introduction to the groundbreaking *All The Women Are White, All the Blacks Are Men, But Some of Us Are Brave: Black Women's Studies:*

> Clearly, then, if one looks for "hard data" concerning curriculum relating to Black women in the existing studies of academic insitutions, we are seemingly nonexistent. And yet impressionistically and experientially it is obvious that more and more study is being done about Black women and, even more importantly, it is being done with an increasing consciousness of the impact of sexual-racial politics on Black women's lives. One thinks, for instance, of Alice Walker's groundbreaking course on Black women writers at Wellesley College in 1972, and how work of all sorts by and about Black women writers has since blossomed into a visible Black female literary "renaissance." (xxvi)

As progress was being made in the schools, the courts, the hospitals and the living rooms in the 1970s, right-wing men and women grew more and more nervous, and a powerful backlash ensued. Feminists emerged as enemies of the family and terrorists undermining the basic fabric of American life. In 1977, poor women's access to abortion was severely curtailed by the passage of the Hyde Amendment, legislation that only accelerated the antiabortion movement in the years to come. The Equal Rights Amendment was attacked as the harbinger of such disasters as homosexual marriage, women in combat, and unisex public toilets. Gradually, initial support for the legislation eroded as it was challenged by the Daughters of the American Revolution, the National Council of Catholic Women, fundamentalist Protestant preachers, and lobbying organizations such as the Eagle Forum and smaller groups such as Utah's HOTDOGS (Humanitarians Opposed to the Degradation of Our Girls), which is affiliated with the John Birch Society (Hartmann, 135). Meanwhile, in municipalities around the country, lesbian and gay rights legislation was being defeated by homophobic activists. No doubt much of the antifeminism was fueled by the collective male ego wounded in our defeat in and withdrawal from Vietnam. In every phase of personal and public life, feminist gains were being eroded by what Susan Hartmann calls the "Countermobilization."

If the 1960s was a period during which women activists participated in and faced the contradictions of their unfair treatment in the New Left and Civil Rights movements, the 1970s was a decade when many women looked more closely at misogyny, and began to name and organize against numerous forms of violence against women. The FBI reported that every thirty seconds an American woman was raped and every eighteen seconds a woman was battered. Police observed that rape was increasingly accompanied by whippings, beatings or mutilation (Miner, 1981, 48). In 1970, New York Radical Feminists called a "Rape Speak Out." NOW started a Rape Task force in 1973. All over the country, as women were alerted to the dangers of rape, they tried to raise the consciousness of the courts, started self-defense courses and established rape crisis centers. By the end of the decade, forty states had new or revised rape statutes. Likewise, women made battery a public issue. The first feminist shelter was established in St. Paul, Minnesota in 1971, the product of a consciousness-raising group. As with rape, the public understanding of battery came about through feminist community organizing, educational panels, electoral lobbying, in-service training for police and hospital workers, and the establishment of sanctuaries for women who had been battered. By 1980, there were three-hundred shelters nationally (Hartmann, 122–124).

By the late seventies, it had become apparent that the decade would bring both gains and losses, and that feminist strengths were threats to the orthodox of all stripes. Emblematic of this tension was the extravaganza of the National Women's Conference held in Houston in November, 1977. Two thousand delegates came from all over the country to discuss and vote on a national action platform. Issues affecting women of color and lesbians were well-represented. One of the most dramatic moments in the conference was when Betty Friedan, who had often been antagonistic to lesbians, spoke about the importance of homosexual rights. The delegates articulated strong support for child care, welfare reform, and abortion rights. Meanwhile, the streets outside the conference hall were a carnival of right-wing protest. Born-again Christians carried signs warning about eternal damnation. Phyllis Schlafly held a flag-draped press conference. And the national press had a field day.

At the end of the decade, the ground was laid for feminist advance and misogynist attack. In striking contrast to the large gains made with relative speed at the beginning of the 1970s by women inside and outside the academy, feminists now found increasing friction in every sphere. Women's rights activists began with the impetus and organizational tactics used successfully in the Civil Rights and Anti-War movements. Over the years, the New Right had learned to emulate some of these same strategies. Many feminists underestimated the deep and enduring nature of conservative resistance, and miscalculated the Right's material means to support that resistance. Perhaps some of us expected consciousness to be contagious. Perhaps a more philosophical aspect of the problem is related to the rhetorical limits of the discourse of equality. To a conservative, this abstract liberal ideal is vulnerable to all sorts of panic-ridden interpretations. Its generously unspecific nature invites abusive misrepresentation, such as the notion that affirmative action is "reverse discrimination" and that gay and lesbian civil rights ordinances are calling for "special rights." In the academy, once-amused male colleagues were now responding more seriously and sourly to the growth of feminist books, articles, journals, and classes. Antifeminist harassment was being launched in the form of censorship, ridicule, job discrimination, and personal threat. Then, in 1980, U.S. voters elected Ronald Reagan, and fell into a long sleep.

* * *

The culture wars of the 1980s and 1990s include among their various targets feminism and feminists. U.S. culture is in the midst of an antifeminist rebound (unfortunately not the first time in U.S. history), directed against feminism as a theoretical approach and against feminists personally. The contemporary version has its own particular "New Right" face, even a grimace, that differs from those of the 1920s, or the 1940s but evokes older rallying forces such as laissez-faire economics and the glorification of family values, of femininity, and of motherhood within traditional nuclear models. However, feminism has an activist impulse. This enables constructive alliances with other oppressed groups, and brings feminism's goals in the 1980s and 1990s into conjunction with those of ethnic and multicultural studies. Hence, we witness that antifeminism in this period is accompanied often by antagonism to ethnic and multicultural studies. Negative reactions to feminism in academia, popular culture, and mass media today are camouflaged, even mystified, by wider attacks on women's studies, ethnic studies, and affirmative action policies. Further, such antiprogressive stances take refuge in the popular slogan of "political correctness," which is evoked in order to undercut modest progress in the educational and cultural life of the U.S.: the varied impacts of feminist thought inside and outside the academy, the establishment of women's studies and ethnic studies programs in academic institutions, and social welfare programs.

Antifeminism takes a variety of overt and subtle forms—intellectual devaluing and ridicule of feminist ideas, political baiting of feminists, and at times, physical threats. Antifeminist backlashes are targeted against feminism as a discipline and on feminists personally, often against the *perceived* power of feminists in contemporary times. Adherents of a traditional gender status quo portray a few well-established and visible feminist scholars as threatening. Such "threats" severely misrepresent the majority of women, who continue to endure vast gender inequities in this democratic nation. The attacks may be directed against women self-identified as feminists or those labelled with hostile intent as "feminists." A case in point is the man who gunned down fourteen women in a University of Montreal classroom because they were "all a bunch of fucking feminists."

It is important to recognize that these cultural wars are not simply academic matters. Part of a national debate, they seep into our daily lives through popular culture and mass-media rhetoric against poor people, gays and lesbians, immigrants,[5] and against safe abortions and other reproductive rights,[6] as well as, increasingly, in opposition to affirmative action. These negative messages against women and minorities enter both private and public spaces, broadcast into our living rooms via radio and television, discussed in our classrooms, reported in newspapers and magazines.

Susan Faludi provocatively discusses some of these issues in her book, *Backlash: The Undeclared War Against American Women.* Her introduction, ironically titled, "Blame It on Feminism" demystifies the many "grievances that contemporary American women have about their private and public lives" (ix). Popular media both celebrates and undercuts women's successes, often facetiously blaming feminism for women's unhappiness. "It must be all that equality that's causing all that pain," remarks Faludi, tongue in cheek. "Women are unhappy precisely because they are free."

In academia, Faludi cites how certain "experts" in legal studies, economics, sociology, and demography uphold that "equality doesn't mix with marriage and motherhood." And joining this bandwagon of attacks on feminism are some women who nonetheless consider themselves "feminist," and who are welcomed particularly by the mainstream publishing industry. What better than one of our own to condemn our goals, such as a successful career woman who bemoans the shortcomings of feminism (similar to non-white Dinesh D'Souza, who does the dirty work against minorities even better than a William Bennett or an Allan Bloom)? Let us call them gender insiders, these antifeminist feminists who are given increasing attention by a mainstream media that made Camille Paglia, "an embittered antifeminist academic ... [into] an overnight celebrity, landing [her] on the cover of *New York* and *Harper's* the same month, soon after launching a vitriolic attack on 'whining' feminists in her 1990 book *Sexual Personae: Art and Decadence from Nefertiti to Emily Dickinson*" (Faludi, 319).[7] The press merrily cashes in on Paglia's "antifeminist zingers," such as "If civilization had been left in female hands, we would still be living in grass huts." In her Preface to *Sexual Personae,* she notes, "My method is a form of sensationalism: I try to flesh out intellect with emotion.... Whenever sexual freedom is sought or achieved, sadomasochism will not be far behind.... Sex is a far darker power than feminism has admitted" (xiii, 3).

A few deriders of feminism such as Paglia receive much publicity, whereas among women in general, "75 to 95 percent credit the feminist campaign with improving their lives," states Faludi. "In public opinion surveys, women consistently rank their own inequality, at work and at home, among their most urgent concerns" (xv). Sadly, economic and social equality between men and women is hardly a reality when women constitute "two-thirds of all poor adults," and when "American women face the worst gender-based pay gap in the developed world" (Faludi, xiii). The fact that women still have to fight for an Equal Rights Amendment, for reproductive rights, maternity leave, affordable child care, and safe abortions[8] demonstrates that social, economic, and political equality for women is a long way off.

The 1980s backlash has a particular history, as do earlier ones in U.S. history. Each wave of antifeminism—1920s, 1940s, late 1970s—arises after certain gains in women's rights, and aims to erode such successes. Lois W. Banner remarks how the 1920s antifeminism, though "extensive ... rarely denied women the right to live their lives as they saw fit. But the anti-feminism of the postwar 1940s held women responsible for society's ills— either because they were failures as mothers or because they had left home for work" (212).[9] After the war, "'Rosie the Riveter' was replaced by the homemaker as the national feminine model." Women were bombarded by jingoistic psychologists who declared with dubious "scientific" evidence that women working outside the home were playing havoc with their children's mental states.

Contemporary antifeminism began in the late seventies among the religious Right. This fundamentalist thinking moved into the White House in the eighties with Reagan, and, by the mid-eighties, it had become socially acceptable to challenge women's struggles for equality. In her discussion of "Ironies of the 1980s," in *Born for Liberty,* Sara M. Evans notes that although "political feminism found hard times [during the Reagan era] ... cultural transformations gave it advantages it had never had before.... [Reaganomics could not] significantly alter the gender shifts that had already taken place.... The real battle was over the meaning of those changes both for individuals and for society" (307).

The eighties saw substantial gains and losses for women. Support for ERA was very high in 1981, yet the amendment was struck down in 1982. Rather than the goal of equality being achieved, it was precisely the fear of women moving towards it that was perceived as a threat. Women's advancement in the workforce, however minimal in terms of actual numbers, was regarded with hostility—more than one woman (or minority) was often too many.[10]

Antifeminism of the 1980s and 1990s has operated in often insidious ways. Its uniqueness lies in its clever use of the very hard-earned *gains* of the feminist movement against women; women's successes are turned around as the very reasons for women's *losses.* The particularity of our current backlash lies in the increased power and capabilities of the media, including computerized information superhighways, electronic international mail networks, and other access into virtual realities that can ignore, negate, or render invisible the real conditions governing people's ordinary lives. Hollywood movies, popular psychology, conservative talk radio shows have found ways to turn on their head such goals as autonomy and independence that feminism struggled for, as if these gains in women's self-reliance are responsible now for all of women's ills, whether depression, unemployment, or teenage pregnancy. Publications, as different as the *New York Times, Vanity Fair, The Nation* have issued indictments against the women's movement with such headlines as "When Feminism Failed or The Awful Truth About Women's Lib"; "Professional women are suffering 'burnout' and succumbing to an 'infertility epidemic'"; "Single women are grieving from a 'man shortage'" (Faludi, ix). These myths, which ascribe women's woes to feminism, wish to do away with this "obsolete" feminist "thing." Other periodic outbursts of antifeminism are evident in increased incidents of violence against women (anti-abortionists, for instance, firebombing clinics, or threatening and killing doctors); culturally legitimized, even valorized violence in popular films; Rush Limbaugh's vastly popular radio shows with his humorous jibes at "femi-Nazi feminists."

One deleterious effect of contemporary antifeminism is that it has created a huge wedge between the very few celebrity women who have "made it," some of whom divorce themselves from the Women's Movement, and the vast numbers of working-class and working women who are still struggling for equal wages. Another tactic deployed by antifeminists is to pretend to be apolitical. On the contrary, attacks on feminism, whether in academia, popular culture, or mass media, are rooted in the conservative political climate of the eighties and nineties. These decades may well be remembered as a period of mean-spiritedness, of simplistic assertions of "individual rights and responsibilities" divorced from social and civic conscience. Attempts to dismantle affirmative action are veiled, often dishonestly, as "re-evaluations of an imperfect system." The loudest opponents of so-called reverse discrimination (beleaguered white men who feel that America for Americans—read "white"—is slipping away from their grip) have found new scapegoats in the nineties—immigrants, gays and lesbians (ballot initiatives in Oregon and Colorado), women and children (congressional debates about cutting off school lunchs and aid to welfare mothers).

Contemporary antifeminist attacks are similarly launched by conservative upholders of ostensibly "value-free" scholarship and "pure" literary traditions. These adherents of a Western canonical tradition of humanistic learning are hostile not only to women's studies, but also to ethnic and multicultural studies. Their intellectual assaults are mounted often on the rhetoric of "political correctness," colloquially known as "PC." This anti–PC campaign undertakes overt and covert attacks on feminism as an ideology, with exaggerated claims of the power of feminists.

The difficulties of delineating the parameters of political correctness lie in the fluidity of the concept and its problematic appropriation by right-wing demagogues. Ironically, the loudest protestors who claim to be "silenced" by progressive aspects of feminism and multiculturalism invoke political correctness as a slogan to cut off debate and discussion. The most vociferous protectors of "free speech" see no contradiction in shutting up the voices of women and minorities.

Since antifeminist attacks are often couched in the rhetoric of accusations of political correctness, it is useful to examine two documents with opposing viewpoints—one by the conservative National Association of Scholars (NAS), and the other (formulated in response to NAS) by the liberal/progressive Teachers for a Democratic Culture (TDC). Patricia Aufderheide's *Beyond PC: Towards a Politics of Understanding* presents a provocative selection of voices for and against this concept. Aufderheide's introduction attempts to define this slippery term:

> Is the issue, as *Newsweek* charged in the December 1990 cover story that triggered the media onslaught about PC, "totalitarian ways of teaching on American campuses?" Or, is it, as some in this anthology charge, largely a figment of the right-wing imagination, a strategy aimed at junking such programs as affirmative action? (1)

The National Association of Scholars has grown since 1987 to nearly 1,700 members with affiliates in twenty-five states. This Princeton, New Jersey-based group of traditionalists see themselves as "a disenfranchised minority within the academy." Many of their projects are funded by conservative foundations such as John Olin.[11] NAS puts forward its manifesto objecting to any kind of preferential provisions for women or minorities in recruitment, hiring, and retention. NAS believes that such "policies and practices involve either the application of a double standard or the repudiation of appropriate intellectual criteria.... Safeguarding intellectual freedom is of critical importance to the academy" (Aufderheide, 8). NAS objects to forms of "discriminatory harassment" that involve "punitive codes restricting 'insensitive' speech ... requirements that students take tendentious courses dealing with groups regarded as victimized" (8). The inclusion of race, gender, and class "relentslessly ... in preference to all other approaches to assessing the human condition" leads to increasing division on campus. NAS proposes that ethnic or gender studies courses should be allowed only if "they have genuine scholarly content and are not vehicles for political harangue or recruitment" (10); it opposes "trendy methodologies" that include feminism. Its goals of fostering objective, humanistic knowledge are based on the claim that each individual be evaluated "on the basis of personal achievement and promise." A journal called *Heterodoxy: Articles and Animadversions on Political Correctness and Other Follies* also includes women's studies and feminists among its attacks. In a cover story, "Women's Studies Imperialists," conservative anxieties are vented about "queer studies" and about women's studies' attempts to get "integrated" and to transform the curriculum rather than stay in their own "female" ghetto. Prominent feminist scholars like Johnnella Butler, Catharine Stimpson, Bettina Aptheker are ridiculed, whereas Camille Paglia, who derides women's studies as upholding "unchallenged groupthink," or Christina Hoff Sommers, who finds "quack scholarship" in the discipline, are applauded. The article also lambastes the Ford Foundation for supporting women's studies enterprises.[12]

In response to the concerted NAS campaign to malign the gains of diversity, feminism, and multiculturalism, and to present "an alarming picture of the state of contemporary education as a catastrophic collapse," a group called Teachers for a Democratic Culture (TDC) was formed.[13] TDC supports "curricular reforms influenced by multiculturalism and feminism," and asserts democratic principles of discussion and debate that are valued in U.S.

education. TDC notes that, given the political changes of the last twenty years or so, women and minorities are present in increasing numbers in institutions of higher learning, and that their presence has inspired and often instigated curricular reforms. TDC contests the many "false claims" made by alarmists who believe that race and gender issues are taking precedence over the classics of Western civilization, "that teachers across the land are being silenced and politically intimidated; that the very concepts of reason, truth, and artistic standards are being subverted in favor of a crude ideological agenda." Rather, counters TDC, NAS and media supporters "are endangering education with a campaign of harassment and misrepresentation." A conservative trajectory similar to NAS's is evident in certain disturbing questions raised in Karen Lehrman's campus interviews with students: "Is women's studies failing women? Is feminist education limiting her potential?" (Lehrman, 45–51, 64–68).

Whereas TDC supports open discusion and debate "about the relations of culture, scholarship, and education to politics," NAS touts objectivity and humanistic knowledge, and insists that the "'truths' of 'Western civilization' should be the basis for our educational system." Manning Marable, in his column, "Along the Color Line: Why Conservatives Fear Multiculturalism," contests this claim to truth:

> As a professor of history, I know that there is no "truth" in anyone's history or textbooks. The history books in the past always reflected the interests and perspectives of people in power in America. That's why, until recently, Native Americans, Latinos, and African-Americans were excluded from all textbooks, and our achievements were ignored or stolen. When oppressed people successfully struggle for their democratic rights, the textbooks inevitably are changed.... Why are conservative intellectuals and foundations so frightened by multiculturalism? Behind their public rhetoric are several political realities.... By attacking multicultural education and affirmative action, they are deliberately manipulating racial and gender symbols to mobilize their supporters. (11)

The neoconservatives claim fallaciously that their educational goals of objectivity and truth as embodied in traditional humanistic teaching are devoid of political intent. As Catharine Stimpson remarks, "The attack on diversity is a rhetorical strategy by neoconservatives who have their own political agenda. Under the guise of defending objectivity and intellectual rigor, which is a lot of mishmash, they are trying to preserve the cultural and political supremacy of white heterosexual males" (quoted in Taylor, 32–40).

NAS grew out of a group who felt that they could not speak freely on issues such as affirmative action or feminism. They wanted the freedom to express racist or sexist views. John Taylor's essay, "Are You Politically Correct?" lumps together, in his own words, "the new fundamentalists" who include "an eclectic group" comprised of "multiculturalists, feminists, radical homosexuals, Marxists, New Historicists. What unites them ... is their conviction that Western culture and American society are thoroughly and hopelessly racist, sexist, oppressive" (34). Taylor cites several sensationalized examples, such as the incident at Harvard University when Professor Stephan Thernstrom was criticized for "racial insensitivity" in his course "Peopling in America." Faced with these "new fundamentalists," Thernstrom felt branded and accused, and he dropped the course. More recently, Rutgers University President, Francis Lawrence, was caught in a storm instigated by his comment that African-American students performed poorly on standardized tests because of their "genetic, hereditary background." Calls for Lawrence's resignation were averted not only because of his record as "a longtime civil rights advocate," but by evoking political correctness: Did he "accidentally stumble into a controversial topic" asks Helaine Olen, "and is now falling victim to the vengeful winds of political correctness?" (A5).

In this climate of political conservatism, any criticism of racist or sexist views is regarded as silencing by a politically correct "thought police." Rather, as Stimpson points out, it is useful in our diverse society to develop greater sensitivity to language and to take "insulting language seriously." But such attempts are seen as trampling on freedom of expression, and on demanding "intellectual conformity enforced with harassment and intimidation." Taylor cites Camille Paglia, who likens this harassment to "fascism of the left," and Thernstrom, who characterizes it as "a new McCarthyism." In a similar victimology, Taylor translates the claims of the "gender feminists," who argue that "Western society is organized around a 'sex/gender system,' characterized by male dominance," very quickly and glibly into misanthropic attacks on males, the family, and heterosexuality. His discussion on date rape makes a mockery of the hard-won gains in defining the parameters of sexual assault. To give a legal name to social violence, whether it be "date rape," or "sexual harassment," named some thirty years ago, or what today we call antifeminist harassment, is threatening to the sexual status quo upheld by writers like Taylor.

The kinds of policing perpetrated blatantly by bodies such as NAS, however, are considered acceptable, the kinds that appear in NAS's journal, *Academic Questions*, which, as Jacob Weisberg notes, harps on "a few themes": "Academic feminism, in its various manifestations, is attacked in almost every issue. An article by Boston University sociologist Brigitte Berger equates the work of feminist Evelyn Fox Keller with Nazi physics. Peace studies, Critical Legal Studies" also come under attack (Weisberg, 83). Rather than desperately enforcing "a common culture" (à la Allan Bloom and E.D. Hirsch), Henry Giroux's suggestion from the opposite pole is worth considering—we need "a common ground for dialogue" within a truly democratic educational space. No master narratives with an *a priori* authority. Democracy, according to Giroux, "is expressed not in moral platitudes but in concrete struggles and practices that find expression in classroom social relations, everyday life, and memories of resistance and struggle" (8, 13). In its frenzied protection of a narrowly defined academic freedom and the sanctity of Western civilization, NAS has no compunction about attacking feminists. NAS's closed-mindedness would not even stop to consider that opening up the canon to the voices of women and minorites does not necessarily displace and silence canonic figures. As Stimpson explains, "To expand the canon is to enhance culture, not destroy it" (quoted in Weisberg, 86). Further, NAS's much-touted value of "objectivity" vanished when Lynne Cheney, head of the National Endowment for the Humanities, persuaded the Senate "to approve eight of her nominees, at least half of them members of the conservative National Association of Scholars" (Thompson & Tyagi, xv).

The extent to which neoconservative demagogues direct affairs, as university trustees or lawmakers, was demonstrated in a recent fracas when Angela Davis received a prestigious professorial award of $75,000 from the University of California, Santa Cruz to develop new ethnic studies courses at that institution over two and a half years. Republican lawmakers, uncomfortable with Davis's past (when she was wanted by the FBI, then tried and found *not* guilty of "murder and kidnapping [when] guns belonging to Davis were used in a shootout in Marin County" [Wallace, A27]), asked University of California President Jack W. Peltason to revoke the award. Senator Bill Leonard commented, "At a time when we're trying to reconcile racial and gender differences, here's a person who's made a career of exacerbating those differences." He goes on to make a horrific analogy: honoring Davis is like celebrating a professor "who happened to have a side life as a grand dragon of the Ku Klux Klan. I see her as the leftist equivalent of that." Racist and sexist slurs, harassment of an intellectual, a feminist, are all part of "a concerted assault," as Davis herself put it, "against multicultural education." More specifically, neoconservatives also intend to attack the kind of research that this grant will support—Davis will use half the stipend "to create a Research Cluster on Women of Color in Collaboration and Conflict, which will develop curricula and host conferences" (Wallace, A3).

The conservative reaction to the increasing presence of women and minorities and to ethnic programs on campuses hardly recognizes facts and statistics, and dramatically exaggerates shifts in power. As Becky Thompson and Sangeeta Tyagi note: "Most college and university faculties in the United States still include less than 5 percent people of color. Only 13 percent of the full professors are women (of any race) compared to 10 percent in 1974, and 2.2 percent of full professors are African-American men or women" (xvi). These cultural wars over multiculturalism and political correctness are, as Troy Duster puts it, "about the shifting sands of racial privilege" (32). Ideologues such as Dinesh D'Souza propagate several myths about affirmative action and multiculturalism, namely that they create more divisiveness on campus, and that they dilute standards.[14] Countering these myths, Duster provides concrete historical reasons for affirmative action:

> It exists because over the past two hundred years, blacks and Latinos have had a difficult time entering higher education, and that legacy hasn't gone away.... The gap isn't closing; the economic barriers that restrict minority access to college aren't disappearing.
>
> But Americans' cultural memory lasts about five years, so the idea that affirmative action exists to redress past grievances doesn't resonate with today's students—of all colors. The notion that black people have a past of slavery and discrimination, that this is a fact of American history, is buried so deep in the consciousness of most students that it doesn't surface. The right wing says that if you bring that fact to the fore and teach it, that's called Oppression Studies, or "political correctness," and by telling people of color they should feel good about themselves, you're making white people feel bad about themselves. (32–33)

Dinesh D'Souza is a classic example of a race insider, a person of color aligned with a conservative, mainly white belief structure: like Linda Chavez, Clarence Thomas, and V.S. Naipaul, he has been lauded by mainstream media. D'Souza himself has a formidable right-wing record—as a former domestic policy analyst of the Reagan administration, managing editor of the neoconservative *Policy Review*, a founding editor of the *Dartmouth Review*, and a research fellow at the American Enterprise Institute.

D'Souza's essay "The Visigoths in Tweed" sets out the "dangers" that students face in a feminist liberal arts education: "brainwashing that deprecates Western learning and exalts a neo-Marxist ideology promoted in the name of multiculturalism" (12). D'Souza objects to the transformations in core curricula "in the name of diversity and multiculturalism," changes that are "imposed by a university elite, not … voted upon or even discussed by the society at large." His rhetoric and others from NAS have portrayed the "dangers" of multicultural education as though studies of race and gender mark the end of Western civilization.

Conceding limited ground to the need for changing core curriculum—for no other reason than in response to changing student demographics—D'Souza advocates replacing Western by non-Western classics. Hence, the root concept of challenging domination, whether Western, or non-Western, completely escapes him. Further, he objects to various support services for minorities on college campuses, and presents an ahistoricized claim about the necessity of such services for disadvantaged groups. He complains as well about "other groups such as feminists and homosexuals" who "typically get into the game [by] claiming their own varieties of victim status."

Even as D'Souza is zealous in calling for scholarly facts and substantiation, he makes inaccurate claims—for instance, that "a contrived multiculturalism … frequently glamorizes Third World cultures…. In many of them feminism is virtually nonexistent, as indicated by such practices as dowries, widow-burning, and genital mutilation" (19). The fact that these oppressive practices exist does not discount the presence of feminist consciousness, and of numerous women's activist groups that exist all over the Third World. D'Souza would do well to gather scholarly data and facts on these life-and-death matters for women, though such feminist knowledge falls beyond the purview of his educational ideals. He also critiques certain prominent feminist scholars, quoting them simplistically and out of context: Alison Jaggar "denounces the traditional nuclear family as a 'cornerstone of women's oppression,'" and Eve Sedgwick's work seeks to demonstrate "the homosexual bias in Western culture … through papers such as 'Jane Austen and the Masturbating Girl'" (21).

In this conservative climate, which threatens to roll back the hard-won gains of feminist and ethnic studies in the academy and in U.S. culture, it is still important for progressive people to be aware of the pitfalls and problems in the practical implementations of inclusive feminisms and multiculturalisms that respect difference even as they forge coalitions in working towards social change. In other words, given a powerful right-wing onslaught, progressive voices should not be silenced in engaging with troubling issues within well-meaning attempts at diversity in college curricula. So, even as we endorse tolerance, respect for, and knowledge of diverse cultures—some of the goals of a multicultural curriculum—we also recognize that multiculturalism has become a buzzword, and is used by different groups for their own ends. When multiculturalism is fashioned outside a progressive political context, it can be co-opted and appropriated under various "diversity" agendas. Exclusionary practices are common—for instance, white-woman bias in women's studies, or male bias in ethnic studies. As Thompson and Tyagi rightly argue, it is important to include "sophisticated analyses of the simultaneity of oppressions. These analyses absolutely depend upon accounting for multiple identities and sources of power" (xxv).

1994 has seen the ushering in of New Right politicians at the helm of the current Congress, who issue daily declarations of self-serving notions of "individual responsibility" that threaten to cut off assistance to the most vulnerable members of society—the poor, women, children. The Speaker of the House's (Ging)rich followers have no compunction about balancing the budget on the back of the Social Security Trust Fund; Congress can declare war quite blithely on affirmative action, under the subtle and dangerous rubric of "reevaluating a flawed system." Preferential treatment for minorities and women has outlived its time, they assert, citing success stories among women and minorities, "truly American creations" such as Clarence Thomas or Oprah Winfrey.

Even in these lean and mean times, women in this U.S. culture continue to make politicians, community leaders, and academics accountable; they insist on working towards socially responsible agendas where citizenship rights go along with duties and responsibilities, not only for the few and privileged but for the vast majority of working people. Feminists must still face the fact that some of the most basic tenets of feminist consciousness—that women define themselves, that they assert their rights as human beings—remain contested notions. Further, we must challenge the multiplicity of antifeminisms that face us in academia and in our daily lives.

Our historical overview of feminism and antifeminism has taken us from the 1960s civil rights struggle to the 1980s and 1990s culture wars. Today, on the brink of the next century, we recognize that antifeminist harassment is multidimensional, and takes overt or subtle forms. As we combat this current phenomenon, we recognize that feminists have to take on new battles, as attacks on feminism trade roles with hostility to ethnic studies, affirmative action, and multicultural education. The essays in this volume explore many of these issues: antifeminism becomes linked with due process and freedom of speech; with matters of academic advancement; with publishing and review; and with discriminations on the basis of age, race, and sexuality. We must make a concerted effort to name antifeminist harassment as such. This will combat the obfuscation of various discriminations under the problematic evocations of political correctness. Our tasks of naming, discussion, and analysis will bring us to possibilities of working towards a more just and humane society.

Notes

Special thanks to Shannon Olson, Rebecca Pierre, and Gretchen Scherer for their research and technical assistance, and to Jenny Putzi for historical research.

1. See Beal, 138–142. See also "A Black Feminist Statement," 13–22.

2. From a personal conversation between Moira Ferguson and Madonnah Thunder Hawk.

3. Katz, 139.

4. Linden-Ward, 8. By 1967, all fifty states had a similar status-of-women commission, which conducted research, held annual conventions, and sometimes published a newsletter.

5. Witness Proposition 187, a ballot initiative against immigrants that passed by a 59-to-41 margin in California. To the credit of the ACLU and the Mexican-American Legal Defense Fund, an injuction was filed late last year against Proposition 187. "Make no mistake," states the *Daily Bruin*'s Thomas Overton. "Proposition 187 is unconstitutional. It represents a fundamental change in the nature of constitutional rights and benefits in that they are to be applied only to U.S. citizens. If you read through the Constitution, you will find no such disclaimer.... To call our respect for minority rights undemocratic is ridiculous." February 16, 1995: 19.

6. Sara M. Evans points out that by 1980, the National Right to Life Committee "had claimed 11 million members.... For right-to-life activists, abortion offended basic values about the meaning of womanhood, of sexuality, and of human life. They quickly became a significant political force because of their single-issue intensity." *Born for Liberty*, 305.

7. Faludi also cites other antifeminist voices that have joined the backlash. The text that could be "the most damaging to the feminist cause," notes Faludi, is Betty Friedan's *The Second Stage*. "The mother of the modern women's movement," who, in her 1963 classic, *The Feminine Mystique,* first expressed "the problem that has no name," Friedan now recants many of those radical feminist positions as "limited and wrong and distorted" (322–323).

8. Witness the recent onslaught on President Clinton's nominee for Surgeon General, Dr. Foster, whose nomination was in jeopardy because he had performed abortions. Although perfectly legal, abortions are portrayed as morally objectionable by right-wing propagandists and conservative politicians.

9. Banner's text also includes some wonderful photographs. See also Susan B. Anthony's *Out of the Kitchen, into the War* (New York: S. Daye, Inc., 1943); and Faludi, chap. III.

10. For instance, John Silber, President of Boston University charged that his English department "had turned into a 'damn matriarchy'—when only six of its twenty faculty members were women" (Faludi, 64).

11. Marable quotes some staggering figures (reported in *The Chronicle of Higher Education*) of grants given by the Olin Foundation to conservative ideologues such as Dinesh D'Souza, who received $98,400; University of Chicago Professor Allan Bloom, $800,000; civil rights critic Linda Chavez, $25,000; and former Education Secretary William Bennett, $175,000. See also Diamond, 89–96.

12. Billingsley, "Women's Studies Imperialists," in *Heterodoxy* 1, 11–12. Other issues of *Heterodoxy* reflect this concerted campaign against feminist and multicultural studies, with racy titles like "Multicultural Mafia" (October 1992); "PC Riot" (June 1992); and "Transsexuals vs. Lesbians: The Last Battle in the Erogenous Zone" (October 1993).

13. "Statement of Principles," Teachers for a Democratic Culture. In *Beyond PC*, ed. Aufderheide, 67–70.

14. Particularly since the Republican takeover of Congress in November 1994, local newspapers and college campus dailies have been presenting debates on the necessity, or abolition, or reevaluation of affirmative action policies. Some recent examples worth reading include Cathleen Decker, "Affirmative Action Is Under Fire," *Los Angeles Times* (February 19, 1995): 1; J. Eugene Grigsby III, "California's Troubled Economy No Fault of Affirmative Action," *Los Angeles Times* (February 26, 1995): D2; and Clifford M. Tong, "Affirmative Action has Not Outlived Need," *Los Angeles Times* (February 27, 1995): B5.

Works Cited and Consulted

Aisenberg, Nadya and Mona Harrington. *Women of Academe: Outsiders in the Sacred Grove.* Amherst: University of Massachusetts Press, 1988.

Anzaldúa, Gloria, ed. *Making Face/Making Soul/Haciendo Caras: Creative and Critical Perspectives by Women of Color.* San Francisco: Aunt Lute Books, 1990.

Aptheker, Bettina. *Women's Legacy: Essays on Race, Sex, and Class in American History.* Amherst: University of Massachusetts Press, 1982.

Aufderheide, Patricia, ed. *Beyond PC: Toward a Politics of Understanding.* Saint Paul, MN: Graywolf Press, 1992.

Bambara, Toni Cade, ed. *The Black Women: An Anthology.* New York: New American Library, 1970.

Banner, Lois W. *Women in Modern America: A Brief History.* New York: Harcourt Brace, 1974.

Bannerji, Himani, et al. *Unsettling Relations: The University as a Site of Feminist Struggles.* Toronto: Women's Press, 1991.

Bataille, Gretchen and Kathleen M. Sands. *American Indian Women: Telling Their Lives.* Lincoln: University of Nebraska Press, 1984.

———. *American Indian Women: A Guide to Research.* New York: Garland Publishing, Inc., 1991.

Beal, Frances. "Double Jeopardy: To Be Black and Female." *Women and Womanhood in America*, ed. Ronald W. Hoagland. Lexington, MA: D.C. Heath, 1973.

Beers, David. "PC? B.S. Behind the Hysteria: How the Right Invented Victims of PC Police." *Mother Jones* 16:5 (September/October, 1991): 34–35, 64–65.

Bell, Roseann, Bettye J. Parker, and Beverly Guy-Shaftall, eds. *Sturdy Black Bridges: Visions of Black Women in Literature.* Garden City, NY: Anchor, 1979.

Billingsley, K.L. "Women's Studies Imperialists." *Heterodoxy: Articles and Animadversions on Political Correctness and Other Follies* 1:6 (November 1992).

Black Women's Liberation Group, Mount Vernon, New York. "Statement on Birth Control." *Sisterhood is Powerful*, ed. Robin Morgan. New York: Vintage, 1970.

Blea, Irene I. *La Chicana and the Intersection of Race, Class, and Gender.* New York: Praeger, 1992.

Bloom, Allan. *The Closing of the American Mind: How Higher Education has Failed Democracy and Impoverished the Souls of Today's Students.* New York: Simon & Schuster, 1987.

Cantarow, Ellen. "Jessie Lopez de la Cruz," *Moving the Mountain: Women Working for Social Change*, ed. Ellen Cantarow. Old Westbury: The Feminist Press, 1980. 94–151.

Cochran, Jo Whitehorse et al., eds. *Changing Our Power: An Introduction to Women's Studies.* Dubuque: Kendall Hunt, 1988.

Cohen, Marcia. *The Sisterhood.* New York: Simon & Schuster, 1988.

Collins, Patricia Hill. *Black Feminist Thought: Knowledge, Consciousness, and the Politics of Empowerment.* Boston: Unwin Hyman, 1990. Reprint Routledge, 1991.

The Combahee River Collective. "A Black Feminist Statement." *All the Women Are White, All the Blacks Are Men, But Some of Us Are Brave: Black Women's Studies*, eds. Gloria T. Hull, Patricia Bell Scott, and Barbara Smith. Old Westbury, NY: The Feminist Press, 1982. 13–22.

Cotera, Martha P. *The Chicana Feminist.* Austin: Information Systems Development, 1977.

———. *Profile on the Mexican American Woman.* Austin: Statehome Publishing, 1976.

Crow Dog, Mary, with Richard Erdoes. *Lakota Women.* New York: Harper, 1990.

Cruikshank, Margaret. *Lesbian Studies, Present and Future.* New York: The Feminist Press, 1982.

D'Souza, Dinesh. *Illiberal Education: The Politics of Race and Sex on Campus.* New York: Vintage, 1991.

———. "The New Segregation on Campus," *The American Scholar* 60:1 (Winter, 1991): 17–30.

———. "The Visigoths in Tweed." *Beyond PC*, ed. Patricia Aufderheide.

Damon, Gene. "The Least of These: The Minority Where Screams Haven't Yet Been

Heard." *Sisterhood is Powerful*, ed. Robin Morgan. New York: Vintage, 1970.

Davis, Angela. "Reflections on the Black Woman's Role in the Community of Slaves," *Black Scholar* 3 (December, 1971): 2–15.

———. *Angela Davis: An Autobiography*. New York: Random House, 1974.

———. *Culture and Politics*. New York: Random House, 1989.

———. *Race and Class*. New York: Vintage, 1983.

Davis, Flora. *Moving the Mountain: The Women's Movement in America Since 1960*. New York: Simon & Schuster, 1991.

Deckard, Barbara Sinclair. *The Women's Movement: Political, Socioeconomic, and Psychological Issues*. New York: Harper, 1979.

Diamond, Sara. "The Funding of the NAS." *Beyond PC*, ed. Patricia Aufderheide.

DuBois, Ellen Carol et al., eds. *Feminist Scholarship: Kindling in the Groves of Academe*. Urbana and Chicago: University of Illinois Press, 1987.

Duster, Troy. "They're Taking Over and Other Myths about Race on Campus." *Mother Jones* 16:5 (September/October 1991): 30–33, 63–64.

Echols, Alice. *Daring to be BAD: Radical Feminism in America 1967–1975*. Minneapolis: University of Minnesota Press, 1989.

Evans, Sara M. *Born for Liberty: A History of Women in America*. New York: The Free Press, 1989.

———. *Personal Politics: The Roots of Women's Liberation in the Civil Rights Movement and the New Left*. New York: Knopf, 1979.

——— and Harry C. Boyte. *Free Spaces: The Sources of Democratic Change in America*. New York: Harper and Row, 1986.

———. "Women in Twentieth Century America: An Overview." *The American Woman, 1987–88: A Report in Depth*, ed. Sara Rix (for The Women's Research and Education Institute of the Congressional Caucus for Women's Issues). New York & London: Norton, 1987.

Faludi, Susan. *Backlash: The Undeclared War on American Women*. New York: Crown Publishers, Inc., 1991.

———. "Blame it on Feminism." *Mother Jones* 16:5 (September/October, 1991): 24–29.

Figes, Eva. *Patriarchal Attitudes*. New York: Stein and Day, 1970.

Firestone, Shulamith. *The Dialectic of Sex: The Case for Feminist Revolution*. New York: William Morrow and Company, 1970.

Fitzgerald, Maureen, Connie Guberman, and Margie Wolfe, eds. *Still Ain't Satisfied! Canadian Feminism Today*. Toronto: The Women's Press, 1982.

Freeman, Jo, ed. *Woman: A Feminist Perspective*, 3rd ed. Palo Alto: Mayfield, 1984.

Friedan, Betty. *The Feminine Mystique*. New York: Dell, 1963.

Fritz, Leah. *Dreams and Dealers: An Intimate Appraisal of the Women's Movement*. Boston: Beacon Press, 1979.

Giddings, Paula. *When and Where I Enter: The Impact of Black Women on Race and Sex in America*. New York: William Morrow and Company, Inc., 1984.

Giroux, Henry A. *Living Dangerously: Multiculturalism and the Politics of Difference.* New York: Peter Lang, 1993.

Glickman, Rose. *Daughters of Feminists.* New York: St. Martin's, 1993.

Green, Rayna. *Native American Women: A Contexual Bibliography.* Bloomington: Indiana University Press, 1983.

Greer, Germaine. *The Female Eunuch.* New York: McGraw-Hill, 1971.

Harley, Sharon and Rosalyn Terborg-Penn, eds. *The Afro-American Women: Struggles and Images.* Port Washington, NY, and London: Kennikat Press, 1978.

Hartmann, Susan M. *From Margin to Mainstream: American Women and Politics Since 1960.* New York: Knopf, 1989.

Hirsch, E.D., Jr. *Cultural Literacy: What Every American Needs to Know.* Boston: Houghton Mifflin, 1987.

hooks, bell. *Ain't I a Woman: Black Women and Feminism.* Boston: South End Press, 1981.

Hull, Gloria T., Patricia Bell, and Barbara Smith. *All The Women Are White, All the Blacks Are Men, but Some of Us Are Brave: Black Women's Studies.* Old Westbury: The Feminist Press, 1982.

Jay, Karla and Allen Young, eds. *Lavender Culture.* New York: Jove, 1978.

———— and Joanne Glasgow, eds. *Lesbian Texts and Contexts: Radical Revisions.* New York: New York University Press, 1990.

Jones, Jacqueline. *Labor of Love, Labor of Sorrow: Black Women, Work and the Family, From Slavery to the Present.* New York: Vintage, 1985.

Joseph, Gloria I. and Jill Lewis. *Common Differences: Conflicts in Black and White Feminist Perspectives.* New York: Anchor, 1981.

Katz, Jane, ed. *I Am the Fire of Time: Voices of Native American Women.* New York: E. P. Dutton, 1977.

Kennedy, Flo. *Color Me Flo: My Hard Life and Good Times.* Englewood Cliffs, NJ: Prentice-Hall, 1976.

Lehrman, Karen. "Off Course: Is Women's Studies Failing Women?" *Mother Jones.* (September/October, 1993): 45–51, 64–68.

Lerner, Gerda. *Black Women in White America: A Documentary History.* New York: Vintage, 1972.

Linden-Ward, Blanche and Carol Hurd Green. *American Women in the 1960s: Changing the Future.* New York: T. Wayne, 1993.

Loeb, Catherine. "La Chicana: A Bibliographic Survey," *Frontiers* 5, 2 (Summer 1980): 59–74.

Longauex y Vasquez, Enriqueta. "The Mexican-American Woman." *Sisterhood is Powerful*, ed. Robin Morgan.

Lott, Juanita Tamayo, & Canta Pian. "Beyond Stereotypes and Statistics: Emergence of Asian and Pacific American Women." Washington D.C.: Organization of Pan Asian American Women and Women's Bureau/Dept. of Labor, 1979.

Marable, Manning. "Along the Color Line: Why Conservatives Fear Multiculturalism." *The Collegian* (University of Massachusetts, Amherst): November 10, 1993: 11.

Milkman, Ruth. *Women, Work and Protest: A Century of U.S. Women's Labor History.* London: Routledge & Kegan Paul, 1985.

Miner, Valerie. "Fantasies and Nightmares: The Red-Blooded Media," *Jump Cut: A Review of Contemporary Cinema* 26, Oakland, CA., December, 1981. 48–50.

———. *Rumors from the Cauldron: Selected Essays, Reviews and Reportage.* Ann Arbor: University of Michigan Press, 1992.

Mirandé, Alfredo and Evangelian Enríquez. *La Chicana: The Mexican-American Woman.* Chicago: University of Chicago Press, 1979.

———. *Mexican Women in the United States: Struggles Past and Present.* Los Angeles: University of California, Chicano Studies Research Center Publications, 1980.

Moraga, Cherríe and Gloria Anzaldúa, eds. *This Bridge Called My Back: Writings by Radical Women of Color.* Watertown, MA: Persophone Press, 1981. Reprint New York: Kitchen Table Press, 1983.

Morgan, Robin, ed. *Sisterhood Is Powerful, An Anthology of Writings From The Women's Liberation Movement.* New York: Vintage, 1970.

———, ed. Introduction. *Sisterhood is Global: The International Women's Movement Anthology.* New York: Anchor, 1984.

Morrison, Toni, ed. *Race-ing, Justice, En-gendering Power: Essays on Anita Hill, Clarence Thomas, and the Construction of Social Reality.* New York: Pantheon, 1992.

Nieto, Sonia. *Affirming Diversity: The Sociopolitical Context of Multicultural Education.* New York: Longman, 1992.

Noble, Jeanne. *Beautiful Also Are the Souls of My Sisters: A History of Black Women in America.* Englewood Cliffs, NJ: Prentice-Hall, Inc., 1978.

Olen, Helaine. "Rutgers Remains Embroiled Over Power of a Few Words." *Los Angeles Times*, February 20, 1995: A5.

Paglia, Camille. *Sexual Personae: Art and Decadence from Nefertiti to Emily Dickinson.* New Haven and London: Yale University Press, 1990.

Rao, Aruna. *Gender Analysis in Development Planning: A Casebook.* West Hartford, CT: Kumarian Press, 1991.

———, ed. *Women's Studies International: Nairobi and Beyond.* New York: The Feminist Press, 1991.

Rich, Adrienne. *Blood, Bread, and Poetry: Selected Prose 1979–1985.* New York: Norton, 1986.

Robinson, Lillian S. *Sex, Class and Culture.* Bloomington: Indiana University Press, 1978.

Rodney, Walter. *How Europe Underdeveloped Africa.* Washington, DC: Howard University Press, 1974.

Rodriguez, Richard. *Hunger of Memory: The Education of Richard Rodriguez.* New York: Godine, 1982.

Rukeyser, Muriel. *The Speed of Darkness.* New York: Vintage, 1971.

Schlesinger, Arthur. *The Disuniting of America.* New York: Norton, 1992.

Schultz, Debra L. "To Reclaim a Legacy of Diversity: Analyzing the 'Political Correctness' Debates in Higher Education." A report prepared by The National Council for Research on Women. 1993.

Shelley, Martha. "Notes of a Radical Lesbian." *Sisterhood is Powerful*, ed. Robin Morgan.

Sill, Geoffrey S., et al., eds. *Opening the American Mind: Race, Ethnicity, and Gender in Higher Education*. Newark: University of Delaware Press, 1993.

Simonson, Rick and Scott Walker, eds. *Multi-Cultural Literacy*. Saint Paul, MN: Graywolf Press, 1988.

Smith, Barbara, ed. *Home Girls: A Black Feminist Anthology*. New York: Kitchen Table Press, 1983.

Spender, Dale. *The Writing or the Sex? Or Why You Don't Have to Read Women's Writing to Know It's No Good*. New York: Pergamon Press, 1989.

Steinem, Gloria. *Moving Beyond Words*. New York: Simon & Schuster, 1994.

Swerdlow, Amy & Hanna Lessinger, eds. *Class, Race, and Sex: The Dynamics of Control*. Boston: G. K. Hall, 1983.

Takaki, Ronald. *A Different Mirror: A History of Multicultural America*. Boston: Little, Brown and Company, 1993.

Taylor, John. "Are You Politically Correct?" *New York* Magazine, January 21, 1991: 32–40.

Thompson, Becky and Sangeeta Tyagi, eds. *Beyond a Dream Deferred: Multicultural Education and the Politics of Excellence*. Minnesota and London: University of Minnesota Press, 1993.

Wallace, Amy. "Angela Davis Again at Center of UC Storm." *Los Angeles Times*, February 20, 1995: A3, 27.

Weisberg, Jacob. "NAS—Who Are These Guys, Anyway?" *Beyond PC*, ed. Patricia Aufderheide.

Williams, Patricia. *The Alchemy of Race and Rights*. Cambridge, MA: Harvard University Press, 1991.

Women's Studies Quarterly. Special Feature: Teaching the New Women's History. 15:1 and 2 (Spring/Summer, 1988).

Zinn, Howard. *S.N.C.C.: The New Abolitionists*. Boston: Beacon Press, 1964.

II

Multiple Jeopardy on College Campuses

3

Talking about Race, Talking about Gender, Talking about How We Talk

Patricia Williams

A White first-grade teacher in Atglen, PA, who asked her only two Black pupils to pretend they were slaves during a class discussion on slavery, recently apologized to the youngsters' parents.

"Teacher put us up on a table," said Ashley Dixon, 6, describing the history lesson by teacher Mary Horning. Ashley said Horning told her that, as a slave, she would be sold for about $10 as a house cleaner.

Zachary Thomas, also 6, said Horning used him to demonstrate how shirtless slaves were chained to a post before flogging.

Horning apologized the next day to the children's mothers and asked them to speak to her class on Black heritage. "I did not view it as racial," she said, adding, "I wanted to teach the children about prejudice. I did not do it with malice or to embarrass anyone."[1]

I was born in the 1950s. While I suppose that makes me a baby boomer, I have always thought of myself as a Little Rocker: my earliest memories include the integration of the schools in Little Rock, Arkansas, by children just about my age. My life's expanse has marked some of the greatest social movements in this country's history: the Civil Rights Movement, the Peace Movement, the Women's Movement, the struggle for the rights of lesbians and gay men, children, the homeless, and the wheelchair-bound, the Cold War, the fall of the Berlin Wall, and the emerging challenge of an ethnically, religiously, linguistically, and economically mixed-up world. My forty-odd years have traversed Motown, Vietnam, liberation from the female necessities of bra, girdle, garters, and straightened hair, the Pill, the spectacular rise of television evangelism, the entire span of Justice Thurgood Marshall's remarkable career, and the terms of presidents Eisenhower, Kennedy, Johnson, Ford, Carter, Reagan, Bush, and Clinton.

My age also places me (along with Clarence Thomas) among the very first affirmative action candidates. In the fall of 1969, I entered college as one of fifty-nine blacks; the class ahead of me had only seven. I entered law school in a class of only twelve percent women; the class four years later had twenty-five percent. While the numbers of black students have suffered real declines with cutbacks in federal tuition support, very few universities have yet retreated to pre-1970s levels. And while women's presence in universities remains largely ghettoized in many disciplines, most professional schools in the country now have student populations that are close to fifty percent female. Though women and minorities still make up a small percentage of this nation's professionals (in law, for example, people of color account for three percent of the total, and all women for only twenty-four percent; in most other disciplines these figures are much worse), the profits of such presence have been resounding. Women's studies and feminist theory have become part of a broad international conversation—even if a halting or absurd one at given moments. Latino and black literature is enjoying a popularity not seen since the Harlem Renaissance. Ethnic studies, Holocaust studies, multiculturalism, and global intercommunication could make this world a better place for all of us.

And yet forty years is still a perilously brief period in the history of social movement. While acknowledging the enormous progress that has been made, I am convinced we are poised at a dangerous political crossroads that could take us back much more than forty years. This threat is clear in the rising rate of bias crime everywhere, the technologizing of reproduction, the escalating rates of gun ownership, and the slick commercialization of "formerly crude" hatemongers from David Duke to Andrew Dice Clay. In academia, this trend has gained an insidious boost from the right-wing attack on what has been labeled "political correctness." From *The Atlantic* to *Newsweek* to "This Week with David Brinkley," there has been a relentless assault on the views of those lumped together hyperbolically as "liberals, black activists, militant homosexuals, and radical feminists," charging them (us! could that really be the gentle-hearted me lurking over there in that fringe?) with "politicizing" curricula, pushing "intellectual conformity sometimes enforced by intimidation," turning "whining" into the science of victimology—and, in excited moments, practicing witchcraft and Nazism promiscuously, even simultaneously.

Perhaps the biggest challenge in these heated times will be just stepping back and grabbing onto a little perspective.

I think that the crisis in universities which is so disparagingly referred to as "political correctness" is one part of an unfortunately predictable national tension based on the institutional digestion process of the beneficiaries of the Civil Rights Movement. The battle that began with the integration of grammar schools in Little Rock, Arkansas, that continued with the integration of high schools in Mississippi, and that reemerged with the integration of colleges in Alabama and law schools in Georgia—that battle is now middle-aged. The generation of children who integrated white schools as a result of the transformative legacy of the Supreme Court's opinion in *Brown v. Board of Education* has grown up and attained the time of life when successful careers make their lasting mark. If my life is representative at all of other first-generation affirmative action Little Rockers, we are just coming into the intellectual tenure and cultural power that could inscribe, or shake, or shift, or build upon that bedrock of consensus rather lavishly called "civilization." It is not surprising, therefore, that the bitter resistance and powerful backlash that have met every step of the Civil Rights Movement's push for inclusion should have followed to the next or current loci of what law professor Stephen Carter calls "affirmative action babies." Nor is it surprising that the successes of the black struggle for equal opportunity should result in a wide, noisy, ever-expanding and, yes, demanding trail of feminists, Hispanics, Jews, Muslims, Vietnam veterans, immigrants, and so on.

This is a lot of cultural foment for one generation to digest—but then, strong-headed fomenting has always been the best feature of American democratic style. While I personally think we should all just sit down and have dinner together, it's not hard to understand how various identity groups might feel threatened by so many newcomers—and the newcomers by each other—all jostling for pie slices without so much as having stopped to wash their hands. It will be a cold day in Hell before any of them—those Others—learn to say "please" and "thank you."

It should not be surprising therefore—lamentable perhaps, but not surprising—that, as these newly participant identity groupings have sent representatives into the workplace, gained tenure in universities, and risen to political office, the frightened holdovers of the 1950s fire-hosing tomato-throwers have shifted their fear, and their aim, and their tactics accordingly.

No longer are state troops used to block entry to schools and other public institutions; segregation's strong arm, states' rights, has found new home in an economic gestalt that has simply privatized almost all of what used to be considered the public sector. Whites have moved to the suburbs, and politicians have withdrawn funds from black to white areas in unsubtle redistricting plans: remedial counterdistricting has been struck down as itself racist. No longer is the law expressly discriminatory (as to race and ethnicity at any rate, if not as to homosexuality), yet the phenomenon of laissez-faire exclusion has resulted in as complete a pattern of economic and residential segregation as has ever existed in this country.

Most of all, the moral currency of the Civil Rights Movement's vocabulary has been under attack. "Integration" itself has transformed in meaning, used glowingly by former segregationists like Jesse Helms and Strom Thurmond—and rejected by many former civil rights activists—as having come to mean a form of assimilation that demands black self-erasure rather than an enfolding of African-American contributions and experience. The rejection of those contributions takes many forms, but harks back to facile deflections whose historical precedents are to be found in both 1830s and 1950s discussions about freedom of association and contract, in which those values were used to block discussions of integration. Then, as now, civil rights activists have had to respond with law suits that focus on equality as a constitutional guarantee, on the promise that certain groups need not suffer unfettered or sanctioned stigmatization of their humanity and of their citizenship. In today's world, such efforts have focused on harassment in the workplace, the academic freedom to include or exclude the histories of minority groups in curricula, and the redefinition of citizenship to encompass the extraordinary linguistic, ethnic, religious, racial, and physical variety of all of us who are American Citizens Too.

While resounding in every aspect of American life, there is no place where this particular battle has been more visible than in universities; there is no fiercer entrenchment than the lines drawn around the perceived property of culture. It is a battle marred by the persistence of prejudice: as women are still trying to overcome presumptions that they really *like* getting fondled in the back office, blacks are trying to overcome presumptions that they really *deserve* to be on the bottom of the heap. It is a battle marred by ignorance and denial. Disastrous experiments in education—such as the slavery lesson whose epigraph began in this chapter—reenact and reinforce a power dynamic in which some people get to *imagine* oppression, and others spend their lives having their bodies put through its most grotesque motions. Yet somehow this is nevertheless described as having nothing to do with racism's history. "Good intentions," however blunderingly destructive in impact, end all further discussion. The merest whisper of the possibility that a little education, a little history, a little forethought might improve things is crudely and immediately translated into electrical blizzards of fear of "fascism," and "hypersensitivity," and "lowered standards."

One cannot but wonder what is implied when the suggestion of more knowledge, more history is so persistently misunderstood and devalued as unscientific unknowledge, as untruthful unhistory. In fact, the upside-down-ness of meaning has become a major bafflement in the ability to address educational inequality in a whole range of contexts. "*Inter*culturalism." said a Swarthmore undergrad, firmly and disapprovingly, when I used the word "multiculturalism" at a tea thrown in my honor not long ago. "Huh?" said I, through a mouthful of chocolate cream and crumbs. "Interculturalism," she repeated. "Multiculturalism has too much negative meaning these days."

I guess she was right. Every generation has to go through a purging of language, an invention of meaning in order to exist, in order to be seen. Renaming as fair turnaround; renaming as recapture from the stereotypes of others. Yet … somehow … it seems as though I am running out of words these days. I feel I am on a treadmill that has gradually but unmistakably increased its speed, so that no word I use to positively describe myself or the scholarly projects of us formerly colored ladies lasts for more than five minutes before someone comes along and knocks it over, spills it out, fills it up with toxins. I can no longer justify my presence in academia, for example, with words that exist in the English language. The moment I find some symbol of my presence in the rarefied halls of elite institutions, it gets stolen, co-opted, filled with negative meaning. As integration became synonymous with assimilation into whiteness, affirmative action became synonymous with "pushing out more qualified whites," and, of course, multiculturalism somehow became synonymous with solipsistically monocultural privilege.

While constant rejuvenation is not just good but inevitable in some general sense, the rapid obsolescence of words, even as they drop from my mouth, is an increasingly isolating phenomenon. In fact, it feels like a storm of intellectual blockbusting. I move into a large, meaningful space, with great connotations on a high floor with lots of windows, and suddenly all the neighbors move out. My intellectual aerie becomes a known hangout for dealers in heresy and other soporific drugs, frequented by suspect profiles (if not actual suspects), and located on the edge of that known geological disaster area, the Slippery Slope.

73

I remember when I was little, in the late fifties, two or three black families moved into our neighborhood, where for fifty years my family had been the only blacks. I remember the father of my best friend Cathy going from house to house, warning the neighbors, like Paul Revere with Chicken Little's brain, that the property values were falling, the values were falling. The area changed overnight. Whites who had seen me born, and baked me cookies at Halloween, and grown up with my mother fled for their lives. ("We'd have to hold our breath all the time because colored people smell different," said Cathy, with some conviction about the pending move. Cathy, who was always a little slow about these things, had difficulty with the notion of me as "colored": "No, you're not," and then, later, "Well, you're different.")

The mass movement that turned my neighborhood into an "inner city" was part of the first great backlash to the Civil Rights Movement. I think we are now seeing the second great backlash, waged against the hard-won principles of equal opportunity (disguised as a fight about reverse discrimination and "quotas") in the workplace and in universities-as-feeders for the workplace.

The crisis that the moral inheritance of the Civil Rights Movement has encountered in the attack on "political correctness" strikes me as just such resistance, even robbery—again, a form of verbal blockbusting. It is a calculated devaluation of political property values, no less than the "white flight" organized by the National Association of Realtors a few decades ago, that left us with the legacy of the "inner city." Universities are pictured as "fortresses" against the "siege" of those who are perceived to be uncivilized heathen. (Wherever three percent or more of us are gathered, it's a siege, I guess.) The cry has been sounded: the standards are falling, the standards are falling.

The story of my inner-city neighborhood would have been vastly different if Cathy and her family had bothered to stick around to get to know the two nice black families who moved in. Similarly, the future of U.S. universities— particularly in the hoped-for global economy—could be a fascinating one if campus communities chose to take advantage of the rich multiculturalism that this society offers. We face a quite disastrous intellectual crisis, however, if our universities persist in the culture-baiting that has brought us the English-only movement, the brazen assumption that any blacks on campus do not deserve to be there, and the mounting levels of verbal and physical violence directed against anyone perceived to be different or marginal.

Given this, it is too easy to spend a lot of time being defensive. We have all heard the silly lameness of the retorts into which these attacks box us: "I am too qualified!" "Vote for me but not because I'm a woman!" But it does not work. Powerful cultural stereotypes are simply not dispelled by waving your degrees in people's faces. (That is precisely ultraconservative Dinesh D'Souza's whole premise in his much-touted book, *Illiberal Education*: that an Ivy League degree just is not worth what it used to be now that the riffraff has moved in.)

It seems to me that the ability to talk about diversity (now synonymous with balkanization) depends, therefore, on a constant clarification of terms, a determination to leave nothing to presupposition, and a renewed insistence upon the incorporation of multiple connotative histories into our curricula, our social lives, our politics, and our law. Our hardest job in these times is not to forget why we are where we are at this historical intersection. We cannot forget the sacrifice that went into our presence in the social world. And we cannot forget that our biggest task in all this is coming together— not merely to overcome the sense of individual or personal diminishment, but to fight collectively the persistent devaluation of all of our humanity and of all of our intellectual contributions.

I recently guest-lectured in the class of a constitutional law professor who was teaching disparate impact classes (that is, cases that consider what, if any, remedies might correct the racially disparate impact of facially race-neutral rules.) As I spoke about shifting demographics and the phenomenon of "white flight," the class grew restless, the students flipping pages of newspapers and otherwise evidencing disrespect. Afterwards, the two or three black students congratulated me for speaking so straightforwardly, and for using the words "black" and "white." I later asked the professor: How is it possible to teach cases about racial discrimination without mentioning race? "I just teach the neutral principles," he replied; "I don't want to risk upsetting the black students." And yet it was clear that those most upset were the white students.

This tendency to neutralize is repeated throughout the law school curriculum: "core" classes carve off and discard some of their most important parts, like welfare and entitlement programs from tax policy, consumer protection law from commercial contract. And even though the civil rights movement was one of the most singularly transformative forces in the history of constitutional law, very little of it is taught in basic constitutional law classes. (When I took constitutional law, we spent almost four months on the Commerce Clause.) Some schools—and by no means all—pick up the pieces by having such optional courses as Poverty Law, Law and Feminism, or Race and the Law. It is no wonder that the Rehnquist court has been able to cavalierly undo what took so many lives and years to build: the process of legal education mirrors the social resistance to antidiscrimination principles. Subject matter considered to be "optional" is ultimately swept away as uneconomical "special" interests—as thoughtlessly in real life as it has been in law schools.

Ironically, the smooth bulwark of "neutral principles" has been turned to the task of avoiding the very hard work that moral judgment in any sphere requires, the constant balancing—whether we act as voters, jurors, parents, lawyers, or laypeople—of rules, precepts, principles, and content. I have always thought that developing the ability to engage in such analytical thought is the highest goal of great universities. Yet even this most traditional of educational missions is under attack. "Should [parents] be paying $20,000 a year to have their children sitting there, figuring out how they feel about how they read?" asked James Barber, founder of the neoconservative National Association of Scholars at Duke University. His question underscores the degree to which so much of the fear of balkanized campuses is in fact the authoritarian's worst nightmare of a world in which people actually think for themselves.

I worry that while the happy universalism of assimilative "neutrality" is a fine ideal, we will never achieve it by assuming away the particularity of painful past and present inequalities. The creation of a sense of false consensus about "our common heritage" is not the same as equality and only delays the unraveling of racism's tangled sociopathology. Even assuming no hostility to the incorporation of issues of race, class, and gender into the curriculum (as the example of the first-grade slave auction with which this chapter began demonstrates) the ignorant—or innocent—perpetuation of oppression, even as we purport to be challenging it, can result in situations where empowered people imagine they are learning, and even end up feeling pretty good about themselves; yet the disempowered end up feeling pretty awful, bearing the burden of the lessons imparted to the more powerful, while learning nothing themselves that is new or helpful. Thus powerful inequities and real social crises are ignored, made invisible, and just get worse.

Does this mean we eliminate the topic of slavery or sexism or homophobia in our classrooms as too "dangerous" or "divisive" or "controversial"? Do we really want to avoid controversy in education? Or is that even the issue? Consider the criminal law scholar who taught a class on rape law in an undergraduate seminar of about fifteen women. The professor asked them to write essays on their experiences with date rape, which they then shared in class. While I have much to say about the pedagogical problematic of such an assignment in the first place, I will hold my tongue here, for by the students' accounts the exercise was a successful one that felt safe, moving, and empowering. The next semester, however, he took those same essays and read them aloud to the snickers of his largely male class of about 150 criminal law students. This time it was clearly an exercise in voyeurism and disempowerment. Several of the women in that class were so upset they cried or walked out. Facing complaints, the professor expressed bewilderment: "Are you saying a man can never teach rape?" "I was just letting the women speak in their own voices." "This was no different from what I did last semester and no one complained."

Learning to see the differences, to understand the pernicious subtlety of what it means to live in a culture of pornography or racism—these are the issues we must be debating in universities. These are the considerations that will best humanize our pedagogy in lasting ways.

As a footnote to this vignette, I daresay it would not come as a great surprise if I mentioned that the question of how this class might have been taught more effectively got sidetracked by a discussion of the professor's First-Amendment rights to academic freedom. As has become all too common in such debates, it was hampered by lots of careless contradictions: self-described First-Amendment "absolutists" who would protect "even the grunt" of a Nazi because it is speech, but who would in the next breath condemn "hissing" from left-wing students because it's "censorship." Those who would defend San Francisco police chief Richard Hongisto's ordering his officers to remove copies of a gay newspaper that made fun of him from newsstands throughout the city because it "restored order" yet who would condemn black university students for removing copies of newspapers that contained insulting racial stereotypes because it "interfered with a free press." Those who would outlaw begging words in the subways because they are a "threat" but not the ability of Political Action Committees to alter the financial decisions of government officials because that's "business." Those who would defend the academic freedom of a teacher to instruct that the Holocaust never existed but not that of Leonard Jeffries to teach arcane theories of Afrocentrism. Those who claim to protect all speech but who in fact make facile, behind-the-scenes, perhaps unconscious flip-flops between what they consider speech and what conduct. Those whose conclusions can only be reconciled by the very content and context-based judgments that they purport to condemn. Yet these judgments, made consciously and ethically, made not individually but balanced and negotiated through our institutions of social consensus, have always been the way our very nonabsolutist First-Amendment jurisprudence has worked, whether in the context of politics, perjury, or more recently and most controversially, pornography.

The First Amendment has never been so absolute that, for example, I can walk into a store, tell the clerk I am you and "speak" your credit card number. It does not permit me to set up a large bullhorn, even on my own property, and shout out my political dissent at the world around me. It does not protect me from being fired if I go into my boss's office and hurl a little gratuitous invective at him. It should not protect my employer, if he hurls certain kinds of gratuitous invective at me, from charges of sexual or racial harassment. The First Amendment does not help me at all if I put an ad in the local paper that my landlord is wanted for heinous crimes of moral turpitude, just to get back at him for raising my rent. If someone proceeds to call out the text of the First Amendment in the middle of a busy office, the First Amendment does not limit the ability to eject him. If someone stands up in the middle of the reading room of a public library and begins to deliver a lengthy political tract, his First-Amendment right to rant and rave does not automatically render subservient every single one of the other contemplative and educational goals that the institution of library implies.

A university student who stands, dead drunk, howling incoherently at the moon at 4:00 A.M. beneath the windows of an occupied dorm and throwing stones at windows will quite likely be suspended or arrested. It confounds me, therefore, that if he manages to embellish his performance with a few clearly enunciated racist and homophobic blasphemes, he will be embraced as a fearless defender of the Constitution.

It is not that there are no issues of free speech on campuses, but that the current much-publicized brouhaha seems exaggerated and misplaced, and with all the blather, not truly about "chilling" the political speech of anyone. Rather, the issue at the heart of this debate is what has always been most challenging about the First Amendment or any other question of democracy for that matter: the endless balancing of one ideal—of free, even if unpleasant or offensive, speech—against other rights—such as the interests in limiting defamation, invasion of privacy, nuisance or harassment.

This debate is not a new one by any means. It can be traced in everything from the original debates over the Reconstruction Amendments, to the arguments in *Brown v. Board of Education.* It can be traced as a tension between a range of variously described freedoms—of speech, of association, of scientific inquiry, of enterprise—on the one hand; and equality on the other, whose purportedly mushy pursuit is depicted as choking out the survival of the fittest, by its supposedly standardless protection of the great undeserving "all."

Yet the irony of the most popularly espoused "absolutist" free speech positions—as espoused by certain neoconservative scholars such as Dinesh D'Souza, Linda Chavez, William Bennett, or Ed Hirsch—is that their conception of speech, and of the university and its curriculum, is premised on a kind of central planning, a universalized model of an Original Fountain of Wisdom, deviation from which is used to summon up visions of cultic repression and truly terrible Stalinist histories repeating themselves. Yet at the same time, these commentors rush to embrace the liberatory potential of late capitalism, whose texture and variety is derived from nothing if not the phenomenon of multiple, shifting identity groups forming coalitions around common language and consumption habits. But the specific issue of line-drawing is not novel, nor is it in and of itself repressive; it is, in fact, central to the democratic administration of all laws; it is at the heart of the relationship between codes and their ethical application.

The fallacy of this form of absolutism is that it ignores the existence of any functioning decision-maker. None of the codes regulating behavior/speech at universities does so without recourse to some jurylike body, which, like all juries, makes specific decisions based on consideration of the specific facts, employing and developing community standards. It is this reference to a consensus of opinion that distinguishes what is happening on campuses from the Draconian illusion created by the new conservatives: no one dictator or martinet makes these decisions; the community that applies the codes is the administration and student body through representative university governance systems which, in all instances with which I am familiar, include hearings and appeals processes. In this way, regulation of either speech or conduct on campus is no different from what all of us engage in and view as a perfectly normal part of legal determinations.

In fact, it is hard to imagine an institution where there is "absolutely" no line-drawing, no ability to regulate and protect certain people against the harassment of others. In fact, workers are protected by their managers, students are protected by their teacher's authority, teachers are protected by administration, and so on. The free speech movement of the 1960s was an effort to allow students to participate in the consensus of community norms; it was not about allowing workers or students or teachers to be hounded out of institutions, with no ability to respond. Hamstringing institutions in this way sends a message to those who either live or work within the institution that some will have *carte blanche* to harass, while others must be its object or bear silent witness. While I share Nat Hentoff's fear, for example, of the state's power to suppress speech, I also fear the opposite: is it not just possible that state action is not the source of all evil all the time, but that, unconstrained by any governmental bounds or any social consensus, state inaction poses risks of its own? Is it not possible that private aggregations of great power, like some monopolistic corporations, could rival or even exceed that power concentrated in public institutions? Is it not possible that state-sponsored terror could come about by the calculated complicity of simply looking the other way? The terrorization of blacks in this country has been accomplished too frequently by the government's turning the other way; by "states' rights" arguments being used to defeat federal antilynching legislation, and then states deciding to do nothing about it.

It is true that the oppression of many groups—most conspicuously in the example of the Holocaust—has been accomplished by inordinate concentrations of state power, and this is a thing devoutly to be guarded against. But in protecting ourselves against that, it is wise also to remember that in the United States we have a history of terror carried out against blacks and certain other minority groups not by the positive acts of the state, not by legislation, not even by the laws of segregation alone, bad as they were, but by individuals speaking, threatening, and acting against blacks suffering the utter lack of access to governmental resources, protection, intervention. It is imperative to remember that in the U.S. we have something of a tradition of laissez-faire terrorism.

Given that history, and given the resurgence of hate crimes across the board in our society—from the White Aryan Resistance to antiabortion murders to, yes, the beating of Reginald Denny—we should be very concerned about hate speech on campuses as part of a broader social pattern. National as well as global tensions about ethnicity, race, and gender pose a profound challenge to educational institutions: How will they formulate their mission in confronting not just the politics of hate speech, but the politics of hate?

I believe that it is this, the politics of hate, that is the real crisis facing our campuses. I am willing to assume, for the sake of argument, that there is a constitutional right to say anything, anywhere, anytime. But this does not answer the dilemma of how to deal with the concerted propaganda of violence that is subverting any potential for creativity in higher education today. I want to know, for example, what to do about a black female colleague who went into teaching after a distinguished career as a civil rights litigator. After one year she quit. Among the myriad horror stories she recounts (and that too many of us can recount): a student came to her and told her that there was a bullet with her name on it. At first I thought she was using some kind of awful metaphor, but it turned out that another of her students, an off-duty police officer, had actually taken a bullet, carved her name on the side of it, and was showing it to his classmates. (Although the dean of the law school casually promised to mention it to a psychiatrist friend, there was absolutely no institutional response of any sort to this incident.)

Predictably, the ability to mount a campaign of harassment depends on muffling the cries of resistance. In campus politics, this has come in the form of efforts to disparage the language of resistance: attacks on "sensitivity" as "mental vegetarianism," on charges of sexism, racism, and homophobia as the products of whining immaturity, and on evidence of victimization as the brewed concoction of practitioners of that dark science, "victimology."

Yet the ability to be, yes, dammit, *sensitive* to one another is the essence of what distinguishes the joy of either multiculturalism or willing assimilation from the oppression of either groupthink or totalitarianism. It is at the heart of diplomacy, and a little well-deployed diplomacy can keep us from going to war with one another. When I was visiting Durham, North Carolina, during the 1990 senatorial race between Jesse Helms and Harvey Gantt (the first black to run for that office since Reconstruction), a friend of mine said she wanted me to see something. Without any explanation, she drove me over to the Chapel Hill campus of the University of North Carolina and dragged me to the center of campus. There, right in front of the student union, was a statue entitled "The Student Body." It was a collection of cast bronze figures, slightly smaller than life-sized. One was of an apparently white, Mr.-Chips-style figure with a satchel of books on his back, pursuing his way. Another was of a young woman of ambiguous racial cast, white or maybe Asian, carrying a violin and some books and earnestly pursuing her way. A third figure was of a young white woman struggling under a load of books stretching from below her waist up to her chin. Then two white figures: a young man holding an open book with one hand; his other arm floated languidly downward, his hand coming to casual rest upon a young woman's buttocks. The young woman leaned into his embrace, her head drooped on his shoulder like a wilted gardenia. In the center of this arrangement was a depiction of an obviously black young man. He was dressed in gym shorts and he balanced a basketball on one finger. The last figure was of a solemn-faced young black woman; she walked alone, a solitary book balanced on her head.

It turned out I was about the only one in the state who had not heard about this statue. A gift from the class of 1985, it had been the topic of hot debate. Some students, particularly black and feminist students, had complained about the insensitivity of this depiction as representative of the student bod(ies). Other students said the first students were just "being sensitive" (invoked disparagingly, as though numbskulledness were a virtue). At that point, the sculptor, a woman, got in on the act, and explained that the black male figure was in honor of the athletic prowess of black UNC grads like Michael Jordan, and that the black female figure depicted the grace of black women. The university, meanwhile, congratulated itself publicly on how fruitfully the marketplace of ideas had been stimulated.

As I stood looking at this statue in amazement, I witnessed a piece of the debate-as-education. Two white male students were arguing with a black female student.

"You need to lighten up," said one of the men.

"But . . ." said the black woman.

"Anyway, black women *are* graceful," said the other.

"But," said the black woman as the white men kept talking. At the end, the black woman walked off in tears, while the white men laughed. There is a litany of questions I have heard raised about scenarios like this: Why should the university "protect" minority students against this sort of thing? Don't they have to learn to deal with it?

Let me pose some alternative questions of my own: Why should universities be in the business of putting students in this situation to begin with? Since when is the persistent reduction of black men and all women to their physical traits "educational" of anything? How is it that these sorts of ignorant free-for-alls are smiled upon by the same university officials who resist restructuring curricula to actually teach the histories of minorities and women?

Syndicated columnist Nat Hentoff represents a popular insistence that the solution to the campus multiculturalism struggle is to just talk about it, one on one, without institutional sanction or interference. Free speech as free enterprise zone. But this solution makes only selected students—those who are most frequently the objects of harassment—the perpetual teachers not merely of their histories, but of their very right just to be students. This is an immense burden, a mountainous presumption of noninclusion that must be constantly addressed and overcome. It keeps us eternally defensive and reactive.

Nor is this issue of legitimacy merely one for students. The respect accorded any teacher is only in small—if essential—part attributable to the knowledge inside one's head. (If that were all, we would have much more respect for street-corner orators, the elderly, and the clear, uncensored vision of children.) What makes me a teacher is a force lent to my words by virtue of the collective power of institutional convention. If faculty do not treat women as colleagues, then students will not treat women as members of the faculty.

An example to illustrate the dimension of this problem: a poetry reading at a school where I once taught, a casual event. A white male student in one of my seminars stood up and read a poem attributed to Rudyard Kipling, comparing the relative lustiness of white, brown, yellow, and "nigger" women. In the silence that followed his reading, I asked to go next. I read a short piece, which later became the core of my book *The Alchemy of Race and Rights*, about my great-great-grandmother having been raped at the age of eleven by her master, my great-great-grandfather. I made no other comment.

The next day, the student went to another faculty member and complained that I seemed unduly upset by his reading: he said he was afraid that I would not be able to grade him objectively, and he would be subjected to the unfairness of my prejudice. The faculty member's response was, "I'm sure you two can work it out."

Now the one thing that this student and I could quickly agree on was that this was a deeply unsatisfactory resolution: in reducing the encounter to one on one, this suggestion ignored the extent to which what was going on was (for both of us) a crisis of power, a dislocation of legitimacy. This was no mere difference of individually held opinion, and it could not be resolved at that level. For the university community to act as though it could be was to abandon its function as a player in the moral debate about the propaganda of human devaluation. The dilemma I face at this moment in the academic world is this: if I respond to or open discussion about belligerent or offensive remarks from students in my classes, I am called "PC" and accused of forcing my opinions down the throats of my students—and of not teaching them the "real" subject matter. If I respond with no matter what degree of clear, dignified control, I become a militant black female who "terrifies" moderate students. If I follow the prevalent advice of "just ignoring it," then I am perceived as weak, humiliated, ineffectual, a doormat.

It is great to turn the other cheek in the face of fighting words; it is probably even wise to run. But it is not a great way to maintain authority in the classroom—in a society that abhors "wimps," and where "kicking ass" is a patriotic duty. In such a context, "just ignoring" verbal challenges from students is a good way to deliver myself into category of the utterly powerless. If, moreover, all my other colleagues pursue the same path (student insult, embarrassed pause, the teacher keeps on teaching as though nothing has happened), we have collectively created that institutional silence that is known as a moral vacuum.

If then, we are not to betray the hard-won gains of the last forty years, one of the subtlest challenges we face is how to relegitimize the national discussion of racial, ethnic, and gender tensions so that we can get past the catch-22 in which merely talking about it is considered an act of war, yet not talking about it is complete capitulation to the status quo, and, indeed, not talking about it is repeatedly covered up with a lot of high-volume substitute-talk about the legalities of censorship and the First Amendment. In the shortfall, more constructive conversations about how we might reinfuse our pedagogy with dignity and tolerance for all are preempted.

In the tabulations that follow, I will try to lay out some of my own thoughts about the pitfalls that even our best efforts at reconciling democracy's challenges seem to encounter, as well as my sense of the urgent necessity to continue our conversations, even when they misfire dismally.

1. Lesson Number One: Jokes, Hypotheticals, and Good Intentions Can Still Impart "Real" Harms. The most frequent refrain in the wake of some of the most virulent and sadistic displays of racism, sexism, and homophobia on campuses has been the dismissive injunction that it is all just good fun, pretend, not meant to hurt anyone. Vast amounts of press attention have been paid to the weak—and ultimately unsuccessful—case brought at the University of Pennsylvania by some black women who alleged that a Jewish student had called them "water buffaloes" and said they belonged in a zoo; yet a far more virulent incident at the College of William and Mary received only passing notice in a small article with the undecided title, "Satire or Racism? Comic Strip Stirs Furor": in a school-funded humor magazine, there appeared a:

> six-panel cartoon featur[ing] a muscular white man, "Mighty Whitie," wearing a caped costume that includes the initials MW, in the reverse style of the WM logo the college uses.
>
> The strip says that Mighty Whitie patrols "the suburban utopia of Cleantown USA, ever vigilant against the incursion of ghetto crime." A white woman screams that she is being attacked by "the Black Man and his gang," whose costumes identify them as "Watermelon" and "Fried Chicken."

> Mighty Whitie beats up the black characters, boasting that "your superior rhythm won't save you." One of the black characters retaliates by summoning "my homeboys, The Yellow Peril and the Turbanator."

The humor magazine's only response to the resulting furor was an editorial, entitled "Tolerance Goes Both Ways," touting the "fundamental right" of a free press.

Similarly, fraternity slave auctions have been explained away as theatrical art, anti-Semitic jokes are justified as attempts to "lighten up" tensions, and classroom hypotheticals involving insulting stereotypes about women are positioned as merely "models" of the subject to be discussed. Yet "theatrical," "light-hearted" "models" have no less potential to reenact the power of hate than anything else. Humor can humiliate, theater teach, and hypotheticals stigmatize. I am confounded by the degree to which this simple observation, so obvious on the one hand, should be so hotly contended as a *possibility* in the arena of the politics of prejudice. (A most literal example of this occurred at a Republican fundraising "roast" in 1993: The banquet joke that had racial overtones was told by a state senator from Northern Virginia, Warren E. Barry. He opened with remarks about the "Clinton fags-in-the-foxhole" policy and then began a joke about how Mr. Parris, when he was in Congress, seemed to be constantly at odds with the officials of the District of Columbia, who are mostly black. He recalled that Mr. Parris had once called a bridge leading from Washington to Virginia "the longest bridge in the world because it connects Virginia to Africa." He went on, with a laugh, to say that Mr. Parris sought to rename the bridge "Soul Brothers Causeway." Yet the attempt to bring home the significance of such statements in terms of the representation of black constituents was dismissed, relying on "humor" and good intentions.)

It bears repeating (endlessly) that I do understand that freedom of expression and the press are precious legacies. I understand that regulating speech is more likely to be used against blacks than whites or the powerless than the powerful, in the long run. And I understand that we must work hardest to protect the speech we hate most. By the same token, speech is a complicated concept. Again, asking money of a stranger might well be speech; it might also be deemed a threat, harassment, or a robbery. If hissing a fellow student is generally conceded to be a silencing mechanism of speech, could not the words "Fried Chicken Man" if chanted in unison to drown out someone else's ideas also fall on the spectrum of that speech we call sound and fury rather than protected? And if political debate is considered serious business, could not the habitual outcasting—in colleges, Congress or the courts—of certain categories of citizens to the realm of verbal tomfoolery have very negative material consequences?

2. Lesson Number Two: Words and Symbols Have Multiple Layers of Meaning. Today's free speech debates are a vital part of the effort to undo what the Reconstruction Amendments called the badges, the incidents, the stigma of slavery. The debate seems to have become snagged on the political content of speech itself, but it is a debate that ranges far beyond speech in its history, visual symbolism, and juridical import. Let me give a complicated example to start with: at an art gallery on the border of an urban college campus near where I live, the display windows recently featured the gigantic black letters "RUPC" and then a stuffed monkey in a suit, seated in an armchair, reading a copy of *National Geographic.* It was an image straight out of D.W. Griffith's *Birth of a Nation*, in which blacks in the Reconstruction Congress were depicted as bestial, formally suited yet shoeless, buffoonish, and pretentious.

I tried hard to imagine what this exhibit was about—I wanted so much for there to be some ironic twist, some play or "joke" that redeemed it from the deafening, slap-in-the-face insult that the painful history of the image summons up in me. I have been treated as a smartly outfitted monkey-in-the-academy more often than I like to think, from the first grade, with explicit primate analogies, onward to the present, when the image is most frequently expressed as "less qualified minorities."

Can I censor this exhibit? Do I want to? Again, is that the issue? What I am sure of is that the relentless discussion of the First Amendment in this context will completely displace any other discussion about the history of blacks as monkeys, gorillas, orangutans, subhuman, animalistic, fit only for zoos. It will completely displace the ability to talk about the enervation and dispossession I feel, or the taunting hostility whose accumulated assertion makes participation in all forms of institutional life so constantly difficult. As I have observed a number of times before, it is as though the First Amendment has become severed from any discussion of the limits of political, commercial, defamatory, perjurious or any other of the myriad classifications of speech. It is as though expressions that contain a particularly volatile payload of hate become automatically privileged as political and, moreover, get to employ the First Amendment as a bludgeon of paradox—"I have my First Amendment right to call you a monkey, so you shut up about it."

Of course, it is worth repeating here that I have no idea what the exhibit was about. And since I have not yet been able to contact anyone who could tell me what it was about, I advance no theory as to what the artist "really" meant, nor as to whether the artist's personal intentions ought to govern the interpretation of a work displayed, without any explanation, in a window on a public street. I offer my observations not necessarily to condemn, but to explore some of the powerful embedded symbolic vocabulary that was drawn upon in juxtaposing that particular question ("RUPC?") with that particular fabled image (monkey, *National Geographic* and its tabled photographs of "primitive" peoples), regardless of whether the artist then embellished that arrangement with an overlay of satire (which I might like), or further ridicule (which might make me even madder). "How can you be upset when you don't even know what it meant?" asked a friend of mine, implying that I was being a tad judgmental. Yet my discomfort was not out of a desire to rush in and destroy: I think that my discomfort was tribute to the overarching power those images commanded in the lexicon of historical parable and black social experience. While we are generally aware that poets, artists, and perhaps advertisers have always employed such imagistic evocation with great consciousness and persuasive, even manipulative, precision, the degree to which these compositional elements are also a part of political debate remains by and large invisible. What Henry Louis Gates has made known as signifying parody is one way of translating the sensation I am speaking of: for example, a colleague of mine told me of his experience at a recently integrated but traditionally white Southern school that had an Old South Day one weekend each spring. Confederate flags, uniforms, swords, horses, bourbon and hoop skirts ruled the day. Black students wondered exactly where they fit in this scheme, and they were told to lighten up, it was just nostalgia, a good excuse for a party. So one of the black students got the bright idea of holding a Nat Turner Day, with fun-filled reenactments of the original event. And coincidentally scheduled for the same weekend as Old South Day. This reversal provided a most instructive symbolic dictionary, with much empathic import for many of the white students.

Let me give one final example of how I think all this has consequences for which we may want to be most vigilant. In a much-publicized incident at Harvard University a few years ago, a white student hung a Confederate flag from her dormitory window, saying that to her it symbolized the warmth and community of her happy Southern home. This act produced a strong series of public denunciations from many other students, blacks in particular, who described the symbolic significance of the Confederacy for them as a *white* community forged against a backdrop of force, intimidation, and death for blacks. Eventually one black student hung a sheet with a swastika painted on it out of her window, with the expressed hope that the university would force both her and the white student to remove such displays. The university did not, and eventually the black student removed her flag voluntarily in view of the fact that it was creating tensions between black and Jewish students.

While the entire debate of this incident focused on predictable free speech issues, what seemed strange to me was a repeated and unexamined imbalance in how the two students' acts were discussed. On the one hand, there was a ubiquitous assumption that the white student's attribution of meaning to the Confederate flag was "just hers," so no one else had any "business" complaining about it. The flag's meaning became a form of private property that she could control exclusively, despite other assertions of its symbolic power. (Those other assertions were just "their opinion"; all's fair in the competitive marketplace of meaning.)

At the same time, there was an assumption that the swastika's meaning was fixed, transcendent, "universally" understood as evil. The black student's attempt to infuse it with "her" contextualized meaning (that is, the translated power of what the Confederate flag meant to her) was lost in the face of the larger social consensus of its historical meaning. This larger social consensus is not really fixed, of course, but its monopoly on the well-educated Harvard community's understanding is tribute both to the degree of its monumentally murderous yet coalescing power in the context of Aryan supremacist movements as well as to our having learned a great deal of specific history about it. The power of that history understandably overshadowed not only that black student's attempt at a narrower meaning, but also the swastika's meaning in aboriginal American religion or in Celtic runes.

The question remains, however, how some speech is so automatically relegated to the free market of ideas, while other expressions remain invisibly monopolized by the channels not merely of what we have learned but of what we have not learned. I do not want to be misunderstood: while I do not question the consensus of negativity embodied in the swastika, I wonder at the immovability of the positive consensus attending the Confederate flag— the sense that as long as it makes some people happy, the rest of us should just butt out. The limits of such reasoning might be clearer if applied to the swastika: without having to conclude anything about whether to censor it, the fact remains that we usually do not cut off discussions of Nazism with the conclusion that it was a way of creating warm and happy communities for the German bourgeoisie.

Let me be clearer still in this thorny territory: I do not wish to compare or relativize the incomparable horrors of the Holocaust and of the legacy of slavery in the U.S. This is not an appropriate subject for competition. What I do worry about is that it is easier to condemn that which exists at a bit of cultural distance than that in which we may ourselves be implicated. And it is easier to be clear about the nature of the evils we know than those whose existence we deny or do not know. The easy flip-flopping between "free" and "monopolistic" signification is a function of knowledge; it underscores the degree to which we all could stand to educate ourselves perhaps most particularly about the unpleasantries of the past: we should not have to rely upon the "shock" shorthand of campus crises, for example, to communicate the experience of black history in the good old days of legalized lynching.

3. Lesson Number Three: We Must Commit Ourselves to Learning the Particular Historical Details of Each Other's Lives. The ability to negotiate the politics of coexistence on college campuses is directly related to how those leaders-of-tomorrow, college graduates, will resolve such problems in "the real world." The fighting in the Crown Heights section of Brooklyn, for example, has been plagued by some of the same symbolic and analytical confusion encountered in the Harvard example. The Crown Heights situation has been relentlessly characterized as a breakdown of friendly relations between blacks and Jews across the political spectrum, which it surely is, but I think that this broad, simplistic characterization, in the context of an infinitely more nuanced encounter, is itself part of the cause of the breakdown. The term "black-Jewish" alliance is, on the one hand, commonly used to invoke a specific history of struggle in the United States, from the turn of the century onward. These struggles, from the labor movement to the Civil Rights Movement, were social settings in which the two groups worked shoulder to shoulder, shoring up and virtually defining the Left in this nation. As was—and still is—appropriate and efficient in the face of the legalized monolith of U.S. apartheid laws, blacks and Jews focused on their similarities, on the commonalities of the Holocaust and the Middle Passage, so incomparable in one sense, yet so filled with the unbounded mandate of never forgetting. Since the successes of the Civil Rights Movement, however, it is clear that the things that divide us demand addressing also. While blacks and Jews may occupy the same symbolic social space when it comes to the

Ku Klux Klan, our divergent histories and daily experiences in the United States make it difficult to presuppose much "sameness" when we deal with each other in more nuanced contexts. For example, while both groups share anguishing issues about members who "pass" as either white or gentile, this assimilative force takes on confusing power as to each other. "You're white," hurled blacks in Crown Heights; "Anti-Semites," Jews hurled back. And of course each side was right in terms of the injurious forays of that verbal war. The Hasidic community used insulting racial epithets and characterizations about blacks, terms whose history goes back hundreds of years in U.S. history. Their employment in this context is testament to the power of even partial assimilation into the ethic of America's race hatred. At the same time, Hasidic Jews are not "invisible" minorities in the sense that most American Jews are; their determination not to blend peaceably into the J. Crew mass of manners, morals, and fashionable dress "marks" them in important and dangerous ways—ways that I think reawaken the sort of unfettered, force-fully unsubtle anti-Semitism that flourished more prevalently only a generation or two ago, when most Jews were somewhat more visible by accent, circumcision in the days before it was widespread, segregation, and so on. And blacks, as participants in this culture, have been no less—nor any more—assimilated into that anti-Semitism than anyone else.

4. Lesson Number Four: It Helps to Consider the Oppositions We Build into a Debate. I cannot help wondering if the Crown Heights tension is really about "blacks versus Jews" at all. That opposition connotes a rather flattened sense of post-civil-rights breakdown, and as well as a certain neoconservative vision in which Jews have become "zealous Zionists" and blacks have "lost" their "transcendent moral claim" on national sympathies. Does the construction of the debate in these stereotyped terms contribute anything to the possibility of accord? In fact, does it not precisely capitulate to the forces that would have us all just give up, get nose jobs and Michael Jackson's skin disease, go to Yale and move next door to Clarence Thomas?

Could not the dispute in Crown Heights more fruitfully be recast as one involving Jews who do not feel "white" yet who occupy the identity space of whites, particularly as the beneficiaries of certain public services like that of police protection: and, at the same time, involving blacks who are unaware of themselves as resonantly Christian in this context, yet who, having evolved a strong survival version of Christianity, are implicated in its history toward Jews indirectly, convolutedly perhaps, but nonetheless.

I daresay it would also help the analysis a lot to take at least some stock of the fact that the steadfastly Messianic Hasidic community in Crown Heights is at odds not just with blacks but with much of the rest of the Jewish community in this country. Similarly, much of the black Caribbean community of Crown Heights is not only at odds with the Hasidic community but also at odds with—in some instances even prejudiced against—blacks whose ancestors were slaves in the United States. The issue, in other words, is, at least in part, whether unassimilated immigrant groups can live in peace not just with one another, but within a culture that resolutely denies their particularity as just too *unpleasant.*

The extent to which constructive conversation becomes derailed under such circumstances is epitomized by a story one of my students told me: at the height of the Crown Heights tension, one of the local television stations thought it would be a great idea to have a group of black and Jewish teenagers having a conversation that would model tolerance, healing, and general we-are-the-worldness. The plan encountered immediate problems, from the fact that the Hasidic boys could not have such a conversation in the same room with girls, and that the black youth of Crown Heights seemed a little, well, sullen. So the producers went about remedying this by fetching a group of reform Jewish students from Long Island, and some pleasant-faced upper-middle-class black kids from private schools—and had them talk about Crown Heights, *in* Crown Heights even, engaging in a "debate" that had less to do with the affected communities than with modeling an imagined melting pot bubbling happily, flavorful and harmonious. But the absurdity of importing people to enact a conversation that the actual neighborhood cannot have is directly akin to the Allan Bloomian nostalgia for an undifferentiated "American" culture flowing seamlessly from the fount of "Western" civilization. Whose anxieties are supposedly redressed by such mythic representations? And is it possible that such representations are not just misleading, but downright oppressive?

5. Lesson Number Five: It Helps to Consider One's Metaphors. When Tina Brown's new *New Yorker* blasted its way into its first national controversy, it did so by meshing—I even want to say mashing—embodied symbols of the violent showdown in Crown Heights. The February 14, 1993 issue featured a cover illustration of a Hasidic man kissing a black woman on the lips. The artist, award-winning cartoonist Art Spiegelman, whose *Maus* books are among the most oddly captivating and powerfully moving accounts of the Holocaust ever published, explained his intentions as a Valentine's Day wish to New York that life's collisions be as simply resolved as kissing and making up.

But the *New Yorker* cover offended everyone, it seemed, and pleased no one; and for all of Tina Brown's protestations that it was meant to spark controversy, the controversy that ensued was hardly one that spoke much to the problems of Crown Heights. As lucidly, even childishly resonant as Spiegelman's wish was on one level, the illustration nevertheless fell into a battleground of complicated symbolic meaning. That battleground is fraught with lessons, I think, about the kinds of conversations blacks and Jews need (and need not) to be having with one another, and about the pitfalls that even our best efforts at reconciliation seem to encounter. It underscores, moreover, the urgent necessity to continue the conversation, even when it misfires as dismally as Spiegelman's kiss.

Frankly, it was hard to imagine to whom Spiegelman's fantasy was addressed. The upscale WASPy Manhattanites or wanna-be Manhattanites who form so much of the readership? Hasidic Jews, who are not permitted to touch any but their own wives—and certainly not with the closed-eyed, mouth-to-mouth eroticism of Spiegelman's depiction? Blacks, whose experience with artistic rendering by whites has always veered to the erotically transgressive? (And imagine *how* transgressive the Jezebel that could lure a devout Hasidic man from his community and the pursuit of piety.)

The act of kissing as the chosen metaphor for the kind of complicated political reconciliation that Crown Heights requires strikes me as a sign of how immensely sexualized our culture is—in particular, how sexualized our racial encounters are. (And the kiss depicted was quite a sexual one: if there is any doubt about that, consider the same pose with, say, a Hasidic man and Al Sharpton. Perhaps then, in our sexually titillated but homophobic society, the raw sex appeal, even pornography, of the pose would have been all too exaggeratedly visible.) Grey babies have become the optimist's antidote to everything, the pervasive antimiscegenist horror that inspires segregation's powerful taboos having time and again been countered by the simplistic antidote of more miscegenation.

But, while political intermarriage may be noble and good, I think this form of romanticism-as-political-solution misses the point. If the whole world were grey tomorrow, I think the situation in Crown Heights would still exist, because it cannot be cured by convincing everyone that we are all related. Crown Heights is about how—or if—we human creatures can live together while observing very different cultural practices. I do not mean to suggest that racism and anti-Semitism are not central culprits in the dispute, but that resolutions based on innocently assimilative, dehistoricized ideals only aggravate rather than assuage. And that maybe a more respectful—yet perhaps ultimately more difficult—vision would depict a Hasidic Jew and a Caribbean neighbor just nodding and saying good morning to one another as they passed each other on the street they share.

It is a kind of heresy, I know, to suggest that the storybook desire for a Montague to marry a Capulet and live happily ever after might be oppressive, and again, I want to underscore the degree to which, like Spiegelman, I personally believe that the streets of Verona will never be calm until there is a little more love between us. But what concerns me is, again, that the West Side Story solution is a blindly depoliticized one, and obscures the possibility that simple cantankerous coexistence may be more like what we should be aiming for in a democracy based on live and let live.

In sum, I think the campus debates that have been so persistently and dismissively lumped under the rubric of "political correctness" are at the center of this nation's resolution of its commitment to the civil rights of all its citizens. This conversation, whether on campuses or in Congress, will require some very hard work, lots of angry participants, and a high threshold for the noise of much wailing and gnashing of teeth. It will necessitate recognition of a fluid view of identity and community, in which the boundaries, phases, and fragments of our lives are always multiply intersecting, constantly shifting, in flux. It will mean that it is not enough for blacks to say we were not at the pogroms or we were not Nazis—the identity of Christianity and the history it imports implicates black Christians whether we will it or not. Similarly, it will mean that it is not enough for Jews to claim that they are not related to white slaveowners, for they, too, are implicated as such in certain black-white controversies. It means learning each other's history, so that Jews will have to resist the temptation to cast black anti-Semitism as something New! Different! and worse than ever before; and blacks will have to resist the characterizations of Jewish racism against blacks as something Ancient! Different! and worse than all other forms of racism.

It will require finding our own words and translating the symbols of each other's suffering. It will require the hard, hard work of sorting out the meanings behind the coopting of words that would keep us divided forever.

Notes

1. "White Teacher Apologizes for 'Enslaving' Two Blacks during Lesson on History," *Jet* Magazine, March 8, 1993: 11, col. 1–2.

4

The Meanings and Metaphors of Student Resistance

Dale Bauer with Katherine Rhoades

The topic of student harassment of feminist teachers is a vexed one, especially given Susan Faludi's *Backlash* and her warning about arguments launched against feminism by way of "impressions" about feminism's deleterious effects. We write with the awareness that some will dismiss this analysis of antifeminism as another form of "impression"-ism or impression management. The danger in doing so is to reject the very real issue of feminism and feminist authority in the classroom, just as it is to misprise how the backlash triggers and shapes students' responses to academic distinctions, especially the mandatory teacher evaluations required for tenure, promotion, and accountability. The following essay examines student comments from introductory writing or women's studies courses—in evaluations and in journals—in order to determine how feminists might transform both their own notions of authority and their students' expectations.[1] Transformative authority entails redefining the classroom as a place of negotiating differences in relation to power, and seeing individual classrooms as less isolated and more interrelated.

Recent pedagogic research has found account after account of resistance to feminists in the classroom and resistance to discussing male privilege and social inequality. In fact, as Elizabeth Grauerholz argues in an essay on "contrapower harassment"—a term coined by K. Benson—a professor's "formal power" over students does not prevent harassment in the form of anonymous sexual or antifeminist comments on student evaluations (789–790). "In some sense, Benson notes, the anonymity of student's behavior serves to reverse the power relationship between the professor and student" (790). Because of differences in authority between students and teachers, antifeminist harassment often takes indirect form. Violent expressions of student resistance occur—heckling, defacing of posters and office doors, public displays of belittling or defamatory material—expressions that are often part of a general distrust of feminist authority. Some examples are more insidious than others, an offensiveness often reflected by the ways evaluations are employed by senior faculty and administrators in tenure and promotion cases. The purpose is to analyze how, in the words of one feminist teacher, "both senior faculty evaluators and students ... have coded this response [of being too feminist] in ways that shift the focus from values (ideology) to value (whether I was a 'good' or 'bad' teacher)" (Heller). This coded shift suggests the link between authority in the classroom and student resistance or harassment, sometimes even faculty harassment of feminists. The focus in the section that follows is on authority and feminist pedagogy: how students' assumptions about authority affect feminist teachers. These assumptions emerge from students' legacies of education, and are reproduced by the demand for mastery and command that teaching evaluation forms often pose and sustain. These forms reinforce the long-held notion that an "authoritative commanding ... model" of teaching, as Tamar Heller argues, is the most effective and hence the most valuable, even though this authoritative style has been vigorously called into question. Theorists of critical pedagogy such as Kathleen Weiler, among many others, have shown the value of alternative pedagogies, and we offer feminist style and authority here as paradigmatic of the difficulties confronting other innovative teaching models. The analysis we offer may prove broadly useful as a way of reading resistance.

Interpreting Student Evaluations

In a large, required, introductory literature lecture course, a feminist professor received the following evaluation: "We read *Frankenstein* last year, and our teacher had nothing to say about a feminist theme in the story. Every story we had this year [the professor] tried to 'feminize.' I don't understand the purpose for this. When these books were written, women were oppressed. But that was then and this is NOW!!" There are two chronologies invoked in this student assessment, both of which are crucial for understanding student backlash against feminists in the classroom. First, the student quoted refers to reading Mary Shelley's novel *last year* and the priority of that initial, ostensibly nonpolitical—or, at least, nonfeminist—interpretation of *Frankenstein*. Second, the student refers to "when these books were written," when women had "real" problems with oppression, in contrast to the liberation women seemingly enjoy now. These assumptions about the status of interpretation and of oppression are interrelated: the first suggests that students perceive interpretation as (or ought to be) a neutral activity and receive some readings as neutral. Behind the second expression of resistance is the assumption that students who read themselves as exterior to politics also resist seeing themselves as part of history. Their senses of knowledge as neutral and of history as the finished past inform their resistance to feminism, whether they see feminism as an interpretive method or as a historical phenomenon.

Teachers who offer counterhegemonic interpretations of the way things are—as feminists do when they instruct students to recognize how knowledge and daily life are based on systems of gender construction—confront students with the generalized diffusion of bureaucratic and institutional power under which we ordinarily operate. Curriculum controversies propelled by certain social movements—feminism among them—bring into focus anxiety about power. Many students resist being wrenched out of the now-comfortable paradigm of liberal humanism, with its rhetoric of positivist science, bourgeois individualism, and capitalist progress. Those resistances are often registered in students' objections to feminist "style," since "style"—as a reductive code for everything feminism represents—is devalued as the substitute for substance, a condemnation linked to the metaphysical distrust of the body, particularly the gendered body (see Bauer and Jarratt, 153).[2]

The range of emotions students employ to describe the feelings that their feminist teacher elicited is telling: upset, in turmoil, exhilarated, exhausted, scared, frustrated, annoyed, troubled, angry, tranquil, and cared for. As one student wrote about an instructor, "Her discussion was warm and comfortable, but I didn't feel like I learned a lot. More of just talking about interesting things." Another student lamented in a journal entry recorded midway through her first feminist course, "The whole aspect of femminism [sic] can begin to wear you out a little." We analyze these student responses in both evaluations and solicited journals, especially as those responses form a kind of student protest against what feminism represents as a pedagogy and as a style.

It is important to start with this range of emotions, from exhilaration to exhaustion, in order to define the issues surrounding many students' struggles with feminist style, and to determine why some feel that they do not "learn a lot" from it. "Feminist style," as Kris Straub describes it, is "a matter of presentation, a mode of action and self-imaging ... a political awareness of the imagery by which the feminist critic represents herself as she analyzes the representation of other women" (153). Surely it would be a mistake to believe that students are indifferent to feminist style, since many feminist courses we know begin with analyzing gender images in the media, a study out of which students learn to deconstruct the codes embedded in the prevailing images of "women" in representations. Not surprisingly, some of these students quickly learn to channel what they have learned about the meanings of these gender images into responses to their instructors' feminist styles. Or, blocked on the subject of feminism, they deflect their anxieties onto the teacher, who is perceived to have robbed them of the easy resource of their prior assumptions about bodies, cultural identities, style itself. These styles include not only dress and appearance, but also behavior.

Although one of the goals of feminist courses is to enable students to join in the dialogue about feminism, feminist professors carry the burden of representing their courses as value-neutral when, in fact, one of the assumptions of feminist pedagogy is that the classroom is value-positive, and that the classroom is the place to negotiate a consensus of values about nonsexist, nonracist, Western culture (see Bizzell). Yet style is not only the realm of gesture, appearance, and dress, but also the classical "dress" of thought. Style, then, is dismissed as the effort "to persuade through deception" (Bauer and Jarratt, 153), but it is precisely the "style" of feminism—its attempt to link the personal with the political, the physical body with the intellect—that is under attack (see below). When a student writes, "You sometimes appear to be too friendly and buddyish with the class," the suggestion is that the instructor has violated the assumed neutrality of the professor in seeking— as a feminist—to establish a relation to her students. Here, the professor insufficiently attends to the hierarchy of power in which aloofness is understood as desirable; remoteness, a sign of strength. Yet feminists are also expected to break down hierarchies of power: "I really enjoyed the way the instructor approached us: ie: sitting on the desk instead of behind it. This brought about an open atmosphere."

Here is the double bind of feminist style: one has to put one's body forward *and* maintain professional distance, while, as one student commented, not being "too professional" or too intellectual, "us[ing] big words that were often unclear." Although professors in other classes are always and everywhere subject to such dismissals or disappointments, they are generally not stereotyped as speakers for a particular ideology. Such professors may "analyze" and "intellectualize" too much, but the fault lies with them—their psychology, their intellects—not the perceived sense of their subject. ("Overreading," or digging out meanings, or finding "conspiracies" are all familiar charges in this vein.)

In rejecting feminist professors, many students also reject the embodiment of the threat of change. Many of the evaluations that are part of this study address the literal embodiment of feminism: the site/sight of the teacher's body. Cheryl L. Johnson concurs that the classroom often invites an "array of responses and expectations, even as [students] challenge [teachers'] authority in the classroom" (418). Writing about her identity as an African-American woman professor, a role "both confused and confusing," she remarks: "Race and gender conspire in the construction of [Johnson's] role as teacher and [her] students' interpretation of an African-American literary text" (410). Whether addressing her clothes, her hair, or her body parts, students often dissect the feminist professor, trying to find something somatic (whether racial or sexual) with which to contain her intellectual difference. The most recurring pattern is one of dismissal, often very plain-spoken (as if to counter the presumably overintellectualized concerns of feminist analysis). For example, "Please stop the *feminist bullshit*. We (the students) don't care about this attitude. Teach some more *interesting* books next time, not the feminist shit like this semester's." Or, as another evaluation put it, "Feminism has its place but not in an English classroom. . . ." This reaction suggests the clash of feminist discourse with some students' notions of appropriate intellectual matters.[3]

The following interpretations of these teaching evaluations do not derogate or reject students' resistance to feminism, but instead take that resistance seriously in an effort to elucidate the significance of individual resistance within a classroom community, since meeting resistance is better than dodging or dismissing it. Lending significance to such opposition or confrontation as part of the feminist course, however, reintroduces the dilemma of teaching-as-persuasion. Student teaching evaluations called for "objectivity," "neutrality," values of individual expression, liberal exchange within communities of knowledge, and objectifiable standards. How could students' needs for transparency be negotiated with feminist pedagogy?

In "The Other 'F' Word," the first of these studies of the meaning of student evaluations of feminist pedagogy, Bauer noted that students:

(1) did not find the political-personal voice an appropriate one for the classroom;

(2) did not want to see the classroom space as ideologically charged but rather as neutral or objective;

(3) did not resist feminisms so much as the negotiation of the public-private split;

(4) did find it possible to negotiate the difference between their inherited cultural values and feminist political ones *if* allowed to ask their own questions; and

(5) did not want to see feminism as a cultural discipline or authority.

Resistance is not something to be overcome, but a necessary component in the "historical attitude" toward feminist pedagogy (see Bauer and Jarratt). In the name of "free expression" and individual right of judgment, we hear arguments against recent changes in pedagogy and the collective values of the classroom. Many students desire to investigate classes and to root out those who violate their assumption of pedagogical neutrality. The complaint is that a new oppressiveness inheres in advancing a truly democratic cultural politics, especially as feminists espouse it. Our fear is that such charges of the tyranny of political correctness have led colleagues and students alike to fashion a new enemy: the feminist as fascist.

Reading evaluations to understand the metaphors and tropes the students use to describe resistance reveals the students' call for an authority in the classroom. We need to revise what that authority means, however. Students often speak with a great deal of authority, the authority of a middle-class orthodoxy. The following teaching evaluations testify to first-year students' notions of authority and what it should be. These evaluations are typical of the language students use to explain their often veiled assumptions about education. Keep in mind that these evaluations are from required courses in which the instructors often teach a dialogue between genders and avoid an emphasis on either strictly male or female voices.

I think the prof. should realize her obligations to the students in regard to teaching English (in the main) and not letting her own opinions ruin an otherwise excellent and informative course.

The lectures, in my opinion, were based too much on the feminist point-of-view. This stand often made the lectures boring and often unbearable. It seems no matter what happens it is always the males [*sic*] fault. At other times, though, the prof. gave very in-depth knowledge.

I didn't like reading works, almost all of which were written by women, about women breaking free from social conventions and breaking away from authority. It got a little monotonous, having this as a running theme through every piece of literature.

100

Note here how authority is aligned in these evaluations with information-giving, in-depth knowledge, and facts. From this professor, the students want "just the facts" and those facts should be "in the main," not letting political opinions "ruin" an "informative," and thus admirable, course. You can read the implicit advice to the professor in the third evaluation quoted above: do not break away (as feminist teacher) from *your* traditional authority, for doing so risks being "monotonous," "boring," "often unbearable." This evaluation is especially telling, since it typifies the kind of responses students have to material that challenges their naturalized or accepted beliefs. There is a contradiction between the claim that the class is both unbearable and "boring," as though the latter were a code word for the shutdown the student must accomplish in order to avoid hearing or internalizing the challenge the material poses.

These evaluations also point to professors' transgression of an assumed professorial style, an inversion against the assumed neutrality many students have come to expect. Students will also focus on teachers' bodies or criticize their speaking voices, because these are the human qualities—the visual and the aural—that cannot be so easily shut out. Feminism here is identified with opinion, point of view, attitude, perspective, style—but not with fact, knowledge, or authority. The students see knowledge and authority as inherited or conferred, not as the result of an activity, or engagement, or work of persuasion. And certainly some professors have withdrawn from exploring the source of the rhetorical power of the classroom.

The students come to the classroom with a very understandable notion from their legacy of education about what constitutes authority and what sort of authority garners power *outside* the academy. But feminist teachers are invested in another sort of power: persuasive power, an exchange model of teaching allied with an ethics. These and other teaching evaluations suggest that we need a different way of negotiating students' cultural authority (inherited after years of education) with feminist authority in the classroom. Clearly, it is not enough to try to convince students to adopt feminism using a traditional teaching model of authority. We *could* use the authority our students are socialized to confer upon us, but it would be wrong and hypocritical, since that authority is so often coercive. Conversely, the early models of feminist decentering of power in the classroom have also failed. Feminist teachers who decentered all authority found that they were undermining themselves: students had trouble granting authority to women when their education had not generally shown women as authorities. Yet relaxing classroom authority is not the same as transforming it.

We need to provide our students with a dialogic model of authority, one which gives students a kind of "constructive authority" (see Greene) and, at the same time, challenges how students see feminist authority as a contending discourse (not just opinion, but informed and ethical authority). It moves them from the monologic model of authoritative voice to an authority in flux. With constructive authority, students can "restructure" their inherited cultural knowledge in a new pattern based on feminist frameworks. They appropriate the feminist context and restructure it for the given rhetorical situation of the classroom or assignment. The notion of constructive or transformative authority gives us insight into ways of modifying the students' sense of authority and our own.

While feminism often contends with exactly the dominant senses of authority students have inherited, we are also concerned about an uncritical acceptance of feminism as a liberatory rhetoric or an ahistorical assumption that the classroom is a place in which all participants are equally enfranchised to enter open dialogue (see bell hooks's response to Diana Fuss in *American Literary History*). We worry about students' too-easy accommodation of feminism, an old identity that may be too readily abandoned for the new feminist one so that a time will come for them when feminism is also a "sell," a fraud. The danger is that the language of bourgeois individualism mediates feminism, producing a feminism without a history and a feminist commodity which is a disposable, ahistorical phenomenon.

Such attacks against the "faddishness" of feminism are crucial to understanding the anxiety underlying the backlash. One example is telling:

> The key questions are thought to be about gender, race and class. . . . What groups did the authors of these works represent? How did their books enhance the social power of those groups over others? Truth and beauty and excellence are regarded as irrelevant; questions of intellectual and aesthetic quality, dismissed. . . . There are an awful lot of "politically correct" positions [in classrooms today].

This critique assumes that feminist pedagogy precludes discussions of ethics and aesthetics. Moreover, it also assumes that such issues are politically neutral and ahistorical. Like the student evaluations quoted above, this response argues for a neutrality that favors an intellectual status quo, that is, nonturbulence. This evaluation of feminism in the classroom does not come from a student, but from Lynne Cheney in the November 14, 1990 issue of the *Wall Street Journal.* Cheney identified the *College English* essay "The Other 'F' Word: The Feminist in the Classroom" as a dangerous piece of criticism (Bauer, 1990), and insinuated that the feminist approach to dealing with resistance to feminism bespoke a desire to discourage debate and make students toe a party line.

Far from being the "conversion narratives" one might cynically expect, the evaluations reported on, in that essay as well as this one, reflect a growing and vocal resistance not so much to feminism itself but to the challenge feminist pedagogy and rhetoric pose to traditional ideologies of education, especially to the banking model and to patriarchal models of pedagogic authority. (As one student put it, "sometimes [student resistance is] merely a defensive reaction against the politicization of very personal experiences" [Klein, 3].) In short, we have to learn to read student resistance to feminist teaching as a nostalgia for an imagined neutrality, a particularly dangerous nostalgia since it fuels the antifeminist backlash we see all around us today.

Feminist Style

Some of the reasons for student complaints remain the same in feminist and nonfeminist courses alike: "drab and boring" lectures, tedious assignments, too much reading, and the insistent temptations to skip class and/or fall asleep. What differs about feminist classes is the added dollop of attack on feminist style, in which students' assumptions about feminism are grafted onto their instructors. And that assault, curiously, mirrors the culture's struggle with feminism.

This resistance, which students share with the media, draws in part on their longing for some sort of cooperative or collaborative structure within which to work, a framework which inevitably contradicts their insistence on individualist values. Ultimately, many students worry that individualism does not work, and that realization terrifies them. Instead of representing their anxiety over individualist models, they assail feminism for the perceived tenuousness of the alternative it represents. That sense of failure is linked to the (over)expectations and anxious projections that students bring to the feminist classroom. Expecting the often-touted "conversion experience" of early feminism, these students are disappointed that feminism has not yet changed the world, and still struggles with resistance to it.

We begin this section, then, with the following questions: What do feminists intentionally adopt as "style," especially as a way of changing or at least addressing the power dynamic in the classroom? And, on the other hand, how much is feminist style, in the current academic scene, constituted by students' expectations about their feminist professors? While we do not know what feminist style *really* is nor how feminist style *should* develop, our motive in focusing on the visual codes many of our students are most interested in—clothes, gestures, age, makeup—is to figure out the mutual expectations about feminism that can be read through the discourse of student reactions and academic writing. All of these codes, and others, are in some way produced by the professor and/or projected by the students in the transactional space of the classroom.

In at least half of twenty journals recorded during an introductory feminist course, students begin by describing their *a priori* fears of taking a feminist class. While these journals are meant as a way of recording reactions throughout the semester, they often serve the same purpose of venting frustration that teaching evaluations often do. The following is among the more descriptive: "I was sure that the class would be filled with four or five hundred raging, die-hard feminists who would men bash telling of all the evils men have created. I guess you could say I was a little nervous." A number of other students share this student's nervousness. Referring to feminists as "big time radicals" and "brutes," who "live and breathe" feminism, they register their fears of and disdain for what they perceive as an alien, angry, overpowering, and dangerous feminist image. Taken together, their descriptions construct feminists as a large, undifferentiated, angry mass of women who are out of control ("raging"); hateful toward men ("male-bashers") and yet masculine themselves ("brutes"); and zealously and exclusively committed to feminist causes ("die-hard," "live and breathe"). These negative appraisals of feminism typically focus on public displays of appearance and behavior that contradict students' allegiances, however controversial and incomplete, to some of the dominant constructions of a feminine ideal.

In several instances, students describe how their initial fears about feminist classes were quelled by feminist style. For example, one student expressed relief when, after the first lecture, she surmised that the professor is "just a normal woman, not a lesbian." This student not only tacitly conflates heterosexuality with being normal, but she also projects complete confidence in her ability to judge the lecturer's sexual orientation solely on the basis of her appearance, speech, and mannerisms. Moreover, she is certain that the lecturer is "normal" (that is, "heterosexual") because she does not "look" like a lesbian. Here lesbianism, like feminism, is judged as an observable performance that projects a certain style, thus confirming a person's positionality.

This student, like many of her peers, grounds her opinions in the belief that an observer can readily draw on a prescribed cultural cartography to chart feminist and lesbian identities. These media constructions castigate feminists less for their political and theoretical positionings than for their behavior and appearance, which are believed to contravene acceptable feminine sensibilities. Not surprisingly, these same concerns for behavior and appearance become the foci for many students, in the course of their attempts to make sense out of their encounters with feminism and with feminist teachers.

One student summarized her overall response to her first encounter with a feminist classroom by stating, "I sort of feel that perhaps women want to be angry about something and therefore are searching for something to take offense to." The following journal entry from another student also reflects this pattern:

> At first I was disbelieving of the readings and the lecture, because I thought people were overreacting and finding excuses to be angry. Then I thought about it a little more, and I think that I am reluctant to believe certain things because they are so aweful [sic] and there seems to be nothing I can do about them.

This student explains her encounters with feminist readings as beginning with disbelief and progressing toward hopelessness. Some of that hopelessness emerges from a sense of feminist style as part and parcel of an overall female complaint, a situation Lauren Berlant describes as "a mode of self-expression," as a "powerful record of patriarchal oppression, circumscribed by a knowledge of women's inevitable delegitimation within the patriarchal public sphere" (243). Insofar as that complaint is powerful, some women students fear its public nature; insofar as it is a record of women's powerlessness, some women students fear its perpetuation. Her hopelessness extends from her sense that she, as an individual, cannot change women's "aweful" situation.

Another student prefaces a journal description by commenting, "I've never interacted with any feminists, but this is what I think they look like":

> Feminists look tough, not feminine. They do not wear makeup, and their hair is straight. They wear clothes in shades of black, plums, olives, and burnt reds. Necklaces and earrings are okay, bracelets are okay if they are beaded.

In this description the student draws on available cultural descriptions to paint a detailed prescription of feminist looks. She describes their material bodies, including precise imaginings of their clothing and adornments, although, as she explains, she has never interacted with any feminists. Cast in this light, the student's comments suggest that feminists violate the cultural boundaries of acceptable women's style. In students' views, feminists stand as a group united in their refusal to persuade by conventional means of feminine deception. Interacting in a society that grants a strong reading to gender, many students perceive this as a dangerous and undesirable strategy.

So comments on "feminist style" may be a red flag that something else entirely is going on in feminist classrooms: yet it is not enough to say that feminist professors are often "screens" for student fantasies.[4] Feminist style has not changed much because feminists are still fending off the same charges against what their style presumably means in the traditional codes of gender. Feminist style, then, seems to amalgamate intentional pedagogic choice with students' politicization of professors' behaviors—as a way of asserting their own politics. To that end, feminist style is complexly related to what it resists: students see it as a betrayal, even a violation of their longing to belong to some sort of community. Students and indeed many colleagues label feminism as "unstylish" (or the alternative, they see it as too faddish), thereby erasing the substance of style that is at the heart of the undermining of feminism itself.

One of the issues that recurs in student responses to feminist style is an unwavering belief in meritocracy. To challenge meritocracy is not to claim, however, a kind of victim feminism, but to suggest that the illusion of meritocracy keeps students from thinking beyond the individual. Meritocracy is so inextricably tied to individualism that dismantling the former necessarily means unravelling the latter. The academy itself is structured on individual competition, and the feminists most students see are those who have been granted merit in the system. So the presence of these feminists' bodies often belies the collective message of resistance to the seeming meritocracy of the university by the fact of the individual feminist success. And when feminists point to the establishment and success of feminist pedagogy as part of their collective project, the various pluralisms that have come to mark these programs also do not suggest any collective solutions, but merely aggregates of individual answers and visionary ideals.

Yet most feminist classrooms strive to help students confront the ironies of women's lives, while folding back the covers of signs and social constructions that may limit as well as lengthen women's strides. One student who comments that she experienced no gender limitations until "the oppression of school had its toll" describes how she attempts to incorporate feminist views into her "real world":

> When I read newspapers and texts from other classes I use my "feminist filter" to see how it applies to me as a woman or how it is being sexist or further oppressing women ... *I become a skeptic.* But also when I read literature from my women's studies classes I use my "real world" filter to take out the thick dubious adjectives—to look at it objectively—*I become a skeptic* and somewhere with the use of these two filters I find somewhat of a marriage between the two, and out of this marriage I am left with only a morsel of truth.

This student's division of the world into "feminist" and "real" is revealing. She identifies those aspects of the world that she considers "real" to be those that objectively counter feminist readings of the world. But she also sees how "feminist" lenses bring different readings to her "real" world. The "real" world is where all that opposes or galvanizes feminism applies. Feminism is still another F word: fantasy—a utopian vision that helps her to modulate and to adjudicate the truth claims of the real world. She extends her analysis by articulating how merging or "marrying" these two faulty lenses still leaves her with partial truths. What emerges as most promising from this student's account is her willingness to question the world and its representations from what she herself terms a *skeptical* point of view. She is unwilling to grant any worldview the position as a trustworthy cache of truth. In this instance, style does not detract from feminist "substance," but is, in fact, constitutive of it.

Cultivating this sort of skepticism is a worthy goal of any pedagogy. An unquestioned, wholesale acceptance of a revised feminist way of thinking is counterproductive to the goals of feminist education. By opening conversations that encourage students to contemplate their constructions of femininity and gender relations from multiple positions, feminist education offers the potential to shift the "ground" of given signs, as Teresa de Lauretis suggests (1984, 179). Perhaps more important, feminist education holds out the potential to reinforce understandings that all knowledge, including that which is inspired by emancipatory fervor, must be questioned.

By addressing how "individualism" operates as a rhetorical strategy in our society, for example, feminist educators might invite students to question their positioning relative to broader social structures and the ideologies that undergird them. Moreover, by identifying how all societies and cultures maintain complex gender arrangements, feminist professors can highlight gender as a transnational, transcultural exemplar that can be used to disclose other differences. These strategies replace the bounded structure of identity politics, relying on a perpetuation of "we" and "them," with an identification politics that encourages students to align, at least rhetorically, with other positions of difference. Given students' rhetorics of individualism, it is no accident that they seize on what they see as a collective feminist style as a manifestation of the failure of feminists to gain individual success or progress. That issue of feminist style is also the target of their anxieties about feminist collectivity and its failure (a failure resulting from feminism's gesture toward pluralism or an overall tolerance of difference). Rethinking feminist style as a politics (and teaching through that style) is one way to shape the inevitability of change within feminist teaching practice.

Feminist Authority

The question of feminist authority in the classroom—how to use it, how to empower students to use their own—is central to discussions of feminisms right now. In this context of empowering students to think critically about their disciplines, Gerald Graff has argued that we need to teach the conflicts, and to do this effectively, we must dispense with our privatized notions of "the classroom" (apparently the only place we can believe we have autonomy) and think dialogically about "classrooms" and interdisciplinarity. Bizzell has also recently written that we need "to promote our own notion of cultural literacy ... an alternative critical literacy" which draws on teaching American political documents about difference (1991, 65). She thus proposes how classroom communities can constitute their own regional and local knowledge about differences in national constructions of identity. Both Graff and Bizzell suggest teaching how we develop identities through inherited social, political, and historical languages. They advocate a rhetorical dimension of the classroom as a place to understand both private and public histories of American selves. Their authority, then, about selves-in-history would guide the student coming to consciousness of her or his position in solidarity with "diverse American groups," a vision of what Henry Giroux calls "democratic dreaming" or social egalitarianism (Bizzell, 1991, 67). Teachers' authority would serve a utopian hope.

Consider, for example, Christina Hoff Sommers' attack in *Who Stole Feminism?* against "advocacy" of any sort, since she imagines that advocacy pedagogy or politics is the method by which feminist professors contaminate the paradise of value-neutral space; that is, the college classroom. The debate over "advocacy" centers on the question of whether the classroom is value-neutral or value-positive. Sommers devotes an entire chapter to "the feminist classroom" in the hopes of deciding this debate. As many critics of traditional pedagogy have argued, students always bring their own assumptions and values to class and assume that their teachers do the same. The class-room, as students see it, is always a place where values—of the students' and teachers' own making—circulate. That circulation, *contra* Sommers, is never *one*-sided, but multisided. Pat Bizzell locates the controversy in "the idea that seemingly objective decisions on what to teach and how to teach it are deeply informed by the teacher's values, which, in turn, the teacher has learned from his or her own education in cultural values, education both in and out of school that includes cultural attitudes about gender, race and social class" (1994, 194). Following Bizzell, many others have come to see the classroom as inevitably brimming with values, while others—like Sommers—want to maintain that the classroom can remain objective and value-free. If some find feminism intimidating, it may only be in its difference from the ego-crushing that the pedagogy of relentless "reasonableness" or objectivity can so brutally practice.[5]

Teaching dialogically involves constructing a classroom climate and curriculum which allow students to generate the questions fueling the course. That is, the classroom becomes the space where authority gets trans-ferred or at least certified as transacted. Students invest in this authority and expect to be legitimated as scholars when, actually, the process is more complex than this. On the contrary, the dialogic model does not reject authority, just authoritarianism as an end in itself. In the banking model of education, personal authority and traditional belief bolster each other: these acts of authority are instrumental in that they rationalize the means (banking) to an end (education). Instead, the feminist role is not as facili-tator but as rhetorical authority, with the goal of transforming what students see as "authority" (criticism, feminism, theory, history) and transforming what they see as their territory—often, as a starting point, popular culture, some realm they suppose to be impervious to intellectual analysis. One of the first steps toward teaching dialogically is to establish common ground, a common history.

Not all of this cultural and historical contextualizing meets with easy acceptance, and the students' resistance is not surprising. What strikes us most about their resistance as embedded in historical resistance to women is that students see "us" (feminists)—almost all feminists hear the complaint sooner or later—as "overreading" or taking an "innocent" or objective text and imputing cultural meaning to it. "Why can't it *just* tell a good story?" students complain, their emphasis on *just* registering the intensity of their frustration or disdain, and the inevitability of their submission. Moreover, textual neutrality or the ideal of classroom objectivity is their refuge. What could be persuasive is a feminist rhetorical and cultural reading that does make sense, even troubling sense, to students who do not want to see the world as invested in political meaning rather than "just the facts." Remember the students' claim for authority in the classroom—an authority they initially see as factually based, not rhetorically based. They do not see culture as intentional or as having designs; instead, they see the feminist classroom as designing, digging out meaning, inventing "conspiracies of/in culture." Because of their legacy of education and the discrete arrangement of knowledge into disciplinary units, they reject not only a knowledge that is interdisciplinary, but also one that turns the "private" realm of values, beliefs, and leisure into a public knowledge. What dialogic teaching does, then, is to negotiate (yet again) the private-public split, a pedagogy that constitutes part of a feminist political strategy in the classroom.

This rhetorical inclination leads us less to fear the indoctrination which might accompany the politicized classroom than to fear more the failure to identify one's politics at all. No political self-identification (for instance, "I'm a white, middle-class feminist who believes . . . ") will convert a whole group of students (see Graff). With persuasive power comes the responsibility of showing what those political identifications might mean in the world, what a collective vision is. It is not to complain, as some people do, that they have no political intentions or persuasive designs. That may be, but they do have philosophical ones, with effects and persuasions of their own that have political ramifications. Given the range of voices within the academy, there is no danger that students will adopt blindly all of the positions to which they are exposed. We trust in their inheritance of a variety of discourses—some more persuasive than others—about how these discourses position them in history and in politics. They may mimic, modify, discard, or distill these positions, but students' active work is crucial to their taking responsibility for their education.

Finally, the charges of "political correctness" and "indoctrination" emerge from the existing confusion about power in general in our nation, and on campuses in particular. The teacher who foregrounds issues of power in the classroom forces students to confront a generalized bureaucratic and institutional power under which we all work daily and, hence, often invites resistance. Speaking openly about (to repeat a student's comment) "difficult politicization of personal experiences" shores up the lack of authority in a huge, diffused power system. Like us, students are anxious about power and the bureaucracy they must confront. But many students still cling to an illusion of democratic individualism—or personal accommodation—as a solution to that anxiety. Perhaps our collective disenchantment with, even resistance to, an overly rationalized and bureaucratic culture, which blocks out any possibility of shared values, will also be the path to a renewed feminist commitment.

Notes

Parts of this essay were published in *Styles of Cultural Activism,* edited by Philip Goldstein (Newark: University of Delaware Press, 1994), 64–76.

1. Bauer has been working on the qualitative meaning of student evaluations of feminist teachers since 1990. By reading evaluations to determine the assumptions students bring to bear in ideologically charged classrooms, Bauer has shown how many students imagine the classroom to be a neutral space when, in fact, feminist and critical pedagogy assumes the opposite about all pedagogical situations (Bauer, 1990). The evaluations analyzed here come from both introductory literature and introductory women's studies courses, most of which were taught by white women instructors who often dealt with questions of race and ethnicity in course content. The data from students' journals is part of a larger ethnographic study of women's studies students at a large, public university in the Midwest (Rhoades, forthcoming). Uncovering some of the complexities of students' identifications with and resistances to women's studies, Rhoades argues for expanded explanations of theories of empowerment, especially as they apply to the politics of difference in educational settings. Students participating in the journal project signed consent forms prepared in accordance with University Guidelines for Research with Human Subjects. These forms authorized use of the journal content in reporting research findings, and assured students' anonymity in that reporting. The group included twenty freshmen and sophomore students enrolled in their first introductory women's studies class. The white instructor incorporated issues related to race, ethnicity, and sexuality into the course. The students came from different class backgrounds, ranging from working- to upper-middle class, and represent regional variation, ranging from small communities in the rural Midwest to urban areas from both U.S. coasts. All of the students describe themselves as heterosexuals. Two students are returning adults, one of whom is a single mother. Four others identify as women of color: one African-American, one Asian-American, and two Chicanas.

2. Susan Jarratt and Dale Bauer take up this devaluation of feminist style in a meditation on "teaching with an attitude."

3. Lynn Keller's essay about the Women of Color in the Curriculum project at the University of Wisconsin-Madison provides a model analysis of student resistance to feminist discourse. She contends that students displaced their "reluctance to address issues of race—and thereby invite charges of racism" onto the

"safer target of feminism (safer especially in this era of anti-feminist backlash)" (33).

4. Kaja Silverman has argued that "the sartorial reticence of North American feminism is also part of a larger reaction against everything that has been traditionally associated with female narcissism and exhibitionism, that it is the symptom of what might almost be called 'The Great Feminine Renunciation.' As I look about me in the mid-eighties, I am forcibly struck by the fact that every current vestimentary code that insists upon women's social and political equality also tends either toward the muted imitation of male dress (jeans and shirts, slacks and jackets, the 'business suit'), or its bold parody (leather jackets and pants, the tuxedo 'look,' sequined ties). Feminism would seem to be in the process of repeating male vestimentary history" (149).

5. See Bauer's response to Sommers in *Democratic Culture*, the Fall 1994 issue devoted to Sommers' attacks on feminist teaching.

Works Cited and Consulted

Anderson, Martin. *Impostors in the Temple.* New York: Simon & Schuster, 1992.

Bartky, Sandra Lee. *Femininity and Domination.* New York: Routledge, 1990.

Bauer, Dale. "The Other 'F' Word." *College English* 52, 4 (April 1990): 385–396.

Bauer, Dale and Susan C. Jarratt. "Feminist Sophistics: Teaching with an Attitude." *Changing Classroom Practices*, ed. David Downing. Urbana: National Council of Teachers of English, 1994. 149–165.

Behar, Ruth. "Dare We Say 'I'? Bringing the Personal into Scholarship." *Chronicle of Higher Education* (June 29, 1994): B1–B2.

Benjamin, Jessica. *The Bonds of Love.* New York: Pantheon, 1988.

Berlant, Lauren. "The Female Complaint." *Social Text* 19/20 (Fall 1988): 237–259.

Bizzell, Patricia. "Power, Authority, and Critical Pedagogy." *Journal of Basic Writing* 10 (Fall 1991): 54–70.

———. "The Teacher's Authority: Negotiating Difference in the Classroom." *Changing Classroom Practices*, ed. David Downing. Urbana: National Council of Teachers of English, 1994. 194–201.

Brodkey, Linda and Michelle Fine. "Presence of Mind in the Absence of Body." *Boston University Journal of Education* 170, 3 (1988): 84–99.

Cheney, Lynne. *Wall Street Journal.* November 14, 1990: A16.

de Lauretis, Teresa. *Alice Doesn't: Feminism, Semiotics, and Cinema.* Bloomington: Indiana University Press, 1984.

Douglas, Susan J. *Where the Girls Are: Growing Up Female with the Mass Media.* New York: Times Books, 1994.

Faludi, Susan. *Backlash.* New York: Crown, 1991.

Genovese, Eugene. "Review of *Illiberal Education.*" *The New Republic* (April 15, 1991): 30–34.

Giroux, Henry. "Schooling as a Form of Cultural Politics: Toward a Pedagogy of and for Difference." *Critical Pedagogy, the State, and Cultural Struggle*, ed. Henry Giroux and Peter McLaren. Albany: State University of New York Press, 1989. 125–151.

Gorra, Michael. "About Men." *New York Times Magazine*, May 1, 1988.

Graff, Gerald. "A Pedagogy of Counterauthority, or the Bully/Wimp Syndrome." *Changing Classroom Practices*, ed. David Downing. Urbana: National Council of Teachers of English, 1994. 179–193.

Grauerholz, Elizabeth. "Sexual Harassment of Women Professors by Students: Exploring the Dynamics of Power, Authority, and Gender in a University Setting." *Sex Roles* 21, 11/12 (1989): 789–801.

Greene, Stuart. "Writing from Sources: Authority in Text and Tasks." *Technical Report* 55 (October 1991). University of California at Berkeley and Carnegie-Mellon University Center for the Study of Writing.

Grossberg, Larry. *We Gotta Get Out of This Place: Popular Conservatism and Postmodern Culture*. New York: Routledge, 1992.

Heller, Tamar. Personal correspondence, January 16, 1992.

hooks, bell. "Essentialism and Experience." *American Literary History* 3,1 (Spring 1991): 172–183.

Johnson, Cheryl L. "Participatory Rhetoric and the Teacher as Racial/Gendered Subject." *College English* 56, 4 (April 1994): 409–419.

Keller, Lynn. Working Paper Series #16: "Full Circle: Women of Color Across the Curriculum Project," University of Wisconsin-Madison, 1995.

Klein, Emily. Student paper, April 11, 1991.

Lather, Patti. *Getting Smart*. New York: Routledge, 1991.

Patai, Daphne and Noretta Koertge. *Professing Feminism: Cautionary Tales from the Strange World of Women's Studies*. New York: Basic Books, 1994.

Rhoades, Katherine. "Women's Studies Students and the Politics of Empowerment." Unpublished dissertation, University of Wisconsin-Madison, forthcoming.

Silverman, Kaja. "Fragments of Fashionable Discourse." *Studies in Entertainment*, ed. Tania Modleski. Bloomington: Indiana University Press, 1986. 139–152.

Sommers, Christina Hoff. *Who Stole Feminism?* New York: Simon & Schuster, 1994.

Straub, Kristina. "Feminist Politics and Post-Modernist Style." *Works and Days* 11/12 (Spring/Fall 1988): 151–165.

Wallis, Claudia. "Onward Women." *Time*. December 4, 1989: 80–89.

5

Anti-lesbian Intellectual Harassment in the Academy

Greta Gaard

"Sexism," according to Suzanne Pharr, "is kept in place by three powerful weapons designed to cause or threaten women with pain and loss"—economics, violence, and homophobia (9). These three elements also constitute the central components of anti-lesbian intellectual harassment. As lesbians in the academy, we are kept from pursuing topics of relevance to us, from holding jobs, from receiving promotion and tenure, and from having our scholarship taken seriously.[1] Anti-lesbian harassment is central to any discussion of antifeminism simply because, to the dominant culture, the lesbian represents the ultimate threat of feminism: a woman who is independent of male approval psychologically, economically, and sexually. As weapons of sexism, homophobia and its correlate, anti-lesbian harassment, serve to keep women and lesbians in their place—whether that be outside the academy and its publications, in the closet, or away from topics involving lesbians or lesbian perspectives which challenge the dominance of heterosexualism.

In practice, anti-lesbian harassment is often difficult to distinguish from more general harassment of women, since "attacks against lesbians exist on a continuum from exclusively anti-woman to exclusively anti-gay" (von Schulthess, 71). When a woman is harassed and does not respond in the way the harasser wants, one way to escalate the attack is to shift the harassment from antiwoman to anti-lesbian remarks. For this reason, researchers tend to consider lesbianism as an extension of gender, and anti-lesbian harassment as an extension and intensification of antiwoman violence (von Schulthess, 71–73). As Pharr has argued, "without the existence of sexism, there would be no homophobia" (26).

Few studies to date, however, have focused exclusively on violence against lesbians, and those that have done so tend to compare lesbians with gay men, rather than placing such incidents of harassment within the larger social context of antifeminism (von Schulthess, 66). In fact, given the postmodern emphasis on the multiplicity of identity, it is rather surprising that most of the available research documents harassment based on an assumed single-ness of identity: either gender, race, or sexuality is studied, but seldom a cross section of these. Nonetheless, it is worth comparing the contexts and find-ings of studies on anti-feminist, anti-gay, and anti-lesbian harassment, since these studies reveal certain similarities with regard to the purpose and targets of harassment, the characteristics of the aggressors, and the victims' percep-tions of harassment, frequency of reporting, and aftereffects. Such studies also offer a background against which anti-lesbian intellectual harassment may be defined.

Harassing Women, Harassing Lesbians

Most commonly, sexual harassment is described as involving escalating levels of assault, ranging from gender harassment (generalized sexist remarks and behavior) and seductive behavior (inappropriate and offensive sexual advances), to sexual bribery, sexual coercion, and sexual assault (Till). Sexual harassment has been said to occur in situations where "the offender has power over the victim, the behavior is unwanted (as perceived by the victim), [and] there is some negative harm or outcome such as distress or interfer-ence with activities (usually as perceived by the victim)" (McKinney, 422). As a form of intimidation, sexual harassment is one way for higher-status/power individuals to maintain power and control over lower-status individ-uals. But gender is not the only source of status and power: race and sexu-ality are also categories of status.

Anti-lesbian harassment differs from anti-woman harassment in that anti-lesbian harassment may occur in situations where the harasser has power only in the category of sexuality: in addition to the more predictable categories of harassers, both students and heterosexual women faculty may have the power to harass a lesbian faculty member. One researcher labels these situations "contrapower harassment" (Benson, 516–519). For example, even though a lesbian faculty member may have more position power than her students, she lacks power in terms of her stigmatized status as female and as lesbian; in fact, her stigmatized status may be used as a rationalization for viewing her achieved status as not being legitimate or important. The harassment is further complicated by race: one study found that white lesbians were more likely to experience verbal assault—86 percent of white lesbians, as opposed to 65 percent of lesbians of color—but when physical violence was involved, lesbians of color consistently experienced a higher level of violence (von Schulthess, 70).

Since most of the data on harassment considers the variable of gender separately from sexuality, the research can only be used to show that women faculty are more likely than men to be harassed by both their peers and their students.[2] One study, which focused particularly on harassment of faculty by students, found that 48 percent of female faculty claimed to have experienced at least one form of sexual harassment by a student, ranging from sexist comments to sexual assaults (McKinney, 426). Another study showed a clear pattern of unmarried women as being the more frequent victims of harassment (though the researchers did not make the correlation that most lesbians are unmarried, and make further inquiries regarding the study participants' sexuality) (Rubin and Borgers, 397–411). In fact, the only group more frequently targeted for harassment than female faculty in the academy is female students. Male students, it is reported, are "quite unlikely to be harassed" (Fitzgerald et al.).

Gay men, lesbians, and heterosexual women alike are harassed most frequently by heterosexual men, whose power is derived from their status based on age, sexuality, race, or gender alone (Rubin and Borgers, 407). According to data from San Francisco's Community United Against Violence (CUAV), the general profile of a "gay-basher" is "a young male, often acting together with other young males, all of whom are strangers to the victim" (Berrill, 29). In CUAV's 1990 studies of gay-bashing, 92 percent of the incidents reported overall were perpetrated by males (Berrill, 30). What the perpetrators know is that the categories of woman, lesbian, and gay male are conceptually similar, marginalized, and the authorized targets of harassment and violence in dominant culture.

The way that harassment is perceived also falls along gender lines, with women being more likely to define incidents as harassment, and men being more likely to believe the victims have contributed to their own problems (Rubin and Borgers, 410). As of 1991, the most consistent finding in studies of harassment were these gender differences in perceptions of harassment (Fitzgerald and Ormerod, 282). These findings are important, since the way a victim perceives an incident affects whether or not she will report it: usually, only the most serious forms of harassment are likely to be reported.

Consistently, studies find that, although a large number of female students report experiencing events that researchers define as harassment, only a small percentage of these same women are able to name the events as forms of sexual harassment (Fitzgerald and Ormerod, 283). Comparing the research on gender harassment with that on sexuality reveals a certain consistency: a survey of four hundred lesbians in San Francisco showed that 84 percent reported experiencing anti-lesbian harassment, but only 15 percent reported these incidents to the police, because they did not perceive the harassment as "serious enough" (von Schulthess, 68–69). Minimizing acts of harassment is one example of the way women, lesbians, and other marginalized groups are socialized to protect their abusers.

Whether the victims are lesbian, gay, or heterosexual women, very few individuals report incidents. One study found that only three percent of the women in their sample had attempted to report a sexual harassment experience (Fitzgerald et al.). In study after study, this non-reporting behavior could be traced to a few, very specific problems: a belief that the incident was not "serious enough"; a fear that their story would not be believed, and they would be further victimized through reporting it; a lack of faith in the effectiveness of reporting to change their situation; and a fear of further harassment from their harassers once they were reported (McKinney, 436; Rubin and Borgers, 406). For gays and lesbians in particular, further harassment was especially feared, as was the concern that no action would result from their reports (D'Augelli, 320). As one study focusing specifically on heterosexual women concluded, "University officials should not interpret the lack of reported cases as indicators of the absence of sexual harassment on their campuses" (Brooks and Perot, 46).

At the same time that information on anti-lesbian harassment is desperately needed, it is also especially difficult to obtain. As one campus study reports, "Because lesbians, gays, and bisexuals constitute a relatively closeted, invisible community ... no methodology has yet been developed for drawing a scientifically random sample of lesbians and gays from the general population" (*In Every Classroom*). According to another campus study, although 50 percent of the participants reported experiencing anti-gay harassment, 62 percent of the participants knew of no harassment of lesbians (D'Augelli). The current lack of information may be the result of researchers' failure to focus on lesbians, as well as lesbians' reluctance to report incidents of harassment.

Lesbian faculty in particular have especially strong reasons for not reporting their abuse. Many feel that they are already two laps behind in the "race for tenure," by virtue of gender and sexuality, and must work that much harder to build strong tenure cases; such women are reluctant to spend writing time on telling their stories, when they could be writing for publication. Lesbians who are closeted face a double burden: reporting harassment entails disclosing both their sexuality and the details of their harassment. Finally, many feel that homophobia is institutionalized to such a degree at their university that their harassment is somehow sanctioned by the academic community, and reporting would result only in escalating incidents of abuse (*From Invisibility to Inclusion*). Unfortunately, this silence is a major limitation in studies of anti-gay/lesbian harassment, since they are of necessity based on nonrepresentative samples (Berrill, 39). As some campus case studies show, as many as 70 percent of all anti-gay or anti-lesbian incidents are never reported (Ehrlich, 109).

Whether or not the harassment is reported, however, the victims suffer. The negative effects on work performance and career advancement have been repeatedly documented (Brooks and Perot). Studies of anti-gay/lesbian harassment report serious mental health consequences of victimization, including sleep disturbances and nightmares, headaches, diarrhea, uncontrollable crying, agitation and restlessness, increased use of drugs, and deterioration in personal relationships (Garnets, Herek, and Levy, 208). In his study of anti-gay violence, Howard Ehrlich introduces the term "ethnoviolence," which refers to "an act or attempted act in which the actor is motivated to do psychological or physical harm to another, where the 'other' is perceived as a group representative or is identified with a group, and where the motivation for the act is group prejudice" (Ehrlich, 107). Ehrlich's findings indicate that ethnoviolence has a greater impact on its victim than do other forms of victimization, including higher levels of depression and withdrawal, increased sleep difficulties, anxiety, and loss of confidence.

To date, studies of harassment for both lesbians and heterosexual women have suffered various lapses in analysis. In terms of research scope, for example, a 1990 review essay of research studies investigating sexual harassment focused exclusively on instructor-student harassment, but not faculty-faculty, or student-instructor (Rubin and Borgers). Such focus shows a lack of awareness of contrapower harassment, and the ways that sexuality can be seen to make a person a more likely target for harassment. Researchers in another study described their sample population of women in terms of academic rank, race, and marital status; since sexuality was not considered a variable, however, it seems the researchers presumed all participants were heterosexual (Brooks and Perot). Other studies fall short in terms of the solutions they prescribe. For instance, one study concludes that non-reporting is the real problem in harassment: "Perhaps if the reporting process was demystified and women felt reporting actually improved their situations, they would be more willing to take the risk of making a formal complaint" (Rubin and Borgers, 410). Of course, this solution assumes the system itself will correct what may in fact be a form of institutionalized oppression, and takes the focus away from the harassers by placing responsibility for action on the victims. Its circular logic bypasses the "risk" that reporting currently does not "actually improve their situation."

It is the premise of this chapter that no study of anti-lesbian harassment will be accurate unless the results are seen within the context of a homophobic and heterosexist culture. As Gregory Herek has argued, "anti-gay violence is a logical, albeit extreme, extension of the heterosexism that pervades American society" (Herek, 90). Cultural heterosexism—which means the way that power and privilege are institutionalized based on heterosexuality—is manifested in legal systems, religious systems, academic systems, the health profession, the media, tax laws, and immigration and naturalization laws. The liberal dichotomy of public and private serves to obscure the fact that heterosexuality is very public—billboards, media, retail shops all cater to the sealing of heterosexual relationships, while gays and lesbians are supposed to keep our sexuality "private." But anti-lesbian harassment occurs in very public places—in the classroom, the faculty lounge, in journals and publications, in promotion and tenure hearings, as well as on the streets. It is time to make some of these "private" stories public.

This chapter documents anti-lesbian harassment experienced by graduate students, adjunct faculty, and various ranks of tenured and tenure-track faculty. Anti-lesbian harassment occurs in the United States and abroad, in public and private universities; it can no longer be dismissed as an anomalous occurrence. Instead of interpreting anti-lesbian harassment as a personal problem, it is time that lesbians and heterosexuals alike see it for what it is: a symptom of political malaise within the culture, and the academy.

Telling Our Stories

To solicit statements for inclusion in this chapter on anti-lesbian intellectual harassment, I placed a call in a variety of feminist and lesbian journals, newspapers, and newsletters. In addition, I sent the call to every Department of Women's Studies listed in the National Women's Studies Association directory for 1990. At meetings and at conferences, I described the ongoing project, distributed copies of the call, and answered questions. Over a period of three years, I received approximately fifteen statements from lesbian academics in Canada, the U.S., and Europe. Lacking the space to detail all of the cases, I chose selected stories that seemed to represent a good cross-section of concerns, locations, and outcomes. Each story describes a particular facet of academic life that can be targeted for intellectual harassment.

Like the five escalating levels of sexual harassment, anti-lesbian intellectual harassment, as a manifestation of homophobia and sexism, seems to manifest itself in a range of ways, from the more subtle to the more overt. The harassment may focus on scholarship, by marginalizing lesbian authors or lesbian topics of study, co-opting lesbian perspectives into more mainstream theories, or defining "academic merit" in such a way that its very definition excludes lesbian scholarship. In the classroom, anti-lesbian intellectual harassment may be subtle, compelling a lesbian teacher to perform a heterosexual identity, or it may be more overt, as in the case of a student or students harassing a lesbian teacher (contrapower harassment). Finally, in its most overt form, the harassment may be pervasive, a seemingly coordinated effort among faculty, students, and the academic institution itself to target various professors or even an entire program.

This tentative definition of anti-lesbian intellectual harassment and its various manifestations offered here is, of necessity, based largely on the stories I received. Thus, it is only a beginning. For every statement I received, there is no way to calculate how many lesbians remained silent for fear of retribution. The stories I received were largely the stories of those who had survived the harassment, and moved forward with their careers.

1. Selecting/Silencing: Topics for Research

"Is that all you can do?" The "all" refers to the lesbian topics I pursue in my academic studies. The inquisitors range from professors to advisors to heterosexual graduate student colleagues. I've been asked this question so many times, that now it's almost the "greeting" that appears on my computer screen every time I sit down to start a paper. It's the ghost that haunts me in the hard drive, sits next to me in the seminar, hides in my lecture notes. . . . I have to do a little side-step to disassociate myself from the hate and ambivalence on this campus, in its classrooms, and in its publications. If I let it wash over me, I'll drown.

——Lesbian graduate student[3]

In an age when phrases like "academic freedom" and "politically correct" are abundantly present in the vocabularies of academics, the freedom of graduate students to select lesbian research topics would seem to be entirely unfettered. But the intellectual and political climate of the academy varies from one cultural context to another, from rural to urban, and from country to country. For example, in 1983, a University of California Lesbian and Gay Intercampus Network study found that:

> thirty-six percent of the faculty responding that lesbian/gay topics were appropriate to their fields had refrained from doing research on these topics because of fear of negative reaction from colleagues, while forty-one percent had refrained from including such material in their courses. Forty-four percent of students refrained from doing research or coursework for the same reason, and fourteen percent were actually advised by faculty not to pursue these topics. (Parmeter and Reti, 32)

A decade later, at a university in Germany, where the neofascist movement has been gaining in popularity, lesbians doing research within the modern languages are still at risk.

The fear is more of an ambiance than a tangible manifestation, according to a woman who describes herself as "an openly political lesbian in the academy" since 1987. Although her sexuality is well known, Catherine reports: "In my essays I did not want and/or could not voice lesbian theory as a central part of my understanding of the matter at hand."[4] Whereas in her nonacademic life, Catherine reports thinking and acting as a lesbian, "writing and speaking lesbians into existence in a word-dominated reality (and male-dominated academy) is quite a different procedure." The difference, according to Catherine, lies in the role of male professor as audience, male professor as listener. Immediately Virginia Woolf's image of the professor who watches over her writing in *A Room of One's Own* springs to mind. Perhaps it is no coincidence that, as Catherine observes, Woolf's work has been treated with the same kind of silencing that Catherine experiences: "most of the [German] research to date has left out all questions concerning lesbianism and its importance for Virginia Woolf's creative and intellectual energy altogether." For Woolf, as a scholar and lecturer, the professor-who-censors/silences is a symbol of internalized oppression; for Catherine, as a graduate student, the "listening-professor-who-silences" is all too real.

Bringing lesbian authors or lesbian topics into her essays seems too risky to Catherine: "I have not tried it out," she writes, "because all [the essays] I ever wrote were 'addressed' to male professors and deep inside me I don't really want to tell them, for fear of being hurt or becoming more vulnerable next time." More than self-disclosure, it seems, Catherine fears that lesbian theory in "the wrong hands" (that is, heterosexual/male hands) will be knowledge that is used against lesbians. For example, she reports hearing that a lesbian doing her degree in anthropology received a scholarship from a political party's fund, and along with her pleasure was the equally strong fear: "What do these sponsors want to know about lesbians and why?" At times, Catherine believes "that it is in a certain respect politically unwise to publish this important material about 'us' at all."

Along with a fear of unspecified violence is the fear of co-optation. "I do not want to give them an opportunity to show off," writes Catherine, "by using perhaps the term 'lesbian theory' without having really thought about its political implications against their male heterosexual domination of all space there could ever be for me and 'my kind'." At a time when lesbian scholarship may have a certain kind of fashion to it, Catherine's protective comments caution against co-optation. As we will see, it is a fear that has already been realized for others.

In spite of her fears, however, Catherine concludes with her decision to write a lesbian studies thesis for her Ph.D. Her reasoning is that "lesbians who do themselves not want an academic career per se should do the lesbian studies as theses because the others may not be able to afford it." Can the marginalization of lesbian authors and research topics be defined as a form of anti-lesbian intellectual harassment? From Catherine's perspective at this German university, it certainly can. Aware of the vital need for more lesbian scholarship, along with the potential career costs of creating that research, Catherine has chosen nonetheless to write lesbian. It is a choice which confronts lesbians at every level in the academy.

2. Publishing and Co-optation

Perhaps the most startling testimony I received in answer to my call arrived with a cover letter which concluded, "If you are open-minded enough to use this, fine; if not, given the gang-bang politics of postfeminist/ postmodernism, I won't be surprised." After reading Michelle's story, I understood a bit more about her defensive anger. Her harassment came from two sources she had thought it safe to trust: heterosexual feminists and gay males. In the way that it seems to manifest Catherine's fears about the possible co-optation of lesbian scholarship, Michelle's story provides the link between marginalizing lesbian research topics and co-opting lesbian perspectives in the continuum of anti-lesbian intellectual harassment.

Michelle's story began when she was invited by a gay male friend to submit her paper on the lesbian gaze to a conference panel on art history, sponsored by the gay and lesbian caucus of her profession. After the session, the chair of the panel, a heterosexual feminist, suggested devoting an issue of a journal she edited to publishing these conference papers, and others, on the pictorializations of gender. Michelle solicited comments from colleagues and specialists in art history before submitting her paper. Since she had published essays in *Arts, Art Papers, Art Examiner, Art Criticism, College Art Journal, Woman's Art Journal,* and *Woman Artist News,* such review was merely a formality. And since she had been led to believe the essay was guaranteed publication, she expected at the most only minor revisions; it came as quite a shock, then, when the woman editor rejected her essay outright because it was "not lesbian enough."

The woman based her decision on three readers' reports: a lesbian, who had "recommended publishing the paper on the spot"; a gay man, who "had suggested accepting the paper with several changes"; and a third, anonymous reader, who "had hated it." The editor doubted that Michelle "could do anything to salvage the paper," and warned her that if she did attempt to revise, the editor "was going to get some 'real' lesbians to read it."

As Michelle slowly deduced, the editor made her decision in an academic context which continues to privilege the attitudes, interpretations, and perspectives of men. In her case, the editor chose to privilege theoretical, male-identified definitions (that of a gay man and a heterosexual woman) of what a lesbian is over the lesbian-identified perspectives and experiences of two lesbians (the first reader and Michelle) themselves.[5] "How has it happened," Michelle asked, "that these men and heterosexual women can offer a more 'accurate' definition of what it is to be a lesbian than women who are lesbians?" According to Michelle's own definition—which, she qualified, must always be a "definition-in-process"—a lesbian is "someone who in a particular moment feels completely authentic and whole only in a relationship that is sexual and emotional with another woman." According to the gay male reviewer, however, "there are many lesbian lifestyles, . . . and some of them include men." Apparently, Michelle's focus on specific lesbian lifestyles which did not include men, or included men in a peripheral way, was the real problem. The editor chose to privilege "male fiction over female reality," creating a situation "in which the theory superceded experience"—according

124

to Michelle, a choice which exemplifies the distillation of "unbridled patriarchal 'objectivity.'"

But the story does not end here. Michelle telephoned a gay male colleague to solicit advice and to ask for support. She trusted this colleague because together they had edited a gay and lesbian newsletter, and he had been the first to encourage her to present the paper in question, to (according to Michelle) "risk my career by being an out spokeswoman for gay liberation." But when the situation was revealed, her colleague was less than forthcoming: he told her, "I don't want to get into trouble with her [the editor], it wouldn't be good for my career." Then he asked Michelle to forgive him. After some time, Michelle realized "I had been colluding in my own oppression." The experience showed her "that if we are truly ourselves we have to be willing to bear the consequences of doing so."

A final aspect of the problem deals with the language itself: Michelle's paper did not employ the kind of specialist discourse popular in the academy at the time. She found a hegemonic tyranny in the new "queer discourse," which mandates that "you have to speak in its language in order to be heard—and you must conform to its models in order to be published." According to lesbian philosopher Jacquelyn Zita, queer theory's "polysyllabic turn" is an attempt to gain "institutional legitimacy and approval"—an attempt which shortchanges lesbians (266–267).[6] From Michelle's experience, the discourse was one that "splits feminists, and other free thinking individuals, into bodies and brains existing at the edges of successive tidal waves of empowerment." Her lesbian body of experience, weighed in the balance against the male-identified brain of theory, was found wanting.

3. Hiring and Tenure: Defining "Academic Merit"

> The predominant feeling I have is one of exclusion. Much of the course work and research in which I am currently involved addresses issues of children and families. In most discussions, we're lucky to get a footnote. Professors may comment that families including GLB members do exist, but the discussion revolves completely around the lives of heterosexuals.
>
> ——Lesbian graduate student[7]

As Bettina Huber's painfully informative reports in *Profession* frequently show, job opportunities in the Modern Languages have been scarce for over a decade (Huber, 1990, 1992). The long-awaited boom of openings expected to result as a top-heavy profession enters retirement has resulted not in new positions but in retrenchments. Whereas three decades ago, an all-but-completed dissertation was sufficient to land one a teaching post, in the 1990s job markets, candidates are expected to have the completed degree in hand, along with a few publications in reputable journals, and possibly even a book contract for the dissertation. During times of scarcity, definitions of qualifications can be finessed to suit the needs—or the politics—of each particular department. Angela's story shows that shaping popular and institutional definitions of academic merit so that they exclude lesbian teaching and research is yet another form of anti-lesbian intellectual harassment.

An assistant professor in a Canadian university, Angela offered her credentials for scrutiny: "B.A. *summa cum laude*, first in my class; Woodrow Wilson fellowship, 1969; M.A., 1971; Ph.D., 1981; first permanent entry-level job, 1990, age 42; rate of publication in refereed journals in the last six months since I was diagnosed with breast cancer, five and still counting...." Though she had served as editor for a nationally known feminist journal, and received overwhelmingly positive teaching evaluations from her students, Angela was released from her contractually limited position because she was not perceived as having "academic merit." She was unaware of the basis for her termination until she assumed a tenure-track position at another institution.

Once she was hired, a feminist colleague alerted her to the fact that there was a "bomb" in her employment file. When she had applied for the job, her former employer (unasked by her) had sent a letter detailing the reasons she had been let go. Angela writes that, according to her former chair, "while my teaching evaluations had been superlative, it must be understood that I taught mainly 'special interest' courses, and therefore the evaluations he himself termed 'delicious' must be inflated; he could not comment favourably on my research potential, in spite of my abundant productivity, since I had devoted most of my energies to editing a scholarly journal of 'marginal interest.'" According to her former chair, the journal was "mainly lesbian in content," and "his institution had decided to keep on another feminist scholar, whose work on Canadian women writers was more 'mainstream.'"

The letter's intent was clearly to prevent Angela from obtaining a job. Moreover, her scholarship was defined as lacking in academic merit because of its supposedly lesbian content. As Angela concludes from this equation, academic merit has been determined in such a way that "the bottom line is that value has a price as well as that certain values are prized. I paid a price for not having certain values." Effectively, such definitions of academic merit entail a form of compulsory heterosexuality—the insistence that all women be, or appear to be, heterosexual (Rich). Scholarship on "mainstream" women writers is worthy of academic merit, since the authors and the scholars appear to be heterosexual;[8] scholarship that is "mainly lesbian in content" is not.

Angela's story brings up the question of whether and when to go public with discrimination, since breaking silence can involve a revictimization. As Richard Mohr writes in *Gays/Justice*, there is a "difficulty even to complain of discrimination. For if one is gay, to register a complaint would suddenly target one as a stigmatized person, and so, in the absence of any protection against discrimination, would in turn invite additional discrimination" (27). As an untenured professor, Angela has taken a bold position nonetheless: "It seems that at least some of the time, negative private documents can be used to further the understandings, if not the careers, of academic feminists and lesbians who go public with these texts which would have silenced them." Angela has chosen to go forward and "use the letter and the dismissal as a provocation to theorize lesbian resistance." She acknowledges that when printed, such essays on this topic will be added to her tenure file of publications, and concludes, "I want to use my textual experience and my interpretation of its theoretical and political implications to further my academic career and possibly my notoriety, as well as to scare homophobes from thinking they can continue to get away with this behavior." Publications such as these are one way of fighting back.

4. *Compulsory Heterosexuality and Contrapower Harassment in the Classroom*

> If I am to teach whole, if I am to have the power of my own voice, I need to be able to acknowledge that it is a lesbian voice. Anything less than that is death to the spirit.
>
> ——"Judith," a lesbian professor

What kind of intellectual harassment is in effect when a teacher cannot bring an authentic self to her teaching? Rather than emanating from a single source, this type of harassment springs from the institution itself, and inheres in its organizational structure. According to Judith, a tenured professor at a Catholic university in the urban Midwest, being out to her colleagues is acceptable; being out to her students could cost her her job.

In spite of Catholicism's official stance on homosexuality, many Catholic colleges and universities are unofficially tolerant or even welcoming of diverse sexualities, provided that these expressions do not violate the freedom of others on campus, irritate the church, or interfere with their flow of funding from private donors. Lesbian faculty at these institutions serve a critical function in providing positive role models for gay and lesbian students, and in combatting homophobia in the classroom. To serve those students and yet preserve her position, Judith says, is "to walk a very demanding tightrope—to teach in a way that makes me visible to those students who need to know that I am a lesbian while allowing those who need to ignore it to do so." The cost, of course, is a kind of split self, as Judith reports: "Trying to teach in a lesbian voice ... while remaining partially closeted in the classroom is an exercise in schizophrenia."

The locus of the problem, according to Judith, lies in "the heterosexist notion that one's sexual orientation ... is a private matter." And indeed, if sexuality could be reduced to what one does in bed, then the liberal division of public and private could be applied. But once one steps outside the dominant discourse of heterosexuality, the very public position that sexuality occupies—from newspapers and billboards to greeting cards, holidays, and P.T.A. meetings—is inescapable. More than silencing discussion of specific sexual practices, institutionalized anti-lesbianism, Judith reports, requires that "I obscure and deny one of my own sources of insight into and information about lesbian texts—as well as one of my sources of insight into heterosexist literature—and one of my sources of insight into what it means to be marginalized and alienated." In a word, says Judith, "I don't say 'we.'" If this omission does not seem significant, imagine the context of oppression as being racism rather than heterosexism: imagine the absurdity of an African-American professor teaching James Baldwin or Toni Morrison while talking about African Americans as "they." Such positioning of the teaching self as invisible is a form of intellectual harassment, for it requires a silencing of the intellectual and physical knowledge of the totality of self.

Of course, simply being "out" does not solve every problem—in fact, it may mean one becomes the target for other forms of harassment. For instance, lesbian faculty who do come out in their classes may be more likely to face contrapower harassment, a form of harassment wherein the aggressor is a person normally of "lower status" than the person being harassed. Although an instructor is usually thought to be of higher status than a student in the same classroom, the lower status categories of gender and sexuality can put lesbian faculty at a unique disadvantage. Teaching for six years as a graduate student in a major, East Coast, urban university, Laura had been used to handling such harassment from students at least twice annually; however, she had never received a pornographic poem until she taught a course on "Society and Sexual Diversity." Such a poem from a student to an instructor constitutes both sexual and intellectual harassment: it could be read both as a sexual advance, and a challenge to the academic legitimacy of both the course content and the instructor.

Searching for a method of handling the problem, Laura turned to the teaching assistant's handbook, which suggested that if you were harassed by a student you were supposed to "ask the student into your office, *shut the door and make sure you couldn't be overheard or interrupted,* and discuss the matter rationally." As Laura contended, "I wanted there to be several dozen people in the room with me as witnesses if I ever had to face this girl again." To protect herself, Laura took the matter to the Director of Undergraduate Studies, who arranged a meeting among the three of them. There, the Director informed the student that the poem was "inappropriate" and if she did not stop writing such poems immediately, they would be forced to "take the matter further through the appropriate channels." As Laura observes, this latter statement was a bluff, since there were no "channels" to be pursued.

Although the harassment stopped with this single meeting, Laura felt its effects long after. "For weeks I worried about receiving dead rodents in the mail," writes Laura, and "the next time I had to face [the poem-writer] in class I was literally shaking. One of my other students noticed it, and attributed it to my displeasure with their first papers." For the rest of the semester, Laura struggled with the paradox of trying to avoid her harasser while simultaneously trying not to discriminate against that student in terms of the class. "Students go after teachers a whole lot more than people think," Laura concluded, and "perhaps this is particularly true of those of us who are visible lesbians/bisexuals."

Judith's and Laura's experiences indicate that the classroom itself is a potential site for anti-lesbian intellectual harassment, both subtle and overt. Whether lesbian faculty are closeted or "out," our marginalized status in terms of gender and sexuality means that we may be perceived as acceptable targets for harassment from students. As Michele Barale notes, "The presence of a queer instructor" tends to "eroticize the classroom exchange," and if the topic is sexuality itself, "sexual interest is easily focused on us as instructors as well" (18). "Since the assumption is that we are pedophiles to begin with," according to Laura, this form of contrapower harassment against lesbians has been virtually overlooked. It is another way that lesbians are perceived as especially vulnerable to intellectual harassment.

5. From the Subtle to the Overt: Economics, Violence, Homophobia

> On Friday, 11/18/94, $20,000 worth of journals addressed to gay & lesbian issues and feminism [*Signs, Gender & Society, The Women's Review of Books, Lesbian Ethics,* and others] were destroyed or stolen from the Zimmerman Library at the University of New Mexico. Five shelves of materials were taken & replaced with Nazi books, including titles such as *Pens Under the Swastika.* The journal *Lesbian Ethics* was defaced with a swastika, the title crossed out & replaced with "God's Ethics" and the words "God made women for men" scribbled across it. Some feminist journals were left on the shelves with swastikas and "bitch propaganda" written across the pages. It happened during library hours Friday, so there is a suspicion that it was an inside job. A string of hate crimes have occurred at UNM since late October, [leading to the] arrest of three young men for having explosives & white supremacist literature, and a mural of American Indians was defaced with a swastika. The administration is conducting an investigation.
>
> ——Jane Little, Arizona State University, Women's Studies

Recent assaults such as the one at the University of New Mexico demonstrate a number of connections—between antifeminism and anti-lesbianism, between intellectual harassment and physical violence, between heterosexism and racism. Like the earlier connection between Catherine's fear and Michelle's experience of co-optation, the UNM incidents can be seen as the more overt end of a continuum whose more subtle manifestation appeared twelve years earlier at a university in Long Beach. Destroying lesbian scholarship, whether by defacing the journals themselves or by attacking the academic merit of an entire collegiate program, is a clear manifestation of anti-lesbian intellectual harassment.

The nine-year legal battle for Women's Studies at California State University, Long Beach ended in 1991, but the lessons of this battle live on. For the six Women's Studies faculty who endured the harassment—Betty Brooks, Denise Wheeler, Sondra Hale, Linda Shaw, Diane Wicker, and Sheila Kuehl—the damage lives on as well. In this lawsuit, and the actions leading up to it, the connection between misogyny and anti-lesbianism is blatantly clear. It is such a cliché that it is easy to forget: to the conservative mind, lesbianism is the quintessence and ultimate aim of feminism.

In February of 1982, Jessica Shaver, a fundamentalist Christian and part-time psychology student, visited the Women's Center at CSULB and asked to leave literature there opposing the proposed Equal Rights Amendment to the U.S. Constitution. Students told her she could not, since to do so would undermine the mission of the center. Shaver proceeded to lodge a complaint with the Director of Women's Studies, objecting to the "lesbian bias" of the Women's Studies Program, a charge she based on the use of various recommended texts, the program's failure to espouse traditional American values, and the presence of "too many lesbian faculty members." With the help of right-wing conservatives, fundamentalist Christians, and Eagle Forum members, Shaver's complaint precipitated administrative actions which can only be described as lesbian witch-hunts. On August 4, 1982, a lawsuit was filed by the ACLU on behalf of sixteen women faculty members and three students against the State of California and the University administration. What happened between February and August, 1982, at CSULB?

While the events during the nine-year litigation period are too numerous to detail here,[9] the arguments used against the Women's Studies faculty have a recurring equation that is easy to summarize: "woman" equals "lesbian," and "lesbian" equals "unqualified." As the conservatives claimed, "lesbianism naturally follows from feminist demands" (Hale et al., 40). And the university administration, whether out of fear of "budget cuts, declining enrollments, and other problems," as Hale speculates, or whether out of heterosexism, was all too ready to comply.

After speaking to the Women's Studies Director Hale, Shaver took her complaint to the Vice President for Academic Affairs; as a result, the Assistant Vice President issued the Director of the Women's Center a negative performance evaluation, claiming that the Women's Center did not appeal to a "mainstream" audience, and criticizing her for her "ideological approach, almost dogmatic approach to women's issues." Encouraged by her results, Shaver proceeded to CSULB's President, reiterating her complaints about "lesbian indoctrination" and saying she would take the matter to her state senator. Without investigating the basis for Shaver's complaint, CSULB's Associate Dean wrote to Hale: "If the advocacy of lesbianism is the most imaginative response feminist theory can come up with to solve modern social problems affecting women, then there isn't likely to be much of a future for feminist theory either on this campus or anywhere else."

Ostensibly, these comments can be traced to the vaginal self-examination regularly demonstrated in the course "Women and Their Bodies." According to Sharon Sievers, male administrators and faculty not only did not understand the importance of the self-exam, but felt sure "there was more to it," as if it were "part of a secret lesbian agenda" (Hale et al., 44). In order to enforce their views, and to create a paper trail of negative evaluations, the administration instigated illegal reviews of the Women's Studies Program and faculty.

The first review occurred in April 1982, in violation of CSULB policy prohibiting mid-term curriculum review. In early April, Shaver's complaints resulted in a meeting between top CSULB administrators and conservative state senators, members of fundamentalist Christian groups, and the Eagle Forum; in violation of regulations both academic and legal, no member of the Women's Studies Program or center was invited. As a result, the administrators promised that women's studies would become more "mainstream," and that the course "Women and Their Bodies" would be reviewed, even though it had been favorably reviewed by a well-known outside consultant two years earlier. Nine days after the meeting, the Women's Studies Advisory Committee was ordered to scrutinize whether "Women and Their Bodies" exhibited "a lesbian bias." They did so under protest, and found no such bias.

At the end of April, the Women's Center was placed under jurisdiction of CSULB administration because it was perceived to be "lesbian oriented."

In June 1982, administrators visited the first night of class in Brooks's course, "Women and Violence," and told the approximately fifty students present that the class was cancelled due to low enrollment. This notification violated university policy, which allows up to the third class session to obtain full enrollment, as well as common sense, since more than the sufficient number of students were already enrolled and in attendance.

Later that same month, in a second performance evaluation of Wheeler, the Assistant Vice President complained that "Workshops on self-defense for women and sexual harassment, feminist reading groups and battered women's support groups appeal to a relatively small percentage of campus and community women."

That August, Dean Crowther cancelled one of two fall sections of "Women and Their Bodies" because there was no one "qualified" to teach the course—in spite of the fact that Brooks was not only ready to teach the course, and was already teaching the other section of the course, but had regularly taught both sections of the course in the past. In addition, Crowther cancelled the course "Women and Mental Health" which had been assigned to Linda Shaw, saying that "there was no one in the current pool of Women's Studies Program faculty *qualified*" to teach it—not Shaw, and not Wicker, who was a practicing therapist specializing in women's mental health, and who had taught the course in the past. The Associate Vice President for Academic Affairs had previously stated that Shaw should not be allowed to teach certain courses because she was a lesbian. In fact, Shaw had not only taught the course for many years at CSULB—she was the one who developed the course to begin with.

In the fall of 1982, the Dean struck again, saying that Sheila Kuehl was not qualified to teach the course "Women and the Law," though Kuehl had been a top graduate of the Harvard Law School and had taught the course in the past. Nor was Brooks allowed to teach the course "Women and Violence," though she was a well-known expert on the subject and had taught the course before. In the years that followed, she was repeatedly prohibited from teaching on false pretexts.

The Women's Studies faculty did not take these events lightly, and attempted to "use the system" to fight back. According to the legal brief, however, none of their attempts were successful: both Shaw and Hale attempted to file grievances for the university's failure to reappoint them, and were told that CSULB policy did not allow them to do so. Wheeler filed and lost two grievances, and Brooks filed seven separate grievances with CSULB which, if they resulted in her favor, were overruled by the administration, whose actions violated university, state, and federal laws. If the women had not won their lawsuit, institutionalized heterosexism at CSULB would have remained unchallenged.

The women sued the university for over a million dollars in damages, and received an undisclosed "six-figure" settlement. Of course, the career costs were tremendous: Hale was never able to obtain a tenure-track teaching position, nor was she eligible for many fellowships; Brooks was never able to find a college-level teaching position; Kuehl, Wheeler, and Shaw were unable to find comparable tenure-track positions; Brooks's private consulting and Wicker's private therapy practices suffered considerably. These are the costs which can be counted; but harassment affects both the body and the mind, and the mental health costs are, ultimately, incalculable. As a result of the extreme stress, Hale's blood pressure destabilized, and she suffered insomnia, nightmares, and continual fear. Brooks spent $7,500 in therapy over a three-year period in an attempt to combat insomnia and severe depression; she "awoke in tears every morning and experienced frequent bouts of anger, frustration, and nervousness." Her emotional distress resulted in physical complications, which required her to be hospitalized in December 1982. Wheeler experienced "excruciating back, neck, and head pain," and sought both chiropractic and mental health therapy for two years. No matter how great the settlement, no one can be compensated for such costs.

The harassment endured by the Women's Studies faculty at CSULB illustrates the conceptual linkage between antifeminist and anti-lesbian intellectual harassment. But anti-lesbianism is also linked to ethnocentrism and racism, as both the library vandalism at UNM and the anti-lesbianism of the following and final case will show. When lesbian faculty face institutionalized intellectual harassment, their experiences indicate that the tools we have trusted would protect us are now falling far short of our expectations.

In 1990, when Nancy, an out lesbian poet, accepted a tenure-track position in line for the directorship of the poetry center at an urban Midwestern university, she envisioned the challenge of bringing a multicultural awareness to an already established, nationally known program. The outgoing director was approaching retirement, and professed a readiness to turn over the poetry center to a new administration. "Yes, I accept your invitation and welcome," Nancy had written. "I come with all my energies and resources and enthusiasm to work with you as a colleague." But by July 1994, Nancy was demoted from her directorship after holding the post for little over a year, and her position was divided among the older faculty who had created the program. As in the case of CSULB, Nancy's story shows the evolution of anti-lesbian intellectual harassment to some of its most extreme manifestations.

To accept the position as an associate professor, Nancy had to give up tenure, but was assured of receiving it again in three years. To protect her position, therefore, she had to remain silent about the harassment she experienced. For example, in the first two years of her job, Nancy "brought in over $100,000 in donations, grants, and gifts-in-kind, including computer equipment and software" for the poetry center; however, on the day she handed in her tenure portfolio, Nancy learned that the center had suffered a one hundred percent budget cut from the administration. Immediately, Nancy began a national letter-writing campaign, which generated "over 400 letters of support," articles in the local newspapers, and eventually won back 50 percent of the center's funding. Meanwhile, her salary (in the low thirties) represented less than half of the amount paid each of the two previous directors of the center. In her fourth year, Nancy reported that her salary "as a Poet with a Ph.D. & 17 years of University teaching experience" was "only slightly above the salary awarded to a young Asst. Professor & male colleague" hired just out of graduate school "without a Ph.D. or book published in his field of expertise." Before she set foot in the institution, gender harassment through pay inequity was already against her; once she assumed her position as director, the focus of this economic harassment extended from her salary to her entire program, and from her gender to her sexuality.

In the second year of her job, Nancy herself became the clear target of harassment. For the entire academic year, one male colleague carried on an imaginary and sexually explicit correspondence with Nancy, often leaving sets of the letters for his "very nice cleaning lady" to find. "Thanks for the weekend, darling," were some of the words attributed to Nancy, to which her harasser wrote back, "You were poetry in motion." Attributing such words to a female colleague constitutes gender harassment; attributing such words to an out lesbian poet also constitutes anti-lesbian intellectual harassment. During that same year, fliers portraying a witch under a poetry center sign were circulated in Nancy's department. Although she brought these to the attention of her colleagues and asked that the fliers be taken down, she received no response. The following year, after receiving tenure, Nancy brought these incidents to the dean, making certain she was accompanied by another administrator and a representative of NOW. The dean took no action.

But it was through organizing a women's grant to fund black lesbian poets in 1993 that Nancy learned most directly about the racism and homophobia in her institution. She was somewhat prepared for it, having been earlier approached by a three-time finalist in the university's poetry competition who entrusted Nancy with a copy of her rejection letter, written the year before Nancy arrived. In it, one of the judges had written, "a couple of us termed your vision 'narrow', and I cannot honestly say that a committee of heterosexuals all contentedly married to the same people for more than 25 years was capable of responding fully to your work. Yet we learned from it, and I urge you to submit again." Predictably then, a few days after Nancy received the women's grant to fund black lesbian poets, this same man telephoned Nancy to tell her she "should NOT be using words like that." Nancy explained that if she had not explicitly said "lesbians of color," she would not have received the grant. Three weeks later, however, Nancy was caught off guard by an angry, racist letter from a local poet, championing the history of the poetry center: "It would be a pity to lose all of this in the interest of trying to include minorities and fringe groups simply because you think that's fair, or proper, or popular," she wrote. "Talent alone should be the criterion." Her racism was barely concealed in her concluding metaphor: "I would hate to see the empire crumble because the queen couldn't differentiate between a diamond and a cow pie." As with other stories included here, anti-lesbianism, and in this case racism as well, were masquerading as questions of quality and intellectual merit.

In the fall of 1994, after Nancy's demotion from director to Distinguished Poet, the former director and founder of the poetry center used his own, self-published, concrete poetry to harass Nancy. In contrast to Nancy's frequent use of sheila-na-gig metaphors in her poetry, this man had drawn an upended cornucopia with breasts on the thin end, and legs on the outsides of the horn, and zipped up the opening of the horn. In a context where other male professors refer to Nancy's "cuntalistic poetry," such a drawing invokes references to female circumcision, and constitutes a blatant example of anti-lesbian intellectual harassment. And yet the University failed to respond.

Nancy has retained a lawyer and has received good coverage for her case in the local newspapers. Although she now suffers from "trichotillomania, a condition that has caused [her] to obsessively pull out [her] own hair," Nancy is not giving up. In her cover letter to me, Nancy writes: "What amazes me is that as I take small steps to fight for myself I realize what power is within me, how empowering it is to say NO even to seemingly monolithic institutions. And I realize I'm not just fighting for myself. I'm fighting for and with all of us who are fighting."

Both Nancy's case and the story of CSULB make clear what Audre Lorde warned over a decade ago, that "the master's tools will never dismantle the master's house" (110–113). If we intend to be effective in opposing harassment, particularly when it is institutionalized in the academy and in the culture, it may be time to organize our own institutions and methods for fighting back.

Strategies for Fighting Back

The women whose stories are told here found a number of ways to "get even" with harassers, and have felt empowered by doing so. Publishing stories about their harassment, speaking on the topic of heterosexism and homophobia, and coming out to colleagues and to students all seem effective strategies in various contexts. Studies of gay-bashing have suggested other strategies as well: supporting victims through outreach programs; creating anonymous systems to deal with crises; training local law enforcement officials; requesting that unequivocal statements opposing discrimination based on sexuality be made in institutional policy; working to pass local community ordinances which ban discrimination; and documenting patterns of victimization (D'Augelli, 321). Of course, these suggestions must be adopted in conjunction with the understanding that heterosexism is institutionalized in our culture, and the systems within which we are working are merely a manifestation of this broader cultural malaise. Working to change laws at the same time that we work to change ideas is the most effective strategy available to us. To this end, coordinating local efforts with national organizations, such as the Lambda Legal Defense Fund or the National Gay and Lesbian Task Force, is an effective way to empower isolated or embattled individuals or communities.

Whenever it is perceived safe by the individual lesbian herself, coming out in the classroom is still an expedient method for challenging stereotypes and presuppositions. Not only does it create a culturally diverse classroom, coming out makes lesbian teachers more comfortable because we know our students see us for who we are; it offers straight students an opportunity to become educated on issues of sexuality; and it creates a home at the university for gay and lesbian students (Parmeter). "Don't tell anyone—or else ... " is all too often the threat whispered to victims of harassment. Instead of believing in the threats which would keep us isolated from each other, telling our stories, coming out, and connecting with other lesbians and other feminists around issues of concern to all of us constitute the essential first step in settling the score.

But as the activists in the Lesbian Avengers have noted in their literature, "out is not enough." The stories here detail harassment endured by both closeted and out lesbians, whose attempts to use the system to obtain justice have not always succeeded. It is in cases like these that we may be better served by creating a "Lesbian Avengers of the Academy" association, bringing support and activism from around the country to the persons experiencing the harassment.[10] At the Iowa InQueery Conference in November 1994, flyers were distributed which put forth this very idea, in the form of a hotline.[11] The anti-homophobia hotline was created by Lynda Hart after her own "grueling battle for tenure," during which she "was subjected to the most blatant homophobia" she had ever experienced. The hotline is simply "a network of academics in all fields who are concerned about the rights of lesbian, gay, bisexual, transgendered and otherwise queer people in the academy." Hart envisions it as a "watchdog for the profession in lieu of civil rights legislation to protect our interests." Working in coalitions we choose, gays, lesbians, and feminists must take the initiative in creating institutions and networks for fighting back against harassment. In the words of the Lesbian Avengers, "Think about it. Being nice isn't going to get you anywhere." Being organized, however, might save your job.

Notes

Special thanks to Shirley Garner, Margaret Higonnet, Ketu Katrak, and the two anonymous reviewers from *Women's Studies International Forum,* whose helpful remarks on an earlier draft guided my later revisions. This essay is dedicated to the courage of lesbians everywhere.

1. As a lesbian, I found it untenable to write about lesbians in third person, and have chosen the first person plural to use throughout this chapter.

2. One might speculate that lesbian faculty are more likely to be targeted for harassment than gay male faculty; however, no findings to date explore this question.

3. Statement taken from *Breaking the Silence: Final Report of the Select Committee on Gay, Lesbian, and Bisexual Concerns.*

4. In soliciting statements, I guaranteed anonymity for all respondents. The names have been changed accordingly, except for the women involved in the CSULB case, since it is on public record.

5. This is not to suggest that only lesbians are concerned with topics related to lesbian lives, or that women who are lesbian do authentic and satisfying work only if it directly concerns lesbianism. Michelle's claim is one of authority based on identity—a claim generally disputed by postmodernist theories, which have in turn been criticized for their antifeminism. See Diana Fuss, *Essentially Speaking* (New York: Routledge, 1989); Tania Modleski, *Feminism Without Women* (New York: Routledge, 1991); and Linda J. Nicholson, ed., *Feminism/Postmodernism* (New York: Routledge, 1990).

6. Barbara Christian has also criticized the way that the discourse of elite academic theory silences or co-opts the views of many Others, particularly black women: "The Race for Theory," 335–345 in Gloria Anzaldúa, ed., *Making Face, Making Soul/Haciendo Caras* (San Francisco: Aunt Lute, 1990).

7. Statement taken from *Breaking the Silence: Final Report of the Select Committee on Gay, Lesbian, and Bisexual Concerns.*

8. For a discussion of mainstream women writers and the silencing of lesbian sexuality, see Carol Seajay, "The Backlash and the Backlist," *The Women's Review of Books* 12:3 (December 1994): 18–19.

9. The details in this section are taken from the lawsuit brief itself. The stories of three Women's Studies faculty—Sondra Hale, Sharon Sievers, and Sherna Berger Gluck—may be found in "Three Personal Perspectives on Feminist Education at Cal State, Long Beach," *Frontiers* 8, 3 (1986): 39–49, and the situation itself was described in *Feminist Studies* 9, 3 (Fall 1983): 603–605.

10. The Lesbian Avengers Handbook is printed as an appendix in Sarah Schulman's *My American History: Lesbian and Gay Life During the Reagan/Bush Years* (New York: Routledge, 1994). The Lesbian Avengers have been very successful in supporting embattled communities fighting homophobia. From August through November 1994, they sent eight full-time lesbian organizers from New York to Idaho to organize and defeat the homophobic Proposition One. The Idaho gay and lesbian community is now more organized and better prepared, with plans to create long-term structures for organizing and defending their communities.

138

11. For more information on the anti-homophobia hotline, send an e-mail message to lhart@dept.english.upenn.edu, or write Lynda Hart directly at 119 Bennett Hall, Department of English, University of Pennsylvania, Philadelphia, PA 19104.

Works Cited and Consulted

Barale, Michele Aina. "The Romance of Class and Queers: Academic Erotic Zones." In *Tilting the Tower: Lesbians, Teaching, Queer Subjects*, ed. Linda Garber. New York: Routledge, 1994. 16–24.

Benson, K.A. "Comment on Crocker's 'An Analysis of University Definitions of Sexual Harassment.'" *Signs* 9 (1984): 516–519.

Berrill, Kevin T. "Anti-Gay Violence and Victimization in the United States: An Overview." In *Hate Crimes: Confronting Violence Against Lesbians and Gay Men*, eds. Gregory M. Herek and Kevin T. Berrill. Newbury Park: Sage Publications, 1992. 19–45.

Breaking the Silence: Final Report of the Select Committee on Lesbian, Gay, and Bisexual Concerns. Minneapolis: University of Minnesota, 1993.

Brooks, Linda and Annette R. Perot. "Reporting Sexual Harassment: Exploring a Predictive Model." *Psychology of Women Quarterly* 15 (1991): 31–47.

D'Augelli, Anthony R. "Lesbians' and Gay Men's Experiences of Discrimination and Harassment in a University Community." *American Journal of Community Psychology* 17, 3 (1989): 317–321.

Ehrlich, Howard J. "The Ecology of Anti-Gay Violence." In *Hate Crimes: Confronting Violence Against Lesbians and Gay Men*, eds. Herek and Berrill. 1992. 105–112.

Fitzgerald, L.F., Shullman, S.L., Bailey, N., Richards, M., Swecker, J., Gold, Y., Ormerod, M., and Weitzman, L. "The Incidence and Dimensions of Sexual Harassment in Academia and the Workplace." *Journal of Vocational Behavior* 32 (1988): 152–175.

Fitzgerald, Louise F. and Alayne J. Ormerod. "Perceptions of Sexual Harassment: The Influence of Gender and Academic Context." *Psychology of Women Quarterly* 15 (1991): 281–294.

From Invisibility to Inclusion: Opening the Doors for Lesbians and Gay Men at the University of Michigan. Prepared by the Study Committee on the Status of Lesbians and Gay Men. June 1991.

Garnets, Linda, Gregory M. Herek, and Barrie Levy. "Violence and Victimization of Lesbians and Gay Men: Mental Health Consequences." In *Hate Crimes: Confronting Violence Against Lesbians and Gay Men*, eds. Herek and Berrill. 1992. 207–226.

Hale, Sondra, Sharon L. Sievers, and Sherna Berger Gluck. "Three Personal Perspectives on Feminist Education at Cal State, Long Beach." *Frontiers* 8, 3 (1986): 39–49.

Herek, Gregory M. "The Social Context of Hate Crimes: Notes on Cultural Hetero-sexism." *Hate Crimes: Confronting Violence Against Lesbians and Gay Men.* Eds. Herek and Berrill. 1992. 89–104.

Herek, Gregory M., and Kevin T. Berrill, eds. *Hate Crimes: Confronting Violence Against Lesbians and Gay Men.* Newbury Park: Sage Publications, 1992.

Huber, Bettina J. "Women in the Modern Languages, 1970–90." *Profession '90.* New York: The Modern Language Association, 1990. 58–73.

————. "The Changing Job Market." *Profession '92.* New York: The Modern Language Association, 1992. 59–73.

In Every Classroom: The Report of the President's Select Committee for Lesbian and Gay Concerns. Rutgers: The State University, 1989.

Lorde, Audre. "The Master's Tools Will Never Dismantle The Master's House." *Sister Outsider.* Trumansburg, NY: Crossing Press, 1984. 110–113.

McKinney, Kathleen. "Sexual Harassment of University Faculty by Colleagues and Students." *Sex Roles* 23, 7/8 (1990): 421–438.

Mohr, Richard. *Gays/Justice: A Study of Ethics, Society, and Law.* New York: Columbia University Press, 1988.

Parmeter, Sarah-Hope. "Four Good Reasons Why Every Lesbian Teacher Should Be Free to Come Out in the Classroom." *The Lesbian in Front of the Classroom: Writings by Lesbian Teachers.* 1988. 44–58.

———— and Irene Reti, eds. *The Lesbian in Front of the Classroom: Writings by Lesbian Teachers.* Santa Cruz, CA: HerBooks, 1988.

Pharr, Suzanne. *Homophobia: A Weapon of Sexism.* Inverness, CA: Chardon Press, 1988.

Rich, Adrienne. "Compulsory Heterosexuality and Lesbian Existence." *Blood, Bread and Poetry.* New York: Norton, 1986. 23–75.

Rubin, Linda J. and Sherry B. Borgers. "Sexual Harassment in Universities During the 1980s." *Sex Roles* 23, 7/8 (1990): 397–411.

Till, F. J. *Sexual Harassment: A Report on the Sexual Harassment of Students.* Report of the National Advisory Council of Women's Educational Programs. Washington, DC: U.S. Department of Education, 1980.

von Schulthess, Beatrice. "Violence in the Streets: Anti-Lesbian Assault and Harassment in San Francisco." *Hate Crimes: Confronting Violence Against Lesbians and Gay Men,* eds. Herek and Berrill. 1992. 65–75.

Zita, Jacquelyn N. "Gay and Lesbian Studies: Yet Another Unhappy Marriage?" *Tilting the Tower: Lesbians, Teaching, Queer Subjects,* ed. Linda Garber. New York: Routledge, 1994. 258–276.

6

Female Grotesques in Academia: Ageism, Antifeminism, and Feminists on the Faculty

Mary Wilson Carpenter

This is typical and very strongly expressed grotesque. It is ambivalent. It is pregnant death, a death that gives birth. There is nothing completed, nothing calm and stable in the bodies of these old hags. They combine senile, decaying, and deformed flesh with the flesh of new life, conceived but as yet unformed. "Moreover," he writes, "the old hags are laughing."

——Bakhtin, quoted in Russo

But it probably would be more accurate to acknowledge that the failure of vision I experience emerges at least in part from the panic of *my own aging*.

—— Miller

As Mary Russo explains in her 1986 essay, Bakhtin's description of Kerch's terra-cotta figurines of "senile, pregnant hags" exemplifies for him the grotesque body, as "open, protruding, extended, secreting body, the body of becoming, process and change," and its opposition to the classical body, "monumental, static, closed, and sleek, corresponding to the aspirations of bourgeois individualism" (1986, 219). For Bakhtin, this model of the grotesque body figures not only the "socialist state to come" but "carnival language" or culturally productive semiosis. He reads it as the strongly positive sign of carnival laughter and spectacle. But, Russo notes, "for the feminist reader, this image of the pregnant hag is more than ambivalent. It is loaded with all the connotations of fear and loathing associated with the biological processes of reproduction and of aging" (219).

The ageism women encounter in academia, according to their own perceptions of it as reported in letters and oral testimony submitted to the Modern Language Association (MLA) Commission on the Status of Women in the Profession, continues to be linked to perceptions of the female body—not only to the aging female body but to its reproductive phases.[1] Ageism in the 1990s impinges on women in the academy precisely at these two "moments" of reproduction and aging, which is to say that academic women may be subject to ageist discrimination at all ages and stages of their careers. Moreover, this fear of the "female grotesque" both underpins the fear of feminist power in the academy and can be mobilized as a weapon against it by refusing older women admission to the academy at the various levels of graduate studies, tenure-track positions, tenure, and promotion. Finally, as Nancy Miller's acutely self-aware statement makes evident, ageism as fear of the "female grotesque" now divides both feminism and feminists, producing a generational identity politics, a sense of "mother-daughter" conflicts among feminists in academia, and anxiety about the future of feminism itself.

The intersections of ageism and antifeminism, antiageism and feminism, and feminism and ageism, as they structure academic relations today, are thus far from simple or one-dimensional. Nor do they function identically from one academic institution to another—attitudes toward age and gender are not necessarily the same at the chronically underfunded state institution as at the prestigious and well-endowed private institution.[2] As more men adopt nontraditional career tracks, sometimes as consequence of nontraditional parenting responsibilities, ageism may begin to affect more men in academia. At this time, however, it is the combination of ageism and sexism, or what I have termed *sexagism*, that appears to be by far the more pervasive and disturbing aspect of ageism in academia—and it is unquestionably the aspect of ageism that matters most in the current antifeminist backlash.

Ageism in its most commonly understood form—discrimination against "older" people in favor of youth—has traditionally been accepted as natural, inevitable, and justifiable in academia: hence, the mere citation of age is often a surefire method of keeping an "older woman" (which may mean any woman over thirty) out of a position of power in the academy. As such, ageism automatically tends to limit possibilities for the growth of feminist power even if the woman excluded does not present herself as a feminist. If she is known to be feminist, the acceptance of ageism in academia makes it easy to exclude her without having to dispute feminist research or politics *per* se. As Gayle Greene cogently argues, we should not overlook the seriousness of the fact that "[f]eminism has already disappeared once in this century, and we are now living through the second backlash that's occurred within fifty years" (1993, 12). Greene points out that by the 1950s there were fewer women on faculties than at any time since 1900. The exclusion of the "older woman" may play a very significant part in the current antifeminist backlash by providing a supposedly gender-neutral rationale for limiting the sheer number of women on any faculty. Despite the fact that ageism is so often represented as necessary for the good of the department, academic women's testimony suggests that ageism directed against women continues to exhibit that anxiety about the aging and/or reproductive female body that Mary Russo has so accurately described as fear of "the female grotesque." What academia desires in this day of supposedly equal opportunity for the sexes is the "classical" female body: beautiful, static or nonreproductive, young, modeled on the (masculine) model of bourgeois individualism. Academic ageism is thus inherently misogynist, perceiving the aging female body as grotesque in a way that the aging male is not, and serving the antifeminist backlash by working to exclude as many women as possible, and thus to contain the growth of feminist power in the academy.

Antiageism and feminism should therefore be natural allies. Not only does ageism affect women in general more than men, but it impacts on *academic* women disproportionately in comparison to academic men. Men, like women, may be subject to ageism if they attempt to enter academia at an age perceived as older than "normal." However, not only do fewer men than women enter graduate studies as "returning older students," but once hired, men are unlikely to encounter ageism based on their marital or parental status. By contrast, women are vulnerable to ageism at many stages of the academic career path. Maternity at any age makes it difficult to maintain the conventionally undeviating progression from graduate studies to job candidacy, from hiring to tenure candidacy. Yet any deviation from this path, as I shall demonstrate, is likely to make a woman subject to ageist discrimination. Nor is maternity necessarily the only aspect of feminine sexuality that makes a woman more vulnerable to ageism: some lesbian academics feel that lesbians may be even more targeted by ageist discrimination than heterosexual women, as if the aging lesbian body shares with the older pregnant body an identification as the extreme of the "female grotesque"—a woman who is making a spectacle of herself by flaunting an "unnatural" sexuality at an "unnatural" age.[3]

Yet, though antiageism and feminism should consequently be natural allies, I believe that ageism "between women"—and between academic feminists in particular—has emerged as an important issue, and one that is crucial for feminists on the faculty to address. "Second-wave" feminism has now been around long enough for many feminists to perceive themselves as belonging to an "older" generation. This perception indicates the formation of a generational identity politics which I will suggest is ageist in complex and multifaceted ways, representing not only women's ambivalence about either younger or older women colleagues but ambivalence about the aging of both their own bodies and the "body" of feminist theory. The intersection between ageism and feminism is further complicated by racial, ethnic, and class differences in the perception of the "mother" and of the "daughter's" relation to her. Ageism in feminism, then, constitutes the last but by no means the least important of the intersections between ageism and antifeminism that both undermine and uphold the hierarchical and patriarchal structures of academia.

I. Ageism and antifeminism

In his *The University: An Owner's Manual* (1990), former Harvard Dean Henry Rosovsky discusses a "typical" Harvard tenure case:

> The Economics Department, seeking to attract a new tenured specialist in the field of, say, industrial organization, has reached a preliminary consensus: a scholar in his middle thirties, a full professor at a rival university. Youth is a definite asset because the average age of tenured professors is near fifty-five. A young man or woman will bring fresh views, up-to-date technical training, and the promise of being a mentor to a new generation of graduate students. Innovative approaches to the field and command of the latest research techniques are especially desirable. There is an unstated feeling that our resident experts are slightly beyond their prime. (198)

Feminist academics should note the assumptions in this "owner's manual" very carefully. Although Rosovsky scrupulously avoids explicit sexism—"a young man *or woman*"—he makes no attempt whatever to avoid ageism. "Youth is a definite asset," he assures us, because the other professors in the department are in their fifties and are suspected to be "slightly beyond their prime." Obviously, he assumes that only professors under fifty are likely to be in their prime, and from the description of the candidate, it appears that even professors in their forties are likely to be less "in their prime" than professors in their thirties—*full* professors, that is. The assumption is that an individual who makes full professor at a "young" age is more talented than one who makes it at an older age, an assumption that, needless to say, totally ignores the issue of what is sometimes called an "alternative career track." An individual who makes full professor in the mid-thirties is likely to be male, because that individual is unlikely to have deviated from his career track since he entered graduate school. Although Rosovsky's privileging of youth is billed as nonsexist, such a policy will inevitably have a sexist effect, discriminating against women who deviate from the conventional career path because of maternity or any other kind of family care responsibilities, which continue to fall most heavily on the shoulders of women.

We should also note the negative stereotypes of aging implicit in Rosovsky's "typical case." Faculty in their fifties are likely to be stale, out of date, and unable to mentor the "new generation." Yet it is precisely faculty in their fifties who are likely to have an established research record, pedagogical and administrative experience, and who, for these good reasons, are likely to be named chair of the department or dean of the college. It is precisely these individuals who often are seen as "in their prime" or at the pinnacle of their career.

The United States Age Discrimination in Employment Act of 1967, which later became part of the Equal Employment Opportunity Act, states that it shall be unlawful for an employer "to fail or refuse to hire or to discharge any individual or otherwise discriminate against any individual with respect to his compensation, terms, conditions, or privileges of employment, because of such individual's age." However, this act applies only to those forty years of age or over.[4] In academia individuals may be discriminated against on the basis of being "too old" because they are 35 and applying for a "junior position," or they may be excluded from fellowship and grant applications because of age restrictions.[5] In addition, as Sara Arber and Jay Ginn point out, the ADEA "is of limited value for women because it does not cover sex. That is, it does not specify that employers must be willing to hire older people of *both* sexes. Similarly, the 1964 Civil Rights Act (Title VII) outlaws sex discrimination but does not cover age" (1991, 44). Thus, by hiring older men and young women, as the Older Women's League commented, "many employers can actively (although not openly) pursue a policy of discrimination against older women, yet escape the sting of the law."[6]

Although the ADEA does not bar age discrimination where age is a *bona fide* occupational qualification, many academics still confuse an ageist stereotype of those over forty—or thirty-five or even thirty—as typically out-of-date in their field and lacking in "fresh ideas," with a *bona fide* qualification for the field. This seems so indisputable to some academics that many women have had the experience of being openly told that they were not hired or perhaps even considered for a position because they were just "too old." For example, one woman was told by the chair of a department that:

> the main reason you were not hired is that you are too old. Our department has two people below thirty years of age and the remaining nine are fifty years of age or more. We need to hire someone in the under thirty bracket. "But I am forty!" I replied. "It would seem to me that you need someone in the range of forty years old." The answer: "No, we have to have someone under thirty."[7]

The chair in this case clearly thought not only that telling the candidate she was "too old" would be more acceptable than any other reason for rejection, but that it was a *generally* acceptable reason for failing to hire a particular candidate. Yet since this candidate actually was forty, his remarks could have incriminated him in terms of the ADEA. His bland assumptions not only that ageism is perfectly rational and understandable but that it is not illegal are even more obvious in another case:

> In 1976, I applied for a job teaching English at M.I.T. The department approved me, and I was told I had the job. But I heard nothing further, and when I inquired, was told that Dean Harry Hanham had determined I was too old for it. I had ten years of experience, a book published by Harvard UP, and was a young 46. I never found work in academia again.[8]

Such cases give no indication that feminism or even necessarily the gender of the candidate was significant in relation to the question of age.[9] But at an open session on antifeminism and ageism in the academy at the 1989 MLA, a woman faculty member commented that:

> Last year I was a member of a Search Committee. I am 34 years old and several senior members of the Committee commented in my presence that ... I was the youngest person in my department and that that was terrible because the department was so old and we really had to look for young people. They did not mean young people, they meant young women because in fact the men that we ended up interviewing were older than me and ... we hired some of them ... somehow it is not a disadvantage to be a forty-year-old man.... I really do think it is sexism and ageism together. They want any age man and young women ... what they were offended by was that the women in the department in their ... late 30s early 40s and so on were all very vocal, we were all feminists, and I think they were just hoping that somewhere they would find a seventeen-year-old cheerleading Ph.D.[10]

Such comments strongly suggest that claims about a candidate being "too old" are underpinned not only by fear of "the female grotesque" in the form of an older and semiotically productive female but by an active pedophilic penchant. Consider the remarks of Umberto Eco who, in a 1987 *diacritics* interview, insisted that it was not "normal" for people to study until they reached the age of thirty-five—in his generation, people had to leave the university by the age of twenty-two. Eco begins his remarks in this interview by commenting that he felt like "a lover" when he faced a class, that "you have to make the students love you during the first three minutes of class," and that he had a very similar experience with dogs.[11] That Eco is particularly repelled by the older *female* student is clear from his comments about forty-year-old women who, according to him, entered graduate studies because they "want to preserve or recapture their youth":

> Why should I see forty-five year old women who want to write a thesis in my classes at Columbia University? They are never going to teach; they have eight children and a husband to take care of. If they like to study, let them spend the entire day in the library. (Eco, 48)[12]

Eco says nothing about his own desire to recapture his youth by getting his properly youthful students to fall in love with him. But in a recent article published in *Harper's*, William Kerrigan is even more explicit about the erotic pleasures available to him as the university professor of young students, especially young *female* students:

> I have been the subject of advances from male and female students for twenty-five years.... And there is a particular kind of student I have responded to.... I'm talking about a female student who, for one reason or another, has unnaturally prolonged her virginity.... There have been times when this virginity has been presented to me as something that I, not quite another man, half an authority figure, can handle ... these relationships exist between adults and can be quite beautiful and genuinely transforming. It's very powerful sexually and psychologically, and because of that power, one can touch a student in a positive way.[13]

It seems probable that Kerrigan would be equally "positive" about the advantages of hiring youthful and still "virginal" women on the faculty, and equally negative about hiring postvirginal and middle-aged types, especially those whose feminism might not put them in awe of his "authority." Although Kerrigan's—like Eco's—views are so extreme as to appear absurd, the testimony submitted to the MLA Commission on the Status of Women in the

Profession suggests they should not be discounted as atypical or insignificant in academia.[14] The preference for youth, especially youthful *women*, and the prejudice against age, especially older *women*, is very real. To unpack the intersection between ageism and antifeminism in academia is to unpack a repellantly incestuous sexagism as well as a fear of and hostility toward the "female grotesque"—that figure of a power not only female but feminist.

II. Anti-ageism and feminism

In *Gender and Later Life: A Sociological Analysis of Resources and Constraints* (1991), Arber and Ginn note that "[a]geism does not affect women and men equally; for women it is combined with sexist attitudes" (36). While "[m]ale chronology hinges on employment, ... a woman's age status is defined in terms of events in the reproductive cycle. She is therefore 'valued according to sexual attractiveness, availability, and usefulness to men.' ... The social devaluation of older women occurs regardless of occupation or background, or of the fact that after childrearing they have potentially twenty-five years of productive working life ahead" (42).

Arber and Ginn also note that racism compounds ageism and sexism in some cultures. In American life, "[e]lderly blacks are systematically disadvantaged in terms of financial resources and health status," but in Britain the majority of migrants are still usually young adults, so that ageism does not appear to intersect importantly with racism as yet (16). A similar situation may obtain on academic faculties in the U.S., from which women of color have been excluded until so recently that ageism and sexagism may not yet have had time, so to speak, to function significantly in what bell hooks calls "interlocking systems of domination."[15]

Given the fact that ageism affects women more than men, and that the double impact of this "sexagism" stems from the characteristic evaluation of women's age "in terms of events in the reproductive cycle," regardless of occupation, antiageism and feminism should be natural allies. Academic feminists should recognize that ageism in academia—as elsewhere—does not apply in gender-neutral ways, but is always inflected by attitudes toward the female body. As Susan Sontag has put it, men are "allowed" to age without social penalization, but the aging female body arouses revulsion.[16] The phrase "in his prime," whether intended positively or negatively in the case of a particular individual, is exclusively a convention of *masculine* maturation. The woman in her fifties is commonly characterized as "menopausal" or "postmenopausal," and both characterizations carry an antimaturation connotation. The menopausal woman is not "in her prime" but inevitably past it: she is typically imaged as in a biologically unstable period, subject to hot flashes and mood swings, obviously not a likely prospect for the calm and objective deliberations of the "mature scholar."

But in academia, sexagism is not confined to this conventional prejudice against the older female body. Rather, many women academics perceive that it begins with discrimination against the *reproductive* female body—a discrimination that often merges imperceptibly into ageist discrimination. As one graduate student put it, "I have found a very subtle 'mommy-tracking' at work in our graduate program: the women who bear children during their Ph.D. work are not seen as part of the graduate student 'elite' ... nor are they held to the same high standards during prelims or the dissertation stage...."[17] She noted that her dissertation "timetable" left no time off for pregnancy, delivery, or maternity leave, and she had also noted that of the eight female professors in her department, only two had children. The first child of one of these professors had been born precisely nine months after the professor received tenure.

The posttenure baby is not an uncommon event in the lives of academic women. However, many women feel they cannot take the risk of postponing motherhood to whatever age they might be at the time of tenure, and therefore choose to have babies at an earlier stage in their academic careers. It is at this point that they may find themselves exchanging sexism for ageism, for any time off the tenure track or, even more critically, any gap in the years between Ph.D. and time of first hiring for a tenure-track job, is likely to be taken as *prima facie* evidence of inferior achievement and potential. As another woman reported:

> I listened to the fiftyish male department chairman reviewing applications for full-time positions for the coming year. He read one aloud from a woman in her early forties, who was applying for an instructor or lecturer's level position. He placed it aside, saying that she couldn't be any good as a potential faculty member if she were at such a low level at that age.[18]

The woman who reported this comment had herself made the decision to put off having children until she was ready to write her dissertation. She had her first child and then completed the dissertation, after which she had a second child and tried to go back to full-time teaching. However, at this point exhaustion overcame her: her spouse was not an academic, did not have a flexible schedule, and she could not find day care within driving distance. Accordingly, she made the "mistake" of taking time off from her academic career, combining independent scholarly work with child care until the younger child was old enough to go to school. It was then she found she had joined an "army of academically trained fortyish women trying to get back into academe."

A Federal judge recently found Vassar College guilty of failing to grant tenure to an assistant biology professor whose case was very similar to that described in the letters and testimony submitted to the MLA Commission on the Status of Women in the Profession. Judge Constance Baker Motley of the United States District Court in Manhattan found that Vassar had discriminated against Professor Cynthia J. Fisher "because she was married and older than her peers." Dr. Fisher had been hired at Vassar in 1977 after spending eight years rearing her two daughters. She had also taught part-time during this period at Marist College in Poughkeepsie. When she came up for tenure at Vassar in 1985, she was fifty-three years old. The chairman of the Biology Department admitted at the trial that "the time plaintiff had taken off in order to raise a family was a principal factor in the department's recommendation to deny her tenure" because, despite the fact that she had been awarded several grants and had published well-received articles in academic journals, he "felt that this represented a huge gap in her knowledge which she was unable to rectify." Dr. Fisher's lawyer, Eleanor Jackson Pie, commented that: "This has to do with an idea at the elitist women's colleges in the East that going into academics was like a call to the ministry.... Either women went into academia or they got married, but not both." Judge Motley "noted that in the 30 years before Dr. Fisher's tenure review, no married women had been granted tenure in 'hard sciences' at the school" (Tabor 1994: B1, B5).

Another of the respondents to the MLA Commission on the Status of Women in the Profession observed that when academic *men* became parents, a "reverse sexism"—and ageism—could result. When a male professor in his mid-thirties embarked on his third marriage and first child:

> he was understandably overjoyed and thoroughly relished the role of the liberated male father who proudly changed diapers, walked the baby at three A.M., etc. However, when meetings were held that he did not want to attend, or appointments were made, he often stated that he could not cooperate because he had to see to his infant. Older faculty oohed and aahed about what a terrific father he was and wasn't his wife lucky to have him. Those of us who had children and were struggling to achieve tenure could never have

used this as an excuse. I felt I could not use my children or hardly ever mention them for fear of not being serious about my work and being looked at as not professional. For him it became a badge of courage.[19]

To sum up: it is the point in her "reproductive cycle" that determines the precise mechanism by which ageism will be brought to bear on the academic woman's career—regardless of whether she ever has a child or not. If she is chronologically young, the knowledge of academic ageism will pressure her to postpone maternity. If she postpones maternity, she may never have a child, given the facts of declining reproductive fertility with increasing chronological age. If she postpones or slows down some stage of her academic progress, she may never have an academic career, given the fact of continuing academic sexagism. Whether she does or does not have children, whether she is heterosexual or homosexual, she will at some point be perceived as an "aging" or "menopausal" woman. If she does not already have tenure at this point (or promotion to associate or full professor), she may be denied tenure (or promotion). She is unlikely to be perceived as being either "in her prime" or "slightly beyond her prime," because ageism in her case is sexagism, always inflected by her sexual objectification. The academic woman is perceived as either being in her reproductive years, with all the attendant risks, or past her reproductive phase, with all the implications of decline. The academic male may experience ageism, but he is most unlikely to experience sexagism—he may even, as in the case of the much-applauded middle-aged father above, experience reverse sexagism.

If ageism for the academic woman is always sexagism, it follows that feminists should recognize ageism as a major feminist issue. As Kathleen Woodward puts it, "*We must add age to recent debates on difference*, which have been linked to desire and have resulted in some of the most important criticism in the last few decades in the areas of sexual difference, colonialism, ethnicity, race, and cultural difference" (Woodward's emphasis) (1991, 157). Yet ageism has received comparatively little attention in feminist criticism and theory. While this may stem in part from the fact that ageism *is* a gender issue, and therefore has tended to be less visible in academia in proportion to the lesser visibility of *women* in academia, I believe that ageism among feminists and in feminism is also a factor.[20] Feminism and antiageism should be natural allies, but feminism and ageism may also be linked in an all too "natural" and transparent alliance.

III. Ageism and Feminism

In her essay, "Decades"—one of twenty essays in what appears to be the first collection by and about "middle-aged" feminist literary critics, *Changing Subjects: The Making of Feminist Literary Criticism* (1993)—Nancy Miller concludes that: "Having arrived at this point, I should now adopt a more confident, visionary tone and scan the cultural firmament for signs of things to come: portents for feminism in the nineties.... That would have been a graceful way to end...." (42).[21] But it would be a "little disingenuous too," to speak "as if the matter of generations and the transmission of feminism's body of knowledge were an easy matter; as if I had forgotten the painful ironies of the feminist classroom in which female authority is regularly contested" (42). She traces her uncertainty in part to the "effect of feminism's historicity: its self-critical movement into middle age...."(43). But ulti-mately, she writes, "it probably would be more accurate to acknowledge that the failure of vision I experience emerges at least in part from the panic of *my own aging*" (43).

Miller's candor allows her to acknowledge what many middle-aged femi-nists today tend to repress—that a significant source for her "failure of vision" lies in her own now self-directed ageism. Or perhaps I should say, *sexagism*, for it is "the infrequent stories of *women's* lives after fifty" that leaves her feeling unable to see how both her own "life-writing" and that of academic feminism will turn out (43, my emphasis). Her statement, like others in *Changing Subjects*, epitomizes the struggle of many academic femi-nists formed in the early years of second-wave feminism to reenvision a movement they implicitly identified with the "daughter's" rebellion but that has now been transformed into an age and status more like that of the "mother," and an established one at that. As Jerry Aline Flieger notes, "here we are in middle age, looking back, and forward ... now that we are the older generation of feminists, what do we say to our younger sisters?" (*Changing Subjects*, 253). Although Flieger speaks of "our younger sisters" rather than our "daughters," the challenge faced by academic feminism today appears to many as that of attempting to rewrite the "mother-daughter" script from the other side—to speak as a feminist mother rather than as a feminist daughter. And for many feminist women this is the ultimate grotesquerie: to find your-self inhabiting the very "body" against which you had, in those revolutionary early days of "women's liberation," taken to the streets in protest.

Ann Snitow, for example, comments in an essay published elsewhere that the "emotional throwing off of the mother's life felt like the only way to begin.... We used to agree in those meetings that motherhood was the divide: before it, you could pretend you were just like everyone else; afterward, you were a species apart—invisible and despised" (Hirsch and Keller, 1990, 32). Marianne Hirsch also elaborates on the difficulty of negotiating this "divide" (1989, 26). She speaks of how a discussion group of feminists composed of women who had become mothers found it almost impossible to speak simultaneously as a "mother" and a "daughter":

> when we spoke *as mothers*, the group's members were respectful, awed, helpful in the difficulties of formulating maternal experiences. When we spoke *as daughters* about our own mothers, however, the tone and affect changed and we all giggled knowingly, reverting back to old stereotyped patterns of discussing a shared problem—our "impossible mothers." The sympathy we could muster for ourselves and each other *as mothers*, we could not quite transfer to our own mothers. Although as mothers we were eager to tell our stories, as daughters we could not fully listen to our mothers' stories. This inability, this tragic asymmetry between our own two voices, was so pervasive as to be extremely difficult to discuss. It revealed the depth and the extent of the "matrophobia" that exists not only in the culture at large, but also within feminism, and within women who are mothers. (1989, 26)

Hirsch's comments go directly to the core of the problem: it is not only that ageism operates *between* feminist women in academia; it also operates *in* them. Many academic women, like women everywhere in this ageist culture, panic at the very thought of "middle age," but this thought appears especially disruptive of academic women's self-identification as *feminists*. This internal "divide" has already been written into feminist theory, much of which, as Hirsch notes, "situates itself in the position of the daughter and at a distance from the maternal" (25) A number of the writers in *Changing Subjects* speak to this perception of the dilemma of middle-aged feminism. Coppélia Kahn's essay is simply titled, "Mother": in it she traces the origins of her feminist criticism to some "forty years [of] consciously organizing my personality so as not to resemble my mother...." (1993, 158). Eventually she began to realize that "my book, which traces the problems of achieving male identity in a patriarchal world as a reenactment of the first psychological separation from the mother, crucial in establishing the individual self, was about me as much as about Romeo or Macbeth" (1993, 166).

Kahn does not consider in her essay the ramifications of such a painfully won separation from her mother in her work with feminist students or colleagues young enough to perceive *her* as a mother, but Madelon Sprengnether does. Her essay, entitled "Generational Differences: Reliving Mother-Daughter

Conflicts," sensitively explores the issue of how a feminist who felt "wildly unmothered" herself both at home and in academia, could cope with her difficulties in seeing herself as a mother, again both at home and on the faculty (1993, 202). Although she looked forward to the arrival of younger women colleagues, she found herself running into unexpected snags with them which, she believes, were rooted "in a mother-daughter dynamic so insistent, yet obscured, as to defy all but the most thoughtful and committed efforts to address" (1993, 204). "Academic matrophobia" meant that junior women "projected on to me an image of the mothers who had disappointed them" (1993, 206).

Sprengnether's solution is to urge that older and younger feminists realize that "we owe it to each other not simply to relive our scripts of mother-daughter conflict, but to change them" (1993, 206–207). Perhaps even more crucial, however, to the uneasy matter of dealing with "generations and the transmission of feminism's body of knowledge," is to recognize that its construction as a "mother-daughter conflict" in itself situates it in a generational identity politics that erases other scripts of ageing and ageism, and inscribes feminism in endless cycles of generational reproduction and redestruction. It is notable that, among the academic women of color and/or of working-class origin who contribute to the "middle-aged" perspective on feminism in *Changing Subjects*, none articulates a similar sense of "mother-daughter conflict" or of needing to rewrite that particular script in academic feminism today. The characterization of ageism *in* feminism as an horrific transformation of the daughter's "body" into the mother's needs to be acknowledged as the formulation of a specific race and class, namely of the daughters of white, middle-class mothers, and even more specifically, of those "daughters" who entered graduate school at a particular moment in their own personal histories, that is, while they identified themselves as daughters and not as mothers. Room needs to be cleared for critical analyses of other ageisms "between women" and other constructs of becoming "middle-aged" as feminists.

An "identity politics," as Judith Butler points out, "makes the assumption that there must be a universal basis for feminism, one which must be found in an identity assumed to exist cross-culturally" (1990, 3). The assumption that becoming "middle-aged" means that women identify—and are identified—as "mothers" rather than as "daughters" signals such an "identity politics." It universalizes ageist conflicts between feminist academic women as rooted in their phantasmatic struggles with their own mothers, an oedipal model that, as Jane Gallop points out, inevitably reproduces itself:

> The only alternatives proposed are filial piety or killing the mother. The filial piety model actually reinforces the oedipal structure. Jane Marcus says that our job is to carry forward our mother's text. The daughter graduate student trying to gain a voice for herself must kill the mother if that is the expectation. (Hirsch and Keller, 1990, 355)

The perception of "academic matrophobia" as widespread among "junior women" and also among students, accounting for at least some of what manifests itself as antifeminist backlash, tends to obscure differences in women's experience of becoming "middle-aged" or just growing old as feminists. The perception of matrophobia, as both Kahn's and Sprengnether's essays so eloquently demonstrate, is inevitably a projection of one's own matrophobia onto the next generation. But what these essays also make evident, even more significantly, is that only daughters who perceived their mother's power as complicit with the patriarchal structures against which the daughters rebelled seem to perceive "matrophobia" as a pervasive and dominant impulse structuring relations between younger and older generations of academic feminists.

There is a striking absence of either maternalist or matrophobic metaphors in narratives by women of color and/or of working-class origins in *Changing Subjects*. Gloria T. Hull, insisting on the "personal, unique" and nonrepresentative nature of her story, writes of learning lessons from her "iron-willed, independent mother and my endurance-oriented poor Black southern culture, as well as the strong resourceful and individualistic qualities I perforce developed as an abuse survivor" (Greene and Kahn, 1993, 48). Hull invokes the by-now familiar image of the strong black mother as, in part, responsible for her feminism, but she also emphasizes the importance of growing up in Black culture and of her own strength of independence and individualism. Margo Hendricks speaks of being "provoke[d]" to "reflect on the absence of faculty of color in the English department," and later of being repeatedly struck by "the way in which ethnicity and gender automatically signal an intellectual identity" (Greene and Kahn, 1993, 147, 149). Rather than constructing her feminist identity as organized in relation to a struggle with her mother, Hendricks suggests that the discovery that her ethnicity and gender automatically slotted her into a particular intellectual identity served as primary motivation for her academic feminism. For Barbara Christian, the belief that young black women were "free enough to be all we could be, at least in the Struggle," was soon eclipsed by the discovery that "we were enclosed, even in our own communities, in cages of misrepresentations as to who a black woman should be" (Greene and Kahn, 1993, 196). For Shirley Geok-lin Lim, although she describes herself as the abandoned daughter of a mother who sought her own pleasure and freedom first, becoming a feminist was nevertheless a process of recognizing multiply organized "colonizations." Geok-lin Lim displays a concomitant skepticism about a political agenda that imagined the correction of wrongs for *all* women, and that also imagined the origin of those wrongs largely in relation to the figure of the mother (Greene and Kahn, 1993, 242–244). And like Gloria Hull, Linda S. Kauffman, who worked from the age of eleven, credits her feminism to her strong mother's "fierce insistence that I escape the traps that thwarted her" (Greene and Kahn, 1993, 131).

These accounts of becoming middle-aged as feminists suggest important differences from those written from the perspective of psychoanalytic models of generational relations between women as either maternalist or matrophobic. In a recent review essay critiquing what she sees as a still-prominent "maternalist ethics," Cora Kaplan states, "white, middle-class girls of my generation who became feminists in the late sixties and early seventies often did so from a perspective of extremely angry and rather unreflective daughterdom, a psychic, social, and political position that bell hooks, among others, reminds us was specific to our class, race, and culture."[22] Kahn's and Sprengnether's essays in *Changing Subjects*, however, are anything but "unreflective": on the contrary, they contribute to that "critique of the family" that Kaplan finds both powerful and important, "estrang[ing] that which seemed most binding, close and familiar, so that it might appear as uncanny, even grotesque, as well as a social construction like any other." Yet these essays do not make "matrophobia" appear to be "a social construction like any other," but rather contribute to a prevailing impression among older academic feminists that matrophobia is, in fact, a widespread if not universal aspect of the antifeminist backlash articulated by younger women in academia. They suggest that matrophobia is an integral part of ageism in feminism, as it was an integral part of their own apocalyptic rebirth into feminism as angry daughters. Yet one has only to consider, for example, bell hooks' account of her mother as finding her work outside the home more rewarding than that of any of her children to understand that matrophobia might have as little to do with ageism among black academic feminists as it has everything to do with a certain age cohort of white, middle-class academic feminists.[23]

Even within that age cohort, however, I believe the mother-daughter model of ageist conflicts in feminism obscures significant differences in the "experience" of becoming middle-aged as a feminist. In particular, it obscures the experiences of those of us who became academic feminists *in* middle age, rather than the other way around. Although the writers in *Changing Subjects* represent a range of differences in race, class, and sexualities among feminists who, as Carolyn Heilbrun notes in her afterword, were all born—with the exception of herself—in the thirties and forties, the one difference not represented is that of women of the same age who returned to school at an unconventional *stage* of their lives. Yet the Women's Lib movement saw the beginnings of a huge wave of such older, returning, women students—one that continues to this day. What does becoming "middle-aged" in feminism mean for the woman who enters graduate school when she is already a mother, or perhaps even a grandmother? I offer my experiences as in some respects representative (in others quite nonrepresentative) of women born into the same age cohort as the writers in *Changing Subjects* but of a different academic feminist generation, since we entered graduate studies at a different stage in our histories and in our formation of feminist "identities."

I restarted my college career in 1972, commuting by subway from our suburban home to the inner-city campus of the University of Massachusetts-Boston, when I was in my thirties and already the mother of three daughters. My decision to return was partly inspired by the women's movement and partly by the desire to find at least temporary relief from a volcanic marriage. I was so afraid of my own anger that it was not until I had completed my first year of college that I dared to read Betty Friedan's *The Feminine Mystique*, published a decade before. I took it for granted that I was a feminist, yet although Mary Ann Ferguson was teaching her groundbreaking course in images of women in literature at Massachusetts-Boston at that time, I did not take the course: I thought of "feminist criticism" as fascinating, but as only one "style" of criticism, whereas in my other literary courses I fancied I was learning many such "styles." I thoroughly enjoyed my literary studies, and much admired my professors, who were indeed committed to their humanist teaching, and all but one of whom were male.

As I neared the end of this uncritical, "feminist," undergraduate career, I developed the daring notion of going on to graduate school. The idea was daring because, although my mother considered her family to be "upper-middle-class," no *woman* in the family had ever received a doctoral degree: I was thus stepping out of the proper line of daughters in my family, who were supposed to be educated but not to become, as my grandmother—herself a product of the first antifeminist backlash of this century—would have put it, like "those awful bluestockings."[24]

It was also daring because of the cost. The University of Massachusetts-Boston, dedicated to the education of working adults, had a tuition so low that we could afford it even on the sole income of a librarian, but graduate school tuition was unthinkable. My honors thesis adviser, obviously steeling himself to ask an equally unthinkable question, inquired gently as to how old I was. Thus I discovered that I was already too old to qualify for a traditional Danforth Graduate Fellowship, which at that time was limited to those under thirty-five. Fortunately, the Danforth Foundation—doubtless also inspired by the women's movement—had just instituted a special fellowship program for women who had been out of college for a period of at least three years (I had been out for fifteen), and my receipt of that fellowship solved the money problem for the time being.[25]

At that point, my husband insisted on sweeping the family off for a year in Japan, where he had an exchange position. This was a prospect regarded by most as an unprecedented privilege, but which entailed for me a most unwilling reconfinement to the role of housewife and mother. (Japan in the 1970s was in no way a feminist culture.) By the time we returned, and I was able to begin the commute to Brown University (a three-times-a-week, five-hour round-trip by subway and Amtrak), the kids were all in junior high and high school, and I was nearing forty. Like Judith Kegan Gardiner in *Changing Subjects*, I thought of my feminism at this time (1976) as in some part the product of my being a mother, of wanting to "do feminism" not only *as* a mother but *for* my daughters (Greene and Kahn, 1993, 87). My ambition, however, was baffled by the generally traditionalist approach to literary studies in the Brown English department at that time, but even more so by my own unwillingness to be identified *as* a mother—especially as a nearly-forty mother.

I had good reasons for this, for a subtle "mommy-tracking" of *older*, married, graduate students was being carried on—often, I think, with the best of intentions—in the department. One of my advisors announced that although he was willing to take on more than one "geographically limited"— for which read "mother of kids too young to be left behind"—woman as advisee, he could only support one of us for jobs in our field. Despite his generally feminist politics, it appeared that middle-aged mothers were inter-changeable. Another male faculty member wrote me letters praising me to the skies as a superlatively "mature" candidate for jobs which, unsurprisingly,

I never got. Only Barbara Lewalski openly confronted the problem she knew I would have with ageism and sexagism, warning me not to put anything on my c.v. that would give away my age. That way, she told me, I would at least have a chance to get to the interview stage. (She was right.)

I had the good fortune to be at Brown when the Pembroke Institute for Research on Women was founded: it was in this rigorously theoretical seminar, under the brilliant leadership of Joan Scott and Elizabeth Weed, that I not only received my first introduction to feminist theory but, in effect, a complete, second, graduate education that worked to slowly undermine and rewrite the first. Here I began to understand *theoretically* how the valorization of motherhood confined women to the private, the domestic, the biological, the "natural," that is, the heterosexual.

But it was in a feminist collective I was invited to join at this time that I both personally confronted the mother-daughter divide in feminism for the first time, and actually *became* a feminist in something more than an enthusiastic but rather distanced affirmation.[26] The collective membership desired to be as diverse as possible: some were straight and some were lesbian, and there was fervent discussion of how to become racially diverse, although this never happened. With the inclusion of myself, the collective took on a diversity of age and maternal status that was, I realized, unexpectedly problematic. I was ten to fifteen years older than the other members, though many of them were, like me, graduate students. I was also the *only* mother, a generational identity that stuck out like a sore toe in a group whose collective ethos was largely that of angry daughters. You could say that I wanted to take on the identity of rebellious "daughter" myself at this point, but it was hardly against *mothers* that my rage was directed, being engaged daily in the confusions and frustrations of attempting to deal with three daughters who were by now in college as well as high school. The hetero/homosexual divide in the group, which at first had seemed to me by far its most radical element, came to seem less risky than the combination of "mother" and "daughter" generational identities. But it was in those very awkward moments of destabilization of any attempt to construct my own identity politics as *either* a mother or a daughter that I believe I "became" a feminist—intensely engaged in what it meant to "do" feminism. And for me that "feminist movement" meant being a "middle-aged" feminist in more than one sense, always between generations, divided, split, perpetually *in medias res*. Motherhood was permanently—and usefully—grotesqued for me.

I continue to be in perpetual motion across boundaries. In 1986, when I began teaching as assistant professor in the English department at Queen's University in Kingston, Ontario (an eight-hour *one-way* trip by subway, plane and ViaRail), it seemed entirely appropriate that my first graduate student—now holding down a tenure-track job—should be a grandmother. When I finally "came of age" as a feminist academic—that is, was tenured and promoted—I also became an expectant grandmother (the grand-daughter was born, nicely timed, in my sabbatical year). My experience with students of all ages and stages of parental status, and all degrees of feminism and antifeminism, reinforces my conviction of the importance of avoiding the construction of a monolithic and binaristic model of ageism between feminists as conflicts between "mothers" and "daughters." As Cora Kaplan concludes, "Mother-daughter relations are but two of many constituents of *every* moment of feminism, and they cannot be abstracted from the multiple historical meanings which determine the precise staging of such a tableau" (1994, 165).

Growing "middle-aged" in feminism, becoming "female grotesques," should be grasped and turned against the ubiquitous ageism and sexagism of our culture, as queer theorists have confronted homophobia in their delib-erate appropriation of a term used to vilify and marginalize lesbian and gay people. Far from promoting a vanilla maternity—a sacred obligation to pass on our mothers' texts and be good-enough mothers to our daughters—fem-inists should promote pregnant hags, menopausal and postmenopausal feminist academics who persist, like the extraordinary writers in *Changing Subjects*, in a prolific, horrific, semiotic, and political performance that continues way beyond the usual limits of a foreseeable "prime." But we must also work to dissect and expose the multiple intersections of ageism with antifeminism, for it is at these thousand points of greyness that much of the power of feminist movement in academia can be rendered short-lived.

Notes

1. The Modern Language Association Commission on the Status of Women in the Profession held an open-mike session on the subjects of antifeminist harass-ment and ageism at the 1989 MLA conference held in Washington, D.C. The CSWP also solicited letters on these topics in notices published in the *MLA Newsletter*.

2. Nor, needless to say, does ageism function *outside* academia as it does inside. The academic institution of tenure has virtually eliminated the ageist practice most common in the business world, that of firing or laying off the over-fifty worker, who is then likely to find him- or herself up against the kind of ageism most common in academia: resistance to hiring older workers. Although the U.S. Equal Employment Opportunity Commission recognizes nearly two dozen types of age discrimination, Robert Lewis states that "[f]ired workers account for 50 percent of all complaints" (1991, 10).

3. I refer here both to a letter written in response to the CSWP appeal for personal testimony on the subject of antifeminism and ageism, describing discrimination on the basis of a combined homophobia and "deep-seated ageism," and to the recent uproar over the birth of twins from a donor egg to a fifty-nine-year-old British woman. A former chairman of the British Medical Association said that the event "'bordered on the Frankenstein syndrome,'" and members of both the Italian and the French governments called for bans on artificial insemination of postmenopausal women (Miller, January 4, 1994). Numerous respondents pointed out that no one would think anything (negative) of a *man* becoming a parent at such an age.

4. Beverley Baines points out that although the Canadian Charter of Rights and Freedoms guarantees equality and the right to protection against discrimination based on race, national or ethnic origin, color, religion, sex, age or mental or physical disability, the Charter does not define "equality," nor does it discriminate in its use of the term "sex" between advantaged and disadvantaged groups, i.e., between men's sex equality claims and women's sex equality claims (Burt, Code, Dorney, 245, 246, 269).

5. This situation may be changing as academic institutions become more conscious of ageism. In 1989, for example, the President of the Woodrow Wilson National Fellowship Foundation said that the Mellon Fellowships and Javits Fellowships are "designed to provide special opportunities for the very best young women and men" (*Woodrow Wilson National Fellowship Foundation Newsletter*, Spring 1989, 3). But in 1991, an article in the *WWNFF Newsletter* reported that, "[a]bout 41% of the new Fellows graduated from college a year or more ago, and as such tend to display the benefits both of greater maturity and of perspectives gained by working for a time outside the academy" (Spring 1991, 4). Such a shift from emphasis on *young* men and women to "greater maturity" and diversity of perspectives is indeed encouraging.

6. As quoted in Arber and Ginn, 44.

7. Letter to MLA Committee on the Status of Women in the Profession from Anne Eggebroten, dated March 28, 1990. All writers quoted from testimony submitted to the MLA Committee on the Status of Women in the Profession have given permission to quote from their letters or oral testimony in this article.

8. Letter to the MLA Committee on the Status of Women in the Profession from Marilyn French, dated January 9, 1990.

9. In fact, in the first case the chair had told the candidate that they "wanted someone with more feminist theory and practical experience in something like

women's shelters, but you were a great candidate otherwise." The position was for a candidate qualified in medieval studies and feminist theory, and the chair's formulation that the candidate should also have practical experience "in something like women's shelters" sounds as if the department wanted a female candidate who could be all things to all men.

10. Maureen Reddy, 1989 MLA open session. Professor Reddy also suggested that the committee wanted not only a young but a "malleable" woman. The same requirement may well have applied in an experience of my own in which, after a friend of mine had attempted to put in a good word for me with the chair of a department where I had applied for a beginning tenure-track position, the chair retorted that he would not dream of hiring a woman over forty for a junior position.

11. "Interview: Umberto Eco," 48, 46. I responded to Eco in *diacritics* (1990).

12. Women have, in fact, been traditionally barred from university libraries, as Virginia Woolf's beadle points out in *A Room of One's Own*. The Widener Library at Harvard University confined undergraduate women students to a special reading room, and it was not until 1966 that women at Harvard were admitted to all Harvard Libraries (Carpenter, 1986, 186–189).

13. Botstein, Boswell, Blythe, and Kerrigan, 35–36.

14. It is equally true, of course, that some academic individuals and some academic institutions are less ageist and pedophilic or are even actively antiageist. In this instance, for example, Leon Botstein replied to Kerrigan's remarks with the comment that, "What comes to my mind is, one, a sense of relief that you're not on the faculty at my college. And two, I'm not certain anyone wants to make a virtue of a private act" (36). A letter to the MLA Committee on the Status of Women in the Profession notes that the "University of California at Davis where I am presently enrolled (entered at age 45) should be *applauded* for their record on this issue," whereas she strongly suspected another well-known California university of practicing ageist discrimination at the level of admissions to graduate school (Letter from Susan Skov, November 17, 1989).

15. hooks, 1989, 21. No woman of color wrote or spoke about the experience of the triple oppression of racism, sexism, and ageism in the testimony submitted to the CSWP, and in informal discussions with academic women of color, none expressed the view to me that ageism had impacted unfavorably on her career. In a recent article in *Signs*, however, Anne DuCille comments that black women scholars on white college campuses tend to become "icons" and that such "icons" are not automatically granted tenure. Because of the unusual demands on their time and energy made by their iconization, and their simultaneous hypervisibility and superisolation, there are a "startling number of brilliant black women scholars who have produced only one book or no book," and academia does not forgive the lack of publication. "Sympathetic" white colleagues can only "lament their black colleagues' departures from the university" (1994). It seems inevitable that black women or women of color who have thus failed to adhere to the "tenure clock" will find themselves the object of ageism and sexism, intensified by the racist perception of the black female body as always already sexualized. If older women of color attempting to reenter or simply to maintain their place in white academia have not yet experienced an

ageism that compounds the racism and sexism of this milieu, I suspect that it is, unfortunately, only a matter of time before they do.

16. As quoted in Arber and Ginn, 42.

17. Letter to the Commission on the Status of Women in the Profession, December 7, 1989, from respondent who wishes to remain unidentified.

18. Letter to the Commission on the Status of Women in the Profession, November 22, 1989, from respondent who wishes to remain unidentified.

19. Letter to the Commission on the Status of Women in the Profession, December 5, 1989, from respondent who wishes to remain unidentified.

20. In attempting to explain why "feminist sociologists have paid little attention to the stage of life in which women massively outnumber men and in which nearly two-thirds live apart from men," Arber and Ginn point out that "[t]here are parallels between mainstream sociology's current neglect of later life and its gender-blindness until the 1970s. Both stem from a preoccupation with the male-dominated public sphere of paid work, its discontents and its consequences. Feminist experience of the 'selective eye' of sociology lends support to the view that an entrenched masculine bias has been responsible not only for sexism in sociology, but for ageism as well. Gender was invisible in sociology because women were invisible, hidden in the home or subsumed in male pronouns at work" (18, 26).

21. Hirsch and Keller, eds., *Conflicts in Feminism,* might also be considered a collection largely by "middle-aged" academic feminists, but it does not seem to address the issue of *becoming* "middle-aged" in feminism specifically, as *Changing Subjects* does.

22. 1994, n.15, 167. Brenda Daly and Maureen T. Reddy also note that white, middle-class women have been taught to read the mother as complicit with the structures of patriarchal power. They cite Gloria Joseph as arguing that "black daughters, as witnesses of racism directed at their mothers, earlier come to know the real boundaries of their mothers' power in the world and therefore tend to produce fewer victim/powerless daughter narratives—ones that posit the mother as all-powerful and therefore as all-responsible—than do white women" (7).

23. hooks, 1993, 43. hooks writes movingly of the conflicts between black women and their mothers in *Sisters of the Yam,* but it seems evident that those conflicts are not identified with conflicts between women in academia, where the "older woman" is almost always white.

24. To do my grandmother justice, however, she assented to her daughters becoming the first female generation in her family to enter college or university, as many earlier generations of men in the family had done. My mother graduated from Smith College in 1927 and received a Bachelor of Nursing degree from Yale University School of Nursing in 1931. After my physician father's sudden death at the age of 42, she supported the family by returning to work as a registered nurse—a then low-paid occupation in the sexist institution of medicine—and renting rooms to college students. In 1968 she received a Master of Education degree from the University of Maine-Gorham, and in 1989 she was awarded an honorary Master of Arts degree by Bowdoin College.

Then 85, she continues to audit courses at Bowdoin, a "scholar gypsy" undreamed of by Matthew Arnold.

25. Unfortunately, the entire Danforth Fellowship program has ceased to exist.

26. The other members of this radically transformative group were Mary Campbell, Susan Carlisle, Nancy Munger, Helaine Ross, Eve Sedgwick, Deborah Swedberg, Nancy Waring, Carolyn Williams, and Patsy Yaeger.

Works Cited and Consulted

Arber, Sara and Jay Ginn. *Gender and Later Life: A Sociological Analysis of Resources and Constraints.* London: SAGE Publications, 1991.

Baines, Beverly. "Law, Gender, Equality." In Sandra Burt, Lorraine Code, and Lindsay Dorney, eds., *Changing Patterns: Women in Canada.* Toronto: McClelland & Stewart, Inc., 1993. 243–278.

Botstein, Leon, John Boswell, Joan Blythe, and William Kerrigan. "New Rules About Sex on Campus: Should Professors Be Denied Admission to Students' Beds?" *Harper's* (September, 1993).

Burt, Sandra, Lorraine Code, and Lindsay Dorney, eds. *Changing Patterns: Women in Canada.* Toronto: McClelland and Stewart, Inc., 1993.

Butler, Judith. *Gender Trouble: Feminism and the Subversion of Identity.* New York: Routledge, 1990.

Carpenter, Kenneth E. *The First 350 Years of the Harvard University Library: Description of an Exhibition.* Harvard University Library, 1986.

Carpenter, Mary Wilson. "Eco, Oedipus, and the 'View' of the University." *diacritics* 20, 1 (Spring 1990) 77–85.

Christian, Barbara. "Being the Subject and the Object: Reading African-American Women's Novels." *Changing Subjects,* ed. Greene and Kahn. 1993. 195–200.

Daly, Brenda and Maureen T. Reddy. *Narrating Mothers: Theorizing Maternal Subjectivities.* Knoxville: The University of Tennessee Press, 1991.

DuCille, Anne. "The Occult of True Black Womanhood: Critical Demeanor and Black Feminist Studies." *Signs* 19, 3 (Spring 1994) 591–629.

Eco, Umberto. "Interview: Umberto Eco." *diacritics* 17, 1 (Spring 1987): 46–51.

Gallop, Jane, Marianne Hirsch, and Nancy K. Miller. "Criticizing Feminist Criticism." In *Conflicts in Feminism,* ed. Hirsch and Keller. 1990. 349–369.

Geok-lin Lim, Shirley. "Asians in Anglo-American Feminism: Reciprocity and Resistance." In Greene and Kahn, eds., *Changing Subjects.* 1993. 240–252.

Greene, Gayle. "Looking at History." Greene and Kahn, eds., *Changing Subjects,* 1993. 4–27.

Greene, Gayle and Coppélia Kahn, eds. *Changing Subjects: The Making of Feminist Literary History.* New York: Routledge, 1993.

Hendricks, Margo. "Feminism, the Roaring Girls and Me." In *Changing Subjects,* ed. Greene and Kahn. 1993. 147–153.

Hirsch, Marianne. *The Mother/Daughter Plot: Narrative, Psychoanalysis, Feminism.* Bloomington, Indiana: Indiana University Press, 1989.

Hirsch, Marianne and Evelyn Fox Keller, eds. *Conflicts in Feminism.* New York: Routledge, 1990.

hooks, bell. *talking back: thinking feminist, thinking black.* Boston: South End Press, 1989.

———. *Sisters of the Yam: Black Women and Self-Recovery.* Boston: South End Press, 1993.

Hull, Gloria T. "History/My History." *Changing Subjects,* ed. Greene and Kahn. 1993. 48–63.

Kahn, Coppélia. "Mother." *Changing Subjects,* ed. Greene and Kahn. 1993. 1157–167.

Kaplan, Cora. "Fictions of Feminism: Figuring the Maternal." *Feminist Studies* 20, 1 (Spring, 1994): 153–167.

Kauffman, Linda S. "The Long Goodbye: Against the Personal Testimony or, an Infant Grifter Grows Up." *Changing Subjects,* ed. Greene and Kahn. 1993. 129–146.

Lewis, Robert. "Advantage: Bosses. Despite Gains, Age Law Doesn't Always Right Things." *AARP Bulletin* (December 1991): 1, 10.

Miller, Nancy. "Decades." *Changing Subjects,* ed. Greene and Kahn. 1993. 31–47.

Miller, William. "A Charge of 'Designer Babies.'" *Boston Globe* (January 4, 1994): 1, 5.

Rosovsky, Henry. *The University: An Owner's Manual.* New York: W.W. Norton & Co., 1990.

Russo, Mary. "Female Grotesques: Carnival and Theory." In *Feminist Studies/ Critical Studies,* ed. Teresa de Lauretis. Bloomington: Indiana University Press, 1986. 213–229. Reprinted in Mary Russo. *The Female Grotesque: Risk, Excess, Modernity.* New York: Routledge, 1995. 53–73.

Snitow, Ann. "A Gender Diary." *Conflicts in Feminism,* ed. Hirsch and Keller. 1990. 9–43.

Sprengnether, Madelon. "Generational Differences: Reliving Mother-Daughter Conflicts." Greene and Kahn, eds. *Changing Subjects.* 1993. 201–208.

Tabor, Mary B.W. "Judge Rules Vassar Was Biased Against Married Woman Teacher." *New York Times* (May 17, 1994): B1, B5.

Woodward, Kathleen. *Aging and Its Discontents.* Bloomington: Indiana University Press, 1991.

III

Changing Systems of Knowledge:
Feminist Resistance
in the Academy

7

Antifeminism in Scholarship and Publishing

Elaine Ginsberg and Sara Lennox

Hostility towards feminist scholarship? Antifeminism in the publishing and review process? Each season's new flood of publishers' brochures makes that claim seem ever more improbable. Feminist books that address most areas of the humanities and social sciences feature prominently in the offerings of the major academic presses, and the range, variety, and sheer quantity of feminist studies to which the publishers' fliers attest seem to grow exponentially. If there is any arena where academic feminism might seem to be safely ensconced, it is in the realm of publishing. Queried about antifeminism in publishing, one editor of the prestigious feminist series of an academic press replied that she had not seen it; on the contrary, gender studies were the hottest thing in publishing. Though, she continued, when she began her job, the director of her press was not convinced, the bottom line won him over: the books sold. The director of another academic press told us, "Most editors are scrambling to find good feminist work." Publishers, he added, might be faulted for being too commercially inclined, but they want to sell what people want to buy, and feminist scholarship is a lively and vital field. The testimony of these editors suggests that academic presses are virtually prepared to rip feminist manuscripts out of each others' hands. The marketplace, it appears, has conquered ideological recalcitrance. In the face of such evidence, how can we continue to maintain that antifeminism directed against feminist scholarship is a significant problem within the American academy?

Despite the boom in feminist book publishing, we want to argue in this essay that feminist scholarship remains under siege on a number of fronts. Because feminist books sell, it may not be difficult to find publishers for book-length manuscripts. However, in areas where commercial success does not play so central a role, in academic journals for instance, and in disciplines where feminism has made fewer inroads, pockets of old-style antifeminism survive. Even today, such antifeminism may still occasionally take the form of the outright rejection of the legitimacy of feminist approaches or topics. More often, it may express itself in more ambiguous ways that are sometimes difficult to distinguish from a genuine concern about academic standards and quality. Or, finally, it may assume quite complex and coded guises that have the effect of creating barriers to the publication of feminist scholarship but may not derive from deliberate or intentional efforts to block feminist research. In our view, such old-style forms of antifeminism, though important to address, may well be on the wane as older faculty retire and are replaced by younger and more open-minded members of the profession.

But what we find far more worrisome than such traditional antifeminism is the emergence of new forms of antifeminism, both within the academy and outside it, in the wake of the conservative backlash of the late eighties which continues into the present. This new antifeminism appears to be part of a coordinated, well-funded, and highly visible conservative campaign to discredit scholarly and curricular changes in the academy since the sixties. As we assess it, this new antifeminism directed against feminist scholarship appears to have emerged in two waves. The first wave was most spectacularly represented by such works as Allan Bloom's *The Closing of the American Mind* (1987), Roger Kimball's *Tenured Radicals* (1990) and Dinesh D'Souza's *Illiberal Education* (1991) and the media fanfare that accompanied their claims that developments in the American academy since the sixties threatened the values on which the survival of Western civilization depended. While the general target of Bloom, D'Souza, et al., was multiculturalism, especially ethnic studies programs, new scholarly approaches, and affirmative action policies that had changed the face—and the curricula—of American universities, their antifeminism was integral and pervasive. The attack on multiculturalism has subsided somewhat in the nineties, but a frontal assault on feminism and feminist scholarship continues, and is now supported by many of the same forces that underwrote Bloom, D'Souza, and Co.[1] The newest wave of antifeminism cloaks itself in the vestments of feminism: the new antifeminists are women who, claiming to be feminists themselves, now maintain they are rescuing the women's movement from those who have led it astray. "What's 'new' here," Nancy K. Miller has recently argued, "... is the (claim of) protection of women from their feminist sisters" (107). While

170

brandishing their feminist credentials, the new female antifeminists attack the central principles upon which almost all feminist scholarship has been founded. Again accompanied by a great deal of media attention, in many instances gained by gratuitous name-calling, these new antifeminists have been responsible for an outpouring of assaults on scholarship across the political spectrum of feminism. That antifeminist barrage showed no signs of abating as this volume went to press.

Dale Spender's *The Writing or the Sex? or, How You Don't Have to Read Women's Writing to Know It's No Good* (1989) draws on her own research, as well as that of Lynn Spender, Elaine Showalter, Marilyn French, and others, to document the discrimination against and outright dismissal of women writers, critics, and scholars in the 1970s and early eighties. This discrimination and dismissal ranged from a refusal to even read women's work, to overestimation of the representation of women writers and scholars in publishing, to outright hostility. A most egregious example of antifeminism cited by Spender is a review of Casey Miller's and Kate Swift's *Handbook on Non-Sexist Writing* (1981) which commented on the authors' lack (in the reviewer's opinion) of sexual attractiveness, and concluded that Miller and Swift were "disgruntled feminist agitators" (Spender, 68). Novelist Margaret Atwood has also documented numerous instances of unfair reviewing of women's work (see Spender, 73–75, and Atwood). Atwood especially notes the irrelevant emphasis on a woman writer's appearance, as does Naomi Wolf, author of *The Beauty Myth* (1991). Spender's book documents that antifeminism was pervasive and often quite blatant well into the eighties.

In this investigation, we want to show that such old-style antifeminism continues in the nineties, but has frequently assumed more subtle forms. To gather evidence on varieties of antifeminism that academic women mostly experience privately and individually, we pursued a number of avenues. We placed announcements of our project in the *MLA Newsletter;* the *Women's Review of Books; Concerns: The Newsletter of the Women's Caucus of the Modern Languages;* and the *Women in German Newsletter* and posted the announcement on the Women's Studies discussion list and the Women in German discussion list on the Internet. As well, we mailed a description of our project and a request for testimony to the mailing list of the Five College Women's Studies Research Center, located at Mount Holyoke College. Though this is not a scientific sampling (and obviously slights disciplines other than our own), our method of inquiry generated a variety of responses that indicate the various guises that contemporary attacks on feminist scholarship can take. We have promised our informants confidentiality, and will disguise their identities in the accounts that follow.

According to our respondents, antifeminism, in some reaches of the academy, can still take the form of an outright refusal to grant the validity of feminist topics and approaches. Though American literature has been among the fields where feminism has had the greatest impact, one of the first responses to the announcement of our project in the Summer, 1991, *MLA Newsletter* came from a feminist scholar in twentieth-century American literature who, after publishing a prize-winning book on Sylvia Plath, now sought grant funding for a second book on Adrienne Rich. Her grant application was rejected, and one member of the review panel justified his negative evaluation by maintaining that Rich, like Sylvia Plath, was a cult figure whose reputation had been greatly inflated. But such blatant hostility to feminist scholarship is found more frequently at academic institutions or in disciplines where feminism has been slow to find a foothold. Another early submission came from a feminist scholar at a conservative religious college, who sent us a copy of a complaint she had just filed against a colleague to protect herself. In a paper that he circulated to other members of the institution, her colleague compared "hard-core feminism" to Nazism, Marxism, fundamentalist Islam, and certain kinds of Christianity, representing "an irrational kind of thinking that has brought about practically all of the hurt and suffering of this century." He stated definitively: "Gender ... is not important in the discovery and representation of truth." The University Conversion Project reports that this same feminist scholar was fired without warning in June, 1993, for "inferior teaching and scholarship" (Cowan and Massachi, 7).

Feminist scholars in a variety of fields where feminism has had little impact recounted similar wholesale rejections of feminist approaches. A feminist psychologist told us that the results of her work on gender-role egalitarianism were challenged because she was a "lady psychologist," and "participants in the study knew what 'lady psychologists' want them to say." A medievalist testified that readers of her feminist essay on Chaucer "poo-pooed the feminist elements and encouraged [her] to revise the essay in such a way that the decidedly feminist center might disappear." Another feminist scholar reported that the response to his examination of gender issues in Kant's philosophy was the flat assertion: "No, Kant cannot be read that way." And a music historian who submitted a proposal for an anthology of feminist music criticism to the musicology editor of an academic press found that the editor "had no understanding whatsoever of feminism and absolutely no desire to learn about it." When her proposal nonetheless was favorably reviewed, "in every phone call," the author recalls, the editor "continued to counsel me not to let it become 'too feminist'—apparently I was to censor my authors in this regard. Endlessly (as it now seems) I explained to her that feminism was exactly my objective. Needless to say, I sent my manuscript elsewhere."

A particular problem for feminist scholars are fields with connections to cultures where feminism has not gained widespread acceptance. During the time this essay was in preparation, two major German periodicals saw fit to make sexist comments about the personal appearances of two feminist scholars in the U.S.: in a snide attack on campaigns against sexual harassment at American colleges and universities, *Der Spiegel* called one director of a women's studies program a "slightly old-maidish type in her mid-fifties" (*"leicht altjüngferlicher Typ Mitte 50"* [Matussek, 156]), while the *Frankfurter Allgemeine Zeitung* reported on the "overweight lesbian" (*"schwergewichtige ... Lesbierin"* [von Ullmann, 37]) who dared to explore the sexual identity of a major German poet at an American symposium devoted to his work. In October, 1993, in an article on the PC debates in the U.S., *Die Zeit* reported that one of the unspoken premises of political correctness was that masculinity and feminity were not natural, but cultural (*"Daß Männlichkeit und Weiblichkeit nicht Natur, sondern Kultur sind"* [Zimmer, 60]). The sexism and hostility to feminism that pervade Germany give scholars in U.S. German studies permission to continue to reject feminist approaches out of hand. As Ruth-Ellen B. Joeres, a Germanist and editor of *Signs*, wrote in the *Women in German Yearbook*, "My present thinking is that Germanistik and feminism are reasonably unrelatable.... [I]t isn't even a matter of apples and oranges. It is more like elephants and parsley" (248). And that ignorance of feminism, in turn, provides a context where, as one scholar in the field of German studies told us, a reader's report on a feminist essay examining the treatment of gender in the texts of a male author can maintain: "This paper tries to stick [the author's] treatment of the masculine and feminine into the straight-jacket of a feminist approach. The result is that the individual observations are correct but the premise and conclusion are false."

In many fields, however, the astonishing productivity of feminist scholars over the past quarter-century has made such blanket rejections of feminist work more difficult. Antifeminism in those fields is thus likely to take more subtle and differentiated forms, sometimes blurring the line between outright antifeminism and vigorous but legitimate criticism. In a 1989 letter to *PMLA*, twenty-two Shakespeare scholars protested the unfair treatment of feminist Shakespeare criticism in an article by Richard Levin. In their view, his article embodied "precisely those flaws it falsely accuses feminist critics of: arbitrary selectivity, reductive thematizing, misplaced causality, unexamined and untenable assumptions about intentionality, irresponsible slippage from particulars to abstractions" (Adelman, 77). Levin responded that it was only his critics who saw his article as "an attack on 'the approach as a whole'," and "an attack on feminism itself" (Levin, 1989, 79), claiming his objection was merely to one strand of feminist criticism. This *pars pro toto* variant of antifeminism, in which attacks appear to be directed only at particular feminist approaches or topics, makes the assessment of critics' motivation yet the more difficult, since those approaches or topics may likewise be subjects of intense debate within feminism. Radical feminists, for example, regularly complain that their work is reviewed unfairly by non-feminists and feminists alike. In her recent book, *Women as Wombs* (1993), Janice Raymond remarks that "Radical feminist work on the new reproductive technologies has effectively been censored in both the mainstream media and the mainstream feminist press" (xii), and ecofeminists have also noted the unfriendly reception of their work even within feminism (see Gaard). A social scientist with a distinguished publication record reported that her writing on lesbianism found widespread acceptance, while her essays on obesity were regularly rejected. "If it weren't for the ease with which my lesbian research gets published (and invited, and reprinted), I wouldn't know how biased the reviews have been about the weight topic."

Feminists whose work addresses child sexual abuse have often met with extreme hostility from skeptical reviewers and readers. One example is the controversy, summarized by Jane Marcus in the January, 1994, issue of *The Women's Review of Books*, about interpretations of Virginia Woolf as a victim of childhood sexual abuse. (Marcus also recounts the dismissal in England of American critics' views of Woolf because of their feminist slant, and notes in passing the absence of British academics, especially male, at a conference on Woolf held in England.) Finally, a covert antifeminist excuse for not publishing feminist work may also be a readership not sufficiently prepared for the topic. We received a report from one scholar that her essay on antiracist feminism in Europe was rejected by a Left journal on the grounds that its focus was too narrow for the journal's readers, who needed something more introductory (though the feminist author was not asked to write it), while another feminist scholar recalled that an academic press turned down an anthology on minority women in Europe by intimating that the volume would confuse its readers. "My advisors and I agree, ..." wrote the press's editor, "that it is muddying the waters to look at this topic purely from the woman's perspective. There is enough 'otherness' in Turks, Africans, Jews, etc, to warrant an investigation per se, without the difficulty of any additional marginalisation owing to their gender being added." In both those cases, it is hard not to conclude that racism, as well as antifeminism, played some role in the decision to reject.

Since even unreconstructed antifeminists know that the rejection of feminist approaches on ideological grounds is no longer *comme il faut,* many negative assessments of feminist scholarship avoid any mention of feminism, and question other aspects of the work instead. As is the case for all authors of engaged scholarship, feminists need to recognize that their rejection is much more likely to be announced as based on "flaws" (real or presumed) in their work than on their ideological stance. A foreign language department at one of our own institutions, under pressure to hire a feminist, was relieved to discover that the feminist candidate made grammatical errors in her presentation to the department during her on-campus interview. "We like her very much," the search committee announced, "but obviously she's just not qualified." At another institution a department rejected a well-known, well-published, lesbian scholar for an endowed professorship because her disciplinary focus was not a traditional literary period. Furthermore, in our observation, women and minorities are generally subjected to an intensified scrutiny that may well be only unconsciously antifeminist. (As Margaret Atwood remarked some years ago, "I believe there is still a tendency for reviewers of all kinds, including women and even feminists, to be somewhat harder on women writers. I think that feminists sometimes expect more from women: I mean, from men, what can you expect?" [152].) The response to mistakes by women and minorities is a surplus indignation or outrage far beyond what a white man would incur. That outrage is intensified, of course, if the individual concerned has unpopular politics as well. Thus antifeminism can conjoin with a legitimate critique of failings in a piece of scholarship, meaning that mediocre feminist scholarship might be rejected where writing of similar quality with an approach more acceptable to reviewers might be accepted. Though feminists may suspect that antifeminism is also at work, it is very difficult to come to the defense of shoddy scholarship.

And finally, of course, it is quite possible that some sorts of feminist scholarship really just are not good enough for publication, and are rejected on that basis, whatever their authors think. The editor of a feminist yearbook wrote us, for instance, about articles submitted to the yearbook:

> whose authors have let us editors know that the article had already been rejected by other journals, and the authors attributed the rejections to hostility to feminism. The articles I'm thinking of all had significant weaknesses that would have justified turning them down—such as inadequate research, ideas not well developed, claims not well substantiated, etc. But I believe that the editors and reviewers who turned down those articles might well have had an antifeminist bias (and at the very least were ignorant about feminist criticism and theory). Because, as far as I can tell, the articles were turned down without the sort of encouragement that could have helped the authors improve them. Probably this kind of antifeminism wouldn't necessarily be widely recognized as such except by feminists. Rather, the people turning the articles down would not even recognize that there was the potential for an interesting analysis there, if the author would do x, y, or z.

As this comment suggests, some antifeminism is not deliberate, but nonetheless may have the (quite possibly unintended) effect of creating barriers to feminist publication.

"Gatekeeping," the final variant of old-style antifeminism in scholarly publishing, is probably also often not motivated by hostility to feminist approaches, though the consequence of gatekeeping is frequently to keep feminist scholarship out. Dale Spender has defined the gatekeepers as "the people who set the standards, produce the social knowledge, monitor what is admitted to the systems of distribution, and decree the innovations in thought, or knowledge, or values" (1981, 187). When feminist scholarship does not conform to the standards and conventions the gatekeepers have established in their various disciplines, it may be rejected, whatever its other virtues. Several sociological studies have shown how such gatekeeping works to the detriment of women scholars (hence also of feminists). Examining the articles in the ten major journals in the field of sociology, Linda Grant, Kathryn Ward, and Xue Lan Rong discovered that female authors are more likely to use qualitative rather than quantitative approaches, but both male and female authors of articles in these mainstream journals are more likely to use quantitative approaches when they address gender. They conclude that "[q]ualitative papers on gender"—those that, statistically, women/feminists might have been expected to produce—"might have represented double nonconformity, reducing the likelihood of acceptance for publication in the journals we reviewed" (181). In another study based on an examination of those same journals, Ward and Grant again show statistically that "being female and writing about gender increase the propensity to produce joint-authored rather than solo-authored work." Since, of all outlets for sociological scholarship, coauthorship is least common in the mainstream journals they surveyed, they conclude that a clash exists "between women's preferred modes and methods of production of scholarly research and the publication patterns of major journals that may disadvantage women scholars and women and men carrying out research on gender issues" (248).

Many studies have also documented that feminists' inclination to pursue cross-disciplinary work creates barriers to the acceptance of their work (see Taylor and Rupp, 121; Caplan, 196), and Paula Caplan argues that "the kinds of academic endeavors that involve applied, practical, action-oriented, 'relevant', political or community based work" are also devalued (196). As Angela Simeone points out, feminist scholarship may also be unacceptable to the gatekeepers because it is different in style from what they consider appropriate (74). Feminist scholarship is thus more often published in specialized disciplinary journals than in a field's leading national journals, and often its options for publication are restricted to a single feminist journal. Gertrude Steuernagel notes that in the period from 1980 to 1985, only three articles concerned with women and politics appeared in the *American Political Science Review*, while current feminist research in political science was confined to women's studies journals like *Signs* or specialized journals like *Women and Politics* (180). An editor of a major feminist journal reported to us that she probably receives an article a week from feminists not able to publish their work in their own fields. (Marilyn French recalls that an article she submitted to a learned journal was returned to her with the scrawled comment, "Tell her to try one of them 'feminist' journals" [Spender, 1989, 199]). Conversely, scholarship on women that makes it into mainstream journals may be very narrow in scope, as the authors of *Feminist Scholarship: Kindling in the Groves of Academe* (1987) remarked of the field of philosophy: "Philosophy's unwillingness to consider analyses focused on women has been largely limited to issues raised by legislation and general publication controversy" (DuBois, 178). Their examination of major journals from the fields of anthropology, education, history, literature, and philosophy showed that, by 1980, articles on women still amounted to only 7.4 percent of all articles published (164). These statistical studies need to be repeated in the 1990s, but if the reports from our correspondents are representative, in a number of academic disciplines the results will not be overwhelmingly different from what they were more than a decade ago.

The important point is that the consequence of gatekeeping is the inability of feminists to find outlets for their scholarship in the major journals of their field; their work thus cannot receive the attention that would be necessary if feminism is to have a hope of transforming the academic disciplines; and feminist scholars are denied the recognition, often critical to academic success, that publication in the key journals of a field brings with it. Like the other varieties of old-style antifeminism we have outlined here, the effects of gatekeeping on the careers of individual academic feminists can be devastating.

Yet if the new conservative opponents of feminism have their way, the damage they can wreak on feminist scholarship as a whole may be incomparably greater. In our view, the new antifeminist effort to delegitimize many of the premises on which all academic feminist research rests is one of the gravest threats that feminists in the academy now confront. The new variety of antifeminism that emerged in the mid- to late 1980s was related to well-funded and well-coordinated attacks on multicultural curriculum initiatives, ethnic studies, and women's studies programs, and efforts to achieve a multiracial and multiethnic mix of faculty and students on college campuses. These attacks flourished "in the conservative ideological atmosphere of the Reagan and Bush administrations" and were supported by conservative foundations, associations, and think tanks (National Council, 7). They claim an "erosion" of the quality of American universities, and date it from the moment when the Civil Rights and feminist movements demanded changes in the structure of the academy and its curriculum. This movement was prominently led by William Bennett, the Reagan-appointed chairman of the National Endowment for the Humanities and later Secretary of Education. Bennett's 1984 defense of the traditional curriculum, *To Reclaim a Legacy: A Report on the Humanities in Higher Education*, argued that the classic texts of Western civilization were being replaced by works of lesser value in an attempt to produce a more inclusive curriculum, and that, as a result, American students were being deprived of their "legacy."

Although Bennett's report received a great deal of media attention, it did not achieve nearly the popularity of University of Chicago professor Allan Bloom's jeremiad, *The Closing of the American Mind: How Higher Education Has Failed Democracy and Impoverished the Souls of Today's Students*. Bloom's book quickly became a conservative manifesto, and Bloom joined with Bennett as the chief spokespersons of their movement to preserve the "Great Tradition." *The Closing of the American Mind* was on the *New York*

Times best-seller list for thirty-six weeks, led nonfiction best-sellers for more than three months, and sold 800,000 copies in the first year. The reviewer for *The Nation* commented that the book was "likely to become the bible of a whole class of righteous intellectuals" (Pattison, 714) and the *Chronicle of Higher Education* characterized the early reviews as not only favorable but "sometimes ecstatic" (Hirschorn, 3). Having initially published a review by Roger Kimball, who called the book "the most engaging intellectual perfor- mance of the past five years" (Kimball, 1987, 7) the *New York Times* recanted when the book was negatively reviewed in many scholarly journals. Most significantly, however, the book evoked literally hundreds of reviews, inter- views, and responses in both academic and mainstream publications, drawing public attention, in a way that Bennett's report did not, to the issues surrounding academic scholarship and curricula.

Apparently deeply affected by the student revolts of the late 1960s when he was teaching at Cornell, Bloom accuses the American professoriate of timidly bending to student demands and, as a result, bankrupting the curriculum, and failing in its mission to guard the intellectual and moral traditions of Western thought. The academy, he claims, has seen a displace- ment of philosophical verities by a trendy relativism, which paradoxically has not opened the American mind but has closed it, has not advanced the goals of democracy but failed it. A major portion of Bloom's book is devoted to a critique of contemporary students who, without traditional standards and guideposts, have succumbed to such evils as rock music and sex without commitment. Today's college students have learned no history; they have no heroes; the family is in decay; religion is in disrepute; *Time* and *Playboy* have replaced the Bible and McGuffey's reader. The culture in general is at fault, as are the high schools, but every failure returns to the failures of higher educa- tion. Thus the high schools are "filled with teachers who are products of the sixties and reflecting the pallor of university-level humanities" (65). Affirmative action programs have filled the universities with large numbers of "unqualified and unprepared" Black students admitted under separate quotas, and have led to the deterioration of relationships between the races. Special admissions and special treatment have resulted in institutionalized separatism and degrees that are "tainted" (92–96). Black studies programs, established in response to militant students' demands, have failed "because what was serious in them did not interest the students, and the rest was unprofitable hokum" (95). Feminists and the feminist movement figure prominently on Bloom's list of major villains. They are the "latest enemy of the vitality of the classic texts" (65), as well responsible for a deterioration of relationships between the sexes and the dissolution of the family. "The women's movement," Bloom claims, "is not founded on nature" (100). Feminism, by freeing women from their traditional roles in the family, has led to their greater oppression by creating conflicting responsibilities for family and career.

For none of these accusations or claims does Bloom provide the support of statistics, research, or any hard data. Nor does he ever define some of his key terms: nature, reason, soul. His is an impressionistic and singular condemnation of the changes in the American academy since 1970, as well as an aberrantly nostalgic view of American social history. Everything would have been fine, he is insisting, had the radicals, feminists, Marxists, and other marginal groups left the American system alone: class distinctions have been disappearing; women have had all the doors of opportunity opened to them; higher education is available to all who qualify; race prejudices are a thing of the past. We need only return in our universities to the tradition of the Great Books and rid the academy of the trivial and frivolous (that is, women's studies and African-American studies) to restore the America of his rosy memory. The problem with Bloom's analysis, as James Thompson points out in *The Journal of General Education,* "is that our cultural patrimony ... is white, male, privileged: Mary Wollstonecraft's *A Vindication of the Rights of Woman* and *Narrative of the Life of Frederick Douglass, an American Slave,* would never be taught in Bloom's university. Those who have traditionally been excluded from the inheritance, blacks, hispanics, women, will continue to be excluded, in perpetuity" (231).

The enormous media attention focused on Bloom subsequent to the publication of his book allowed him to express in a more public arena his views on feminism, especially feminist academics. For example, in a *Time* magazine interview in October, 1988, Bloom noted that "Radical feminism tends to be present in the universities more than within the general society.... This is an agenda, and it has entered the university as a huge theoretical network. It is overwhelming in its power and its very angry passions" (74). (That academic feminists are "radical" and out of touch with mainstream American women is only a minor theme in Bloom's book, but it was to become a major theme of later antifeminism, as will be discussed below.) In numerous speeches, interviews, and articles Bloom reiterated his charges, depicting all white, male academics—himself included—as beleaguered by feminists controlling hiring committees, curriculum decisions, and academic publications (claims certainly not confirmed by widespread evidence to the contrary). Bloom's attacks on multiculturalism, affirmative action, and feminism not only found a receptive audience in the mainstream media and among conservative associations and foundations, they seem to have emboldened others to pursue a similar course. His book was followed by others, including Charles J. Sykes' *Profscam: Professors and the Demise of Higher Education* (1988) and Roger Kimball's *Tenured Radicals: How Politics Corrupted Our Higher Education* (1990). Kimball's thesis is clearly stated in his Preface; he accuses "proponents of deconstruction, feminist studies, and other politically motivated challenges to the traditional tenets of humanistic study," including Marxism and ethnic studies, of "seeking to subvert ... the tradition of high culture embodied in the classics of Western art and thought" (xi). He specifically indicts "radical feminism" as "the single biggest challenge to the canon as traditionally conceived" (15). Among the feminist scholars he explicitly attacks for their scholarship are Barbara Johnson, E. Ann Kaplan, Elaine Showalter, Eve Kosofsky Sedgwick, Mary Anne Doane, and Nancy Chodorow. His targets also include the subjects of scholarly sessions organized by feminists at the Modern Language Association annual conventions.

Dinesh D'Souza, a native of India who came to the United States as a high school exchange student in 1978 and subsequently graduated from Dartmouth College, has (ironically) widely defended the same white, male, Western culture as Bloom, Sykes, and Kimball, and has attacked the same bogies. His 1991 book, *Illiberal Education*, uses case studies of the University of California at Berkeley, Stanford, Howard, Michigan, Duke, and Harvard to condemn a range of structural and curricular changes in the academy. Calling such words as *diversity, tolerance, multiculturalism*, and *pluralism* "slogans" of the "victim's revolution," D'Souza bewails the coming of a "new generation [of academics], weaned on the assorted ideologies of the late 1960's: the civil rights movement, the protest movement against U.S. involvement in Viet Nam, and the burgeoning causes of feminism and gay rights" (17). Among his feminist targets are Annette Kolodny, Donna Shalala, and Gayatri Spivak. Rigoberta Menchu, whom he calls a "consummate victim," embodies, according to D'Souza, "a projection of Marxist and feminist views onto South American Indian culture" (72). D'Souza singles out Professor Alice Jardine's class on French literary criticism at Harvard as typical of women's studies classes, concluding his description with a patronizing comment about "intellectual fare" that he found "so esoteric and yet so vulgar, so free-wheeling and yet so dogmatic, so full of energy and yet so ultimately futile" (210). D'Souza, like Bloom and Kimball before him, repeatedly accuses feminists, African-American scholars, deconstructionists, and other villains of having a "political" agenda—apparently wishing his readers to believe the myth that the academy before the 1960s was not political!

The antifeminism of such critics as Bloom, D'Souza, and Kimball needs to be seen also in the larger context of the strong conservative movement of the Reagan/Bush era and the efforts of such groups as the National Association of Scholars to organize conservative faculty in opposition to structural and curricular changes in the academy.[2] The NAS, founded in 1987, has attacked affirmative action, multicultural curriculum initiatives, and feminism through a network of campus-based chapters.[3] One of its most notorious "victories" was its organization of resistance to the inclusion of race and gender issues in a basic English course at the University of Texas. The text in question, Paula Rothenberg's *Sexism and Racism* (1988), was one of the first "to present an integrated feminist analysis of racism and sexism" (National Council, 16). The NAS has also organized resistance to campus harassment codes and to affirmative action policies. During the Reagan and Bush administrations, prominent members of the NAS were appointed to seats on such bodies as the National Council on the Humanities, the advisory body to the National Endowment for the Humanities. The NAS journal, *Academic Questions,* from its inception "took aim at feminist scholarship, affirmative action, supposed leftist control of Latin American, African and Asian studies programs, and even student evaluations of professors" (Diamond, 47–48). Members of the NAS have been most prominent in leading the charge against what has been inappropriately tagged "political correctness," or "PC."[4]

One effect of this conservative backlash in the 1980s was the drastic decrease in government funding for projects associated with ethnic studies, women's studies, and curriculum transformation projects, funding that had been crucial to the development of these programs. Of particular concern to feminist scholars is the budget of the National Endowment for the Humanities, the agency that is the central source of federal funding for liberal arts research. In the early 1980s, when the agency was headed by William Bennett, the Reagan administration cut the total NEH budget by $20 million. The NEH does not publish full data on its awards; thus while it is possible to calculate the number of awards to specific types of projects, it is not possible to determine whether certain kinds of proposals were underrepresented in the pool of applicants or were eliminated in the selection process.

Nevertheless, from 1985 to 1987, according to one study, "No more than 10 percent of the awards, in numbers and dollars, support projects on women, gender, or feminism, while most of the awards support traditional academic research on religion, classical and canonical texts, and patriotic subjects, as well as comparable subjects of public programming" (Messer-Davidow, 297). Lynne Cheney, who succeeded Bennett as chair of the NEH, spoke publicly on numerous occasions of her fear that "feminist criticism, Marxism, various forms of poststructuralism, and other approaches" would displace "the traditional concept of Western civilization, which has come under pressure on many fronts, political as well as theoretical" (quoted in Messer-Davidow, 297). By 1991 to 1992, under Cheney, projects related to women, gender, or feminism accounted for only 164 of 1,776 projects funded by all NEH divisions, and amounted to only 2 percent of the funds awarded by the NEH Division of Research (National Council, 22–23, and Appendix D). Turning to private foundations, feminist scholars found that some increase in those funds (principally from the Ford Foundation, which has provided two-thirds of the total private investment in women's studies projects in the last twenty years) was not enough to offset the losses in government funding (National Council, 24–25).

Perhaps due to a new administration in Washington, the "PC wars" abated somewhat after 1992, but conservatives now began a new assault that focused more centrally on feminism alone. In addition to open and unabashed antifeminist attacks from the Right which have distorted and trivialized feminist scholarship (and pedagogy, from which scholarship cannot be separated), new challenges also arose from the unlikely ranks of women who claim to be feminists themselves. Delighting in what they took to be feminist intramural squabbles, the popular press has widely publicized these attacks. A case in point is the great amount of media hype that accompanied Katie Roiphe's book *The Morning After: Sex, Fear and Feminism on Campus* (1993). Roiphe, a graduate of Harvard and a doctoral student in English at Princeton, ridiculed campus sex education programs, and, using anecdotal evidence, accused feminists of falsifying statistics to frighten women about a nonexistent plague of sexual crimes. She also commits the error of which white U.S. feminists in the seventies were often accused, extrapolating the experience of white, privileged women to all women. Furthermore, as bell hooks points out, by "cleverly failing to mention the work of feminist thinkers who have critiqued the very excesses she names (Judith Butler, Audre Lorde, Kimberlé Crenshaw, Diana Fuss, to name only a few), Roiphe makes it appear that her ideas offer a new and fresh articulation to feminist 'dogmatism'. In fact, her book draws heavily on critiques that have been continually voiced, respectfully, within feminist circles" (43). That such a poorly documented, poorly researched,[5] impressionistic attack on feminists and feminism would be published by a mainstream publishing house (Little, Brown) is as alarming as the attention the media gave to it and to Roiphe herself.

Dismayingly, even a popular Left journal, *Mother Jones*, was prepared to jump aboard the antifeminist bandwagon. Its September/October, 1993, issue included an "investigation" of women's studies programs written by Karen Lehrman, another self-proclaimed, young (antifeminist) feminist. Lehrman's article "ignited heated exchanges in the women's studies community, the press, and on radio talk shows across the country" ("Backtalk," 4). It drew attention from the *Washington Post*, the *Boston Globe*, and the *San Francisco Examiner*, as well as other newspapers. Lehrman acknowledges that the women's studies classes she visited were giving women students a voice that she herself did not have as a college student, but "the problem is," her article claims, "what they're often talking about." She ridicules women's studies programs for making "mere pit stops at the academic," for "unintelligible poststructuralist jargon" and "consciousness-raising psychobabble," (46) and for encouraging the idea of personal experience as "the only real source of truth" (48). Lehrman's essay, based on visits to only four programs (of a total of almost six hundred in 1993), expresses her concern about the inability of women's studies students to think critically and "the degree to which politics has infested women's studies scholarship" (51). Echoing the PC debates, she claims, "'Diversity' is the mantra of both students and professors, but it doesn't apply to political opinions" (47), and she concludes that "the field's narrow politics have constricted the audience for nonideological feminism [the topic of the book she was writing!] instead of widening it" (68). In suggesting that women's studies classes are too political, Lehrman seems to wish to perpetuate the illusion that other classes and other disciplines are not—an odd position for a Left journal to assume. (As Susan Faludi put it in a letter responding to Lehrman's report, "Feminism in the academy is about more than women getting the right to absorb the male-defined curriculum; it's about challenging the foundations of that curriculum" [4].) Lehrman adds to her concerns the influence of poststructuralism and multiculturalism (shades of D'Souza) on women's studies. In a reductive presentation of poststructuralist theory, she writes: "Perhaps the most troubling influence on women's studies in the past decade has been the collection of theories known as poststructuralism, which essentially implies that all texts are arbitrary, all knowledge is biased, all standards are arbitrary, all morality is subjective." Of discussions of multiculturalism within women's studies, she asserts: "Terms like sexism, racism, and homophobia have been bloated beyond all recognition" (66). As Lehrman portrays them, women's studies programs are academically lax, intolerant, dogmatic, and offensively touchy-feely. Though the directors of the women's studies programs Lehrman visited collectively wrote a letter protesting her distortions, *Mother Jones* never printed it.

As bell hooks noted, and as Lehrman refuses to acknowledge, feminist scholarship is not univocal: respectful disagreement is invigorating to any discipline; most conscientious feminist scholars welcome dialogue, and over the past quarter-century, feminist scholarship has often been riven by contentious debate. Perhaps because the concerns of feminist scholars are not merely academic, debates within the ranks of feminists, more than disagreements in other disciplines, seem to draw attention-getting headlines, such as "Feminist Scholars Ask Whether Their Sparring Marks Healthy Debate or a Splintering 'Catfight'" (*The Chronicle of Higher Education*) and "Feminism's Old Guard Under Fire" (the *Boston Globe*). Such media interest in feminist battles offers a welcome opportunity to those antifeminist scholars who seem more interested in grabbing public attention than in engaging in scholarly dialogue.

The most well known of these is Camille Paglia, a Yale Ph.D. who teaches at the College of the Arts in Philadelphia. Paglia's relatively recent notoriety (after twenty years of academic obscurity) has come in part as a result of her bold and attention-getting "bashing" of feminists and feminist scholarship. Her first published book, *Sexual Personae: Art and Decadence from Nefertiti to Emily Dickinson* (1990), from its very first page expresses her disagreement with what she identifies as feminist positions on sex, beauty, and the relationships between men and women. For example, she writes: "Feminists grossly oversimplify the problem of sex when they reduce it to a matter of social convention" (1); and "Feminists, seeking to drive power relations out of sex, have set themselves against nature" (2); and again, "Feminism has exceeded its proper mission of seeking political equality for women"(3). She has claimed that, if women had been in charge of civilization, we would still be living in grass huts. When her book received some negative reviews from avowed feminist scholars, Paglia fought back in interviews and speeches, resorting to name-calling rather than rationality. In an op-ed piece in the

New York Times, she accused American feminists of being stuck in a "whining" mode, and presented pop star Madonna as an ideal feminist. *The Chronicle of Higher Education,* reporting on a Paglia speech at Harvard, called her "an academic guerrilla, a firestorm of energy, and above all, a performer," and noted that, during her two hours on stage, she "trashed" prominent scholars (naming names), academic conferences, tenure, and French philosophers and literary theorists. "Charlatans, she calls them. Toadies. Conference groupies. Pseudo-feminists. Hustlers. Sleazebags. Ass kissers" (Mooney, A14). That Paglia's tendentious personality and ready wit quickly made her a media personality is documented by Paglia herself in her unabashedly self-promoting second book, a collection of her essays entitled *Sex, Art, and American Culture* (1992). This uneven collection contains brief essays on popular culture figures, pornography, date rape, the Hill-Thomas hearings, and rock music, as well as several book reviews. The longest piece is an essay, written for *Arion,* entitled "Junk Bonds and Corporate Raiders: Academe in the Hour of the Wolf." Beginning as a review of two recent books, the essay metamorphoses into a diatribe against a long list of persons and institutions, including contemporary theory, feminism, academic conferences, and the Modern Language Association. Roger Kimball approvingly called this essay "not a book review ... [but] a full blown assault on the intellectual and moral corruption of contemporary academia" (1992, A14). By far the oddest inclusion in this collection is a "media history" of what the *New York Times* book reviewer called "Ms. Paglia's quarter hour celebrity." What is significant about Paglia's antifeminism is that she gains attention for it while at the same time avoiding the kind of intellectual exchange that might bring feminist scholarship to new insights.

Entering through the door opened by Paglia are several other self-identified academic feminists who are gaining public attention by publishing antifeminist books. The early summer of 1994, for example, saw the publication of a book with the provocative title *Who Stole Feminism? How Women Have Betrayed Women.* The author, Clark University (Massachusetts) associate professor of philosophy Christina Hoff Sommers, has impressive right-wing credentials: the "gracious and generous support" (8) of three conservative corporate foundations—the Lynde and Harry Bradley Foundation, the Carthage Foundation, and the John M. Olin Foundation—funded her two-year research leave to write her book; it was published by Simon & Schuster, Bloom's publisher; and Sommers and her husband are members of the NAS's Boston chapter (which, she claims, "has no distinctive political coloration" [128]). It is a credit to the successes of the American women's movement that Sommers cannot attack feminism head-on; indeed, she claims to be a feminist herself (though one who was prepared to declare in the February, 1994, *Esquire* that "there are a lot of homely women in women's studies" [Friend, 55]), and she ends her book with the cheery assertion that "feminism itself—the pure and wholesome article first displayed at Seneca Falls in 1848—is as American as apple pie, and it will stay" (128). Instead, she tries to divide feminists into two camps: gender feminists, who are angry, strident, and intellectually bankrupt; and equity feminists (such as herself), who care about equality for women, but who refuse to look at the world through gender-colored lenses. Gender feminists, according to Sommers, have taken over the universities, transforming the curriculum, bending administrations to their will, and censoring dissent through intimidation. (She accuses the MLA Committee on the Status of Women in the Profession of making a "preemptive strike" [116] against antifeminist backlash with its announcement upon which this book is based.) *Her* book, she maintains, is written as an effort to save feminism from the gender feminists—aggrieved, resentful, and indifferent to truth—who have "stolen 'feminism' from a mainstream that had never acknowledged their leadership." "But," she admits, "that is not likely to happen without a fight" (18).

It is deceptively easy to discredit Sommers' book. Portraying herself as a muckraker, she employs hyperbole and distortion to depict what she regards as the excesses and failings of feminist scholarship. As Leora Tanenbaum observes, "Instead of critique, she offers caricature, leveling personal attacks against feminist personalities she despises and accusing them of being liars" (32). She is able to identify some unfortunate flaws in some feminist claims (as the *National Review* disclosed with some glee, reprinting the first chapter of her book as the lead article of its June 27, 1994, issue, which proclaimed on its cover: "A Feminist Uses Statistics like a Fish Uses a Bicycle: Why Feminism's Vital Statistics Are Always Wrong"), and then intimates that duplicitous feminist scholars deliberately distort facts to mislead their gullible readers. Her research is largely anecdotal, and her reasoning is, as Nina Auerbach points out in her review of *Who Stole Feminism?* in the *New York Times*, "vitiated by its logical flaws" (13), beginning with the simplistic notion that all feminists can be clearly divided into two "camps." Ann Bryant, executive director of the American Association of University Women, was probably correct to quip that Sommers "wants to be the Rush Limbaugh of academia" (Carton, 74). As Faye Crosby, a Smith College psychology professor put it, Sommers no doubt has her own agenda—which is, "to sell books" (Gordon, E–4).[6]

Yet feminists would err if they did not take the threat that Sommers' book represents seriously. Sommers' book is a powerful volley in a discursive battle over the definition of what counts as feminism. Like Paglia, Sommers brings a right-wing assault on feminist scholarship into the mainstream debate; like Paglia, she is able to reduce complex issues to catchy sound bites palatable to a popular media that is antagonistic to critical scholarship in general and feminist scholarship in particular. Her book launches a major assault on feminist analyses and feminist visions in two respects. First, Sommers claims all that *most* women want is "a fair field and no favors" (78). Though she is forced to acknowledge that women have not always received a fair shake, she refuses to concede that there may ever have been structural or systemic causes for discrimination against women. Since she ridicules feminists' assertion "that the oppression of women, sustained from generation to generation, is a structural feature of our society" (16), she herself is left without an explanation for why women have not always been treated fairly—the most serious conceptual flaw in her book. Instead (like some of her political bedfellows—Paglia, Roiphe, the recent Naomi Wolf), she gives the analytical term "oppression," a central category of feminisms of most every hue, a clever rhetorical spin, portraying feminists' concern with the power men exercise over them as the whiney, self-centered obsession of privileged women with their own imaginary victimization—a defamation of feminist efforts to identify the nature and scope of male dominance that has fared very well indeed in the popular press. And, secondly, Sommers' book may also be read as an effort to construct a definition of feminism that portrays women as wanting no more than equity in the world as it is presently arranged. One of the great accomplishments of American feminism has been its ability to sustain a tension between seeking equality for women in the present social order, and struggling for the transformation of the entire society. ("The root question," as Deirdre English put it in a review of Sommers' book, "is whether women want equality with men as they are, in the world men have shaped, or if women seek change in that world as well as in ... male/female relations" (English, 36). That latter vision is in part a legacy bequeathed to American feminism by the sixties, which Sommers acknowledges as the origin of the kind of feminism her book decries:

> The idea that women are in a gender war originated in the midsixties, when the antiwar and antigovernment mood revivified and redirected the women's

movement away from its Enlightenment liberal philosophy to a more radical, antiestablishment philosophy. The decisive battles of the sexual revolution had been won, and students here and on the Continent were reading Herbert Marcuse, Karl Marx, Franz [*sic*] Fanon, and Jean-Paul Sartre and learning how to critique their culture and institutions in heady new ways. They began to see the university, the military, and the government as merely different parts of a defective status quo. (23)

Sommers' equity feminism repudiates feminism's vision of a larger social transformation; her feminism is content, once women get what men have, to reconcile itself with the world as it is. However one judges the legitimacy of Sommers' claim to being a feminist herself, that is the contribution her book makes to a grander conservative agenda.

In Camille Paglia's opinion, Sommers' book represents "a 'turning point' in the effort of dissident feminists to make themselves heard" (Carton, 74). In this case, Paglia may be right. As *The Chronicle of Higher Education* noted, "the tempest already swirling around her newly published book has exceeded all expectations" ("Hot Type"). In her willingness to attack feminism, Sommers has plenty of distinguished company, including the women she cites as her positive heroes, some of them apostate feminists themselves: Cynthia Ozick, Cynthia Wolff, Mary Lefkowitz, Iris Murdoch, Doris Lessing, Sylvia Hewlett, Elizabeth Fox-Genovese, Jean Bethke Elshtain, Rita Simon, Susan Haack, and Ruth Barcan Marcus (132). The *National Journal* observes that: "When it comes to women's groups, the fastest growth is among conservative and moderate organizations that reject 'feminist' orthodoxy" (Carney, 728), including the Women's Freedom Network (whose members include Elshtain, Simon, and Fox-Genovese), the Independent Women's Forum, the Network for Empowering Women, and others. *Who Stole Feminism?* may well be the opening shot in a much larger campaign against feminism, directed this time by antifeminist women, as the *Boston Globe* reports:

Sommers' book will soon be followed by *The New Victorians: Why Young Women are Abandoning the Women's Movement* (Warner Books) by Portland author Rene Denfeld; *Gender Wars* (Free Press) by Cathy Young, a free-lance columnist and vice chairwoman of the Women's Freedom Network; *Professing Feminism: Cautionary Tales from the Strange World of Women's Studies* (Basic Books) by Daphne Patai of the University of Massachusetts at Amherst and Norette Koertge of Indiana University; and an untitled book on new directions for feminism by journalist Karen Lehrman." (Flint, 14)

Clearly, antifeminism is a hot commodity in the media world of the early 1990s, and feminists will need to muster all their resources to combat it.

189

So what remedies might exist for these various sorts of antifeminisms? Feminist academics whose scholarly credentials are challenged will be able to combat antifeminism only if they recognize it for what it is: an attack founded in an unwillingness or inability to recognize the legitimacy of scholarly analysis undertaken from a feminist perspective. What is crucial to resisting antifeminism is not to take it personally: as Marcia Liebman declares, "The most important thing for you to know is this: They will try to persuade you that you are being denied tenure (or promotion, or reappointment) because of your deficiencies. The argument most certain to take you in is the one that speaks to your self-doubt, so they will tell you that your publications are mediocre, your teaching weak. Don't believe it" (3). The worst of all possible responses, in terms of combatting antifeminism (though sometimes it may be a rational tactical response to insure academic survival) is what Nadya Aisenberg and Mona Harrington have called "the common practice of self-censorship" (69), the decision to modify feminist content or form to gain acceptance and pacify opponents. Whatever tactics they choose, it is likely that individuals will rarely succeed in winning the battle against antifeminist attacks on their work (which does not mean that they should not raise a protest whenever antifeminist attacks occur). Rather, the campaign against antifeminism directed at feminist scholarship needs to be a collective effort on the part of many academic feminists to challenge unfair standards and criteria applied to feminist work, and to demand that top-quality feminist scholarship receive the recognition it deserves.

Against the hard-core antifeminists there may be little recourse. The otherwise optimistic editor of the feminist series of an academic press conceded that her books were not reviewed by *The New York Review of Books*, but declared that they were "old stuffy guys," an "old group of fifties intellectuals, when they die off things might change." Feminist scholars who suspect antifeminism should request readers' reviews of their own work and, to the degree that they can do so without jeopardizing their academic futures, blow the whistle on antifeminism when it occurs. As Joanna Russ, in *How to Suppress Women's Writing* and Dale Spender, in *The Writing or the Sex?* have amply documented, the antifeminist "techniques of containment, belittlement, and sheer denial" (Russ, 17) are ingenious and legion. But there is always safety in numbers, and antifeminists will be far more eager to placate a group of angry feminists, some with academic credentials equal to their own, than a single, aggrieved, junior woman. Feminist protesters should recognize that very frequently they may lose the individual battle, but the fact that they have engaged with the enemy will make him think twice about expending his antifeminist ammunition the next time. Feminist scholars erode antifeminism by challenging it, and they thereby make the path to publication smoother for the feminists who come after them. We also strongly encourage cross-generational feminist alliances. Senior feminists who have already achieved academic security and recognition have more freedom of movement than juniors, and they can take risks that open doors for junior colleagues. We thus urge powerful women to object to antifeminist practices in their own fields. We also hope that they will sometimes venture into areas of scholarship or experiment with scholarly forms that might not be regarded as legitimate by junior feminists as yet without academic status. To preempt challenges to the quality of their work, junior scholars should seek out senior feminist mentors to read their work before they submit it for publication, and in general, feminists are well-advised to read and criticize each other's work to ensure that it meets high feminist standards before it reaches potentially hostile eyes. We also urge the women's caucuses of the disciplines to begin discussion of the unintended barriers to feminist publication in their fields, to explore whether certain types of work still cannot find outlets for publication, and what mechanisms might be utilized to insure equitable publishing opportunities for all scholars in their areas. Finally, we urge feminist scholars in all disciplines to continue their scholarly investigations in their fields, despite the barrage of antifeminist accusations. Well-organized, well-funded and well-publicized attacks, such as those by D'Souza, Paglia, Sommers, et al., can only be countered by well-researched, rational, and dispassionate scholarship, as well as the determined insistence that feminism is neither intractable nor monolithic.

We would like to end our discussion of antifeminism directed against feminist scholarship with an account of our own experience with a complex kind of antifeminism as we worked on this book together with other past and present members of the Modern Language Association Committee on the Status of Women in the Profession. Reluctantly, we have been forced to the conclusion that feminist self-censorship may have been at work when, in the fall of 1992, the Modern Language Association declined to publish our study of antifeminism in the academy, rejecting our prospectus because of what they described as concerns about its quality and focus. Perhaps the MLA's reservations were genuine, but of the ten presses we queried, nine were eager to publish the book. Only the MLA and one other (which said it did not fit their list) declined to review the manuscript. As we reconstruct the history that led to the rejection of our project by the MLA, we think there are lessons to be learned from our experience that may be valuable for other feminist scholars, in what is obviously a time of burgeoning opposition to feminism.

The MLA has had a distinguished record of commitment to equity for academic women and to feminist scholarship. It has been responsible for publishing several pathbreaking manuals on sex discrimination, including *Academic Women, Sex Discrimination and the Law* (1971), *"Unladylike and Unprofessional": Academic Women and Academic Unions* (1975), *Rocking the Boat: Academic Women and Academic Processes* (1981), and *Sexual and Gender Harassment in the Academy: A Guide for Faculty, Students, and Administrators* (1981). Over the years, the MLA has attempted to keep pace with a changing, more diverse membership, and its annual meetings include numerous panels on feminist and multiethnic themes. A number of highly regarded feminist scholars have served as MLA president, and the MLA's present executive director, Phyllis Franklin, is a former member of the MLA Commission on the Status of Women and coeditor of *Sexual and Gender Harassment in the Academy*. In good part because of its demonstrated commitment to feminism and multiculturalism, the MLA came under strong attack from the Right, beginning in the late eighties. In response to the assaults on its members that accompanied the PC debates, the MLA Executive Council broke its usual silence on the manifold approaches its members use in their scholarship and teaching to issue a "Statement on the Curriculum Debate" in May, 1991. "In view of [its almost 30,000 members'] great diversity," the Executive Council protested, "it is unreasonable to suggest that they are imposing a monolithic ideology on the college curriculum.... What is most disturbing in the attacks against the MLA and individual members is the persistent resort to misrepresentation and false labeling. While loudly invoking rational debate, open discussion, and responsible scholarship, these attacks distort evidence and reduce complex issues to slogans and name-calling" (National Council, 49).

The conservative onslaught intensified after the MLA, together with four other major scholarly associations, opposed the nomination of NAS vice president Carol Iannone to the National Council for the Humanities, the advisory committee for the NEH, on the basis of her weak scholarly credentials. Though the MLA was ultimately victorious in July, 1991, when Iannone's confirmation failed by one vote in the Senate Labor and Human Resources Committee, the organization, *Linguafranca* reported, "remains somewhat shell-shocked from a fight it didn't expect, using tactics with which it had little experience. Says Phyllis Franklin, the MLA's executive director, 'We were quite naive'" (Novak, 16–17). Though the battle between the MLA and Iannone supporters initially remained confined to academic circles (including an attack on Franklin's own academic credentials in *The Chronicle of Higher Education*), George Will used his *Newsweek* column to take the issue to the general public, claiming that the MLA was crawling with academic Marxists, feminist literary critics, and other philistines who were "shaping tomorrow's elite" in the academy. According to *Linguafranca*, Lynne Cheney, conservative chairperson of the NEH, orchestrated a skillful campaign that convinced the press that the Iannone nomination battle was an extension of the PC campaign: at least thirty-two editorials and op-ed columns appeared in various newspapers, including a declaration in the *New York Post* that the "intellectual life of this country" was at stake (Novak, 20–21). After Iannone's nomination failed, *Time* magazine subtitled its article on the controversy: "Carol Iannone loses a round to political correctness."

At the height of this controversy in the summer of 1991, we members of the MLA Committee on the Status of Women in the Profession quite innocently published an announcement of our antifeminism project in the *MLA Newsletter*. Our announcement provided the conservatives with more ammunition for their assault on the MLA's "political correctness": now they could aim their sights at feminism. In one letter written to the MLA, its author claimed that there was no better demonstration of the academic totalitarianism that Carol Iannone had fearlessly combatted than in the report of the Committee on the Status of Women in the Profession. Another letter writer maintained that: "The MLA, in uncritically aligning itself with CSWP's agenda of blacklisting criticism of feminists, however laudable in intention, contributes its considerable share toward the creation of an intellectual police state." "How ironic," the writer continued, "that in these post-1984 days, in the land proud to stand for free speech, it is not Big Brother but very possibly Big Sister whom we must be wary of in institutions of higher learning" (Breuer). Sent anonymously to the Committee on the Status of Women was a photocopy of a picture of members (four women and a man) of the Subcommittee on Meetings that had appeared in the same newsletter as the CSWP's announcement of its antifeminism project. The anonymous submitter had typed under the picture: "Poor man! A typical Phyllis Franklin committee"—a prime example of the kind of antifeminist harassment our committee had set out to investigate! A good year later, the battle still raged, and Ward Parks, writing in the "Forum" section of *PMLA*, could maintain that those who protested Richard Levin's criticism of feminist Shakespeare scholarship had actually attacked him: "For having had the gumption to speak the unspeakable—that is, for criticizing academic feminism and Marxism." "Such condemnation," Parks claimed, "has, unfortunately, fallen to the lot of an ever-lengthening list of academics foolhardy enough to stray beyond the pale of currently approved political orthodoxy." "Although," he concluded, "recent critical theory has harped unceasingly on themes of 'marginalization' and 'exclusion', no one is more exclusive or intolerant than those who now dominate the Modern Language Association" (Parks).

It was in this context that our book prospectus came before the Publications Committee of the MLA. Criticized by conservatives within and outside the organization, the MLA confronted institutional boundaries that limited its ability to address politically sensitive issues like our antifeminism project. However legitimate the Publications Committee's concerns about our proposal's quality, circumstantial evidence also strongly suggests that, already besieged by the Right, the MLA rejected our book because, in the prevailing political climate, the topic was too controversial. It appears, that is to say, that the MLA retreated from its previously forceful defense of feminist scholarship in order to protect the organization. Noted feminist scholar Judith Fetterly came to similar conclusions about the MLA's response to conservatives in a letter published in the Spring, 1994, *MLA Newsletter*. Fetterly believed she discerned a disturbing attempt on the part of MLA leaders to distance themselves from feminism in statements made in the Fall, 1993, *Newsletter*. "Taken together," Fetterly observed, these "rhetorical moments lead me to wonder whether our association does not suffer from an alternative mode of political correctness that discourages addressing positively or even addressing at all those issues associated in the public mind with political correctness." She too wonders about the pressures that have produced such positions: "Might the cause be some alternative form of political correctness that requires that a feminist president of the MLA disavow in public the very politics that have brought her to power" (30). Perhaps in response to that charge, the "President's Column" of the Winter, 1994, *Newsletter* reaffirmed the MLA's commitment to addressing a range of social issues, placing this reaffirmation, however, in the context of conservative objections to the MLA's "politicization" (Spacks, 3). As feminists, we welcome this renewed statement of the MLA's social responsibility and its commitment to address issues that, we agree, are of grave and often immediate concern to scholars in languages and literatures. More generally, we urge organizations like the MLA to stand their ground, and we urge feminists and their friends to support them as they do so. Nothing can be gained by attempting to conciliate conservative groups that will never be satisfied by the concessions we make to them. Feminist scholars and others must bring strong counterpressure to bear in order to preserve the access to American institutions they have so laboriously won, and we urge them to mobilize for that struggle.

Notes

1. Acknowledgments prefacing the books by Bloom, D'Souza, and Kimball all mention the John M. Olin Foundation; D'Souza was also supported by the American Enterprise Institute, and Kimball, by the Institute for Educational Affairs. Bloom's 1990 book, *Confronting the Constitution*, was published by the AEI. Christina Hoff Sommers, author of *Who Stole Feminism?* discussed below, was also supported by the Olin Foundation and two other conservative foundations, the Lynde and Harry Bradley Foundation, and the Carthage Foundation. For a discussion of corporate funding of right-wing foundations and right-wing campus groups, see *Guide to Uncovering the Right on Campus*, eds. Rich Cowan and Dalya Massachi.

2. The genealogy of the NAS can be traced to the Institute for Educational Affairs, founded in 1978, which has since changed its name to the Madison Center for Educational Affairs. According to Sara Diamond, writing in *Z* magazine, "IEA-Madison Center is bankrolled by corporate foundations, including Coors, Mobil, Smith-Richardson, Earhart, and Scaife and Olin" (Diamond, 46). These are the foundations that have supported the research and writing of Bloom, D'Souza, Kimball, and Christina Hoff Sommers. Both William Bennett and Dinesh D'Souza are associated with the Madison Center and the American Enterprise Institute.

3. For a basic history of the NAS, see Sara Diamond, "Readin', Writin', and Repressin'." See also Ellen Messer-Davidow, "Manufacturing the Attack on Liberalized Higher Education," *Social Text* 36 (Fall 1993): 40–80; and Messer-Davidow, "Who (Ac)Counts and How," *The Journal of the Midwest Modern Language Association* 27, 1 (Spring 1994): 26–41.

4. This debate and its history are outlined in a report prepared by The National Council for Research on Women, *To Reclaim a Legacy of Diversity: Analyzing the "Political Correctness" Debates in Higher Education* (1993); see also several anthologies on the "political correctness" debates: Patricia Aufderheide, ed., *Beyond PC: Toward a Politics of Understanding* (1992); Paul Berman, ed., *Debating PC: The Controversy Over Political Correctness on College Campuses. The Politics of Liberal Education*, eds. Darryl J. Gless and Barbara Hernstein Smith, is a collection designed as a liberal response to attacks on curricular reform; *Are You Politically Correct? Debating America's Cultural Standards*

(1993), eds. Francis J. Beckwith and Michael E. Bauman, is more conservative than balanced.

5. For a critique of Roiphe, see, in addition to bell hooks's essay, Katha Pollitt's review in the *New Yorker* (October 4, 1993): 220–224, or "Whose Hype?" by Susan Faludi, *Newsweek* (October 25, 1993):61.

6. Additional critiques of *Who Stole Feminism?* may be found in *Democratic Culture* 3, 2 (Fall 1994), the newsletter of Teachers for a Democratic Culture.

Works Cited and Consulted

"A Most Uncommon Scold." Interview with Allan Bloom. *Time* (October 17, 1988): 74–76.

Adelman, Janice, et al. Letter. *PMLA* 104 (1989): 77–78.

Aisenberg, Nadya and Mona Harrington. *Women of Academe: Outsiders in the Sacred Grove.* Amherst: University of Massachusetts Press, 1988.

Atwood, Margaret. "Sexual Bias in Reviewing." In *The Feminine: Women and Words/Les Femmes et les Mots*, ed. Ann Dybikowski et al. Alberta, Canada: Longspoon, 1985. 151–152.

Auerbach, Nina. "Sisterhood is Fractious." *The New York Times Book Review* (June 12, 1994): 13.

"Backtalk." *Mother Jones* (November/December 1993): 4.

Bloom, Allan. *The Closing of the American Mind: How Higher Education Has Failed Democracy and Impoverished the Souls of Today's Students.* New York: Simon and Schuster, 1987.

Breuer, Hans-Peter. Letter. *MLA Newsletter* (Fall 1991): 18.

Caplan, Paula J. *Lifting a Ton of Feathers: A Woman's Guide for Surviving in the Academic World.* Toronto: University of Toronto Press, 1993.

Carney, Eliza Newlin. "A New Breed of Feminist." *National Journal* (March 26,1994): 728–729.

Carton, Barbara. "A Rebel in the Sisterhood: Author Christina Sommers Wants to Rescue Feminism from Its 'Hijackers.'" *Boston Globe* (June 16, 1994): 69, 74.

Cowan, Rich and Dalya Massachi, eds. *Guide to Uncovering the Right on Campus.* Cambridge, MA: University Conversion Project, 1994.

DeSole, Gloria and Lenore Hoffman. *Rocking the Boat: Academic Women and Academic Processes.* New York: Modern Language Assocation of America, 1981.

Diamond, Sara. "Readin', Writin' and Repressin'." *Z* (February 1991): 45–48.

DuBois, Ellen Carol, Gail Pardise Kelly, Elizabeth Lapovsky Kennedy, Carolyn W. Korsmeyer, and Lillian S. Robinson. *Feminist Scholarship: Kindling in the Groves of Academe.* Urbana: University of Illinois Press, 1985.

D'Souza, Dinesh. *Illiberal Education: The Politics of Race and Sex on Campus.* New York: Free Press, 1991.

English, Deirdre. "A Report from the Feminist Fronts." *Washington Post National Weekly Edition* (July 25–31, 1994): 35–36.

Faludi, Susan. Letter. *Mother Jones* (November/December 1993): 4.

Fetterly, Judith. Letter. *MLA Newsletter* (Spring 1994): 30.

Flint, Anthony. "New Breed of Feminist Challenges Old Guard." *Boston Globe* (May 29, 1994): 1, 14.

Franklin, Phyllis, et. al. *Sexual and Gender Harassment in the Academy: A Guide for Faculty, Students and Administrators.* New York: Modern Language Association of America, 1981.

Friend, Tad. "Yes." *Esquire* (February 1994): 48–56.

Gaard, Greta. "Misunderstanding Ecofeminism." *Z Papers 1994* 3, 1: 20–24.

Gordon, Ronni. "Criticizing Feminism: Radicals Lose Sight of Traditional Goals." *Sunday Republican* [Springfield, MA] (July 3, 1994): E1, E4.

Grant, Linda and Kathryn Ward. "Coauthorship, Gender, and Publication among Sociologists." In *Beyond Methodology: Feminist Scholarship as Lived Research*, eds. Mary Margaret Fonow and Judith A. Cook. Bloomington: Indiana University Press, 1991. 248–264.

Grant, Linda, Kathryn Ward, and Xue Lan Rong. "Is There an Association Between Gender and Methods in Sociological Research?" *American Sociological Review* 52 (1987): 856–862.

Hirschorn, Michael W. "A Professor Decries 'Closing of the American Mind.'" *The Chronicle of Higher Education* (May 6, 1987): A3.

hooks, bell. "Dissident Heat: Assessing Naomi Wolf's *Fire with Fire.*" *Z* (March 1994): 26–29.

"Hot Type." *The Chronicle of Higher Education* (June 22, 1994): A10.

Joeres, Ruth-Ellen B. "'Language is Also a Place of Struggle': The Language of Feminism and the Language of American Germanistik." In *Women in German Yearbook* 8, eds. Jeanette Clausen and Sara Friedrichsmeyer. Lincoln: University of Nebraska Press, 1993. 247–257.

Kimball, Roger. Review of *The Closing of the American Mind. The New York Times Book Review* (April 5, 1987): 7.

———. *Tenured Radicals: How Politics Has Corrupted Our Higher Education.* New York: Harper and Row, 1990.

———. "Dragon Lady of Academe." *Wall Street Journal* (September 17, 1992): A14.

Lehrman, Karen. "Off Course." *Mother Jones* (September/October 1993): 45–51, 65–68.

Levin, Richard. "Feminist Thematics and Shakespearean Tragedy." *PMLA* 103 (1988): 125–138.

———. "Reply." *PMLA* 104 (1989): 78–79.

Liebman, Marcia "The Most Important Thing for You to Know." *Rocking the Boat: Academic Women and Academic Processes*, ed. Gloria DeSole and Leonore Hoffmann. New York: The Modern Language Association of America, 1981. 3–7.

Marcus, Jane. "A Tale of Two Cultures." *The Women's Review of Books* (January 1994): 11–13.

Matussek, Matthias. "Hexenjagd auf dem Campus." *Der Spiegel* 20 (1994): 152–165.

Messer-Davidow, Ellen. "Who (Ac)Counts and How." *Journal of the Midwest Modern Language Association* (Spring 1994): 26–41.

Miller, Nancy K. *Getting Personal: Feminist Occasions and Other Autobiographical Acts.* New York: Routledge, 1991.

Mooney, Carolyn J. "Camille Paglia, Academic Guerrilla, Relishes Her Role as Feminist Scourge." *The Chronicle of Higher Education* (April 1, 1992): A14–16.

National Council for Research on Women. *To Reclaim a Legacy of Diversity: Analyzing the "Political Correctness" Debates in Higher Education.* New York: National Council for Research on Women, 1993.

Novak, Viveca. "The Accused." *Linguafranca* 2, 1 (October, 1991): 1, 16–21.

Paglia, Camille. *Sexual Personae: Art and Decadence from Nefertiti to Emily Dickinson.* New Haven, CT: Yale University Press, 1990; New York: Vintage, 1991.

———. *Sex, Art, and American Culture.* New York: Vintage/Random House, 1992.

Parks, Ward. Letter. *PMLA* 107 (1992): 353.

Pattison, Robert. Review of *The Closing of the American Mind. The Nation* (May 30, 1987): 710–716.

Raymond, Janice G. *Women as Wombs: Reproductive Technologies and the Battle over Women's Freedom.* San Francisco: Harper, 1994.

Reuben, Elaine and Lenore Hoffman. *Unladylike and Unprofessional: Academic Women and Academic Unions.* New York: MLA Commission on the Status of Women, 1975.

Russ, Joanna. *How to Suppress Women's Writing.* Austin: University of Texas Press, 1983.

Simeone, Angela. *Academic Women Working Towards Equality.* South Hadley, MA: Bergin & Garvey, 1987.

Sommers, Christina Hoff. *Who Stole Feminism? How Women Have Betrayed Women.* New York: Simon and Schuster, 1994.

———. "Figuring Out Feminism: The New Mythology." *National Review* (June 27, 1994): 30–34.

Spacks, Patricia Meyer. "President's Column: Enlargements of Interest." *MLA Newsletter* (Winter 1994): 3.

Spender, Dale. "The Gatekeepers: A Feminist Critique of Academic Publishing." *Doing Feminist Research.* Ed. Helen Roberts. London: Routledge & Kegan Paul, 1981. 186–202.

———. *The Writing or the Sex? or Why You Don't Have to Read Women's Writing to Know It's No Good.* New York: Pergamon, 1991.

Stein, Harry. "Our Times: A Column about Values and TV." *TV Guide* (July 9, 1994): 35.

Steuernagel, Gertrude A. "'Men Do Not Do Housework': The Image of Women in Political Science." In *Foundations for a Feminist Restructuring of the Academic*

Disciplines, eds. Michele A. Paludi and Gertrude A. Steuernagel. New York: The Haworth Press, 1990. 167–184.

Tanenbaum, Leora. "Who Framed Feminism?" *In These Times* 18, 16 (June 27, 1994): 32–34.

Taylor, Verta and Leila J. Rupp. "Researching the Women's Movement: We Make Our History, But Not Just As We Please." In *Beyond Methodology: Feminist Scholarship as Lived Research*, ed. Mary Margaret Fonow and Judith A. Cook. Bloomington: Indiana University Press, 1991. 119–132.

Thompson, James. "Allan Bloom's Quarrel with History." *Journal of General Education* 39, 4 (1988): 227–231.

Tinsley, Adrian, Elaine Reuben, and Diane Crothers. *Academic Women, Sex Discrimination, and the Law*. New York: MLA Commission on the Status of Women, 1971.

von Ullmann, Jörg. "Schutzengel gegen Autounfälle: Auch Woody Allen bewundert ihn: Rainier Maria Rilke und seine amerikanische Gemeinde." *Frankfurter Allgemeine Zeitung* (May 11, 1994): 37.

Zimmer, Dieter. "PC oder: Da hört die Gemütlichkeit auf." *Die Zeit* (October 22, 1993): 59–60.

8

Transforming Antifeminist Culture in the Academy

Shirley Nelson Garner

Silence has never brought us anything of worth.

——Audre Lorde

Transforming antifeminist culture within the academy means, ultimately, transforming antifeminist culture outside the academy.[1] It also means recognizing the ways it may incorporate biases aligned by race, class, ethnicity, and sexual orientation. Ideally, institutional efforts to resist antifeminism will occur in every reach of the academic community: among students, faculty, administration, staff, and alumni groups. But if we are not to be discouraged by the enormity of what lies ahead, we need to think individually and one-day-at-a-time, as well as collectively, with our sights on larger aims.

My task in writing this section was, in part, to review all of the essays in the volume and glean their ideas for transforming antifeminist culture. I laughed as I told the other editors on one occasion that this section would be more work than I thought, that we were big on resolve, but needed more practical ideas. As I reflected on this thought, however, I realized that it was no small thing to have resolve. It means acting when you are afraid, when it would be easier to sit still and be quiet; giving your time to seek justice for yourself and others; allowing yourself to be distracted from your research and teaching, if necessary; and risking ill will. It also means overcoming the fury you may feel at the high cost you pay only because of your gender or because you want to do the work you care about. In coming to terms with what often feels like a waste of your energy, resources, and creative power, it is probably helpful to remember that many before us have had to engage in equal or more difficult

201

confrontations. In today's economy, in this country and elsewhere, if you have a decent job with reasonable benefits (or prospects for such a position), you must remember to count your blessings. But resolve is a necessary first step. This book is the culmination of many of us speaking first as individuals and now in concert, telling our own stories and those of others. We offer these essays as a commitment to be engaged in struggle.

Individual Action

Audre Lorde's words, "Silence has never brought us anything of worth" (10), speak to the aims of this volume: to recognize antifeminist intellectual harassment when we confront it, to name it, and to work on behalf of change. Speaking in response to and against antifeminism whenever it occurs is something anyone can do when we or those around us become its targets. I have long held Lorde's words in mind as an amulet when I begin to lose courage to speak; I hear her warning, "Your silence will not protect you" (20). It is surprising how great the effect of one voice can be. Occasionally, when I alone on an academic committee have a feminist perspective, I can bring latent intellectual bias to the fore by simply asking: "How is proposal X, which we have just agreed to fund, different from proposal Y (a project involving feminist scholars or feminist methodologies), about which we seem to have doubts?" If there is a case for argument, I am prepared to make it. And often, scholars of good will immediately get the point; others have usually dismissed the project out of hand and are not prepared to argue their position when pressed, and so lose the debate. I do not always win such an argument, but when I don't, I consider whether it's worth asking the opposition to articulate their views for the record; or I might ask that we come back to this discussion when our work is over to review this case since I feel strongly about it. Sometimes proposal Y actually gets funded, but even if it doesn't, there is a point to the strategy I am suggesting. What I hope for is that my words will ring in the ears of committee members, that the next time they review proposals they may hear unfairness or a clear double standard in their opinions.

But talk is not cheap; there is a price. Sometimes you make enemies. If your tone is wrong or if you're too insistent, you sometimes get excluded from important committees. At the least, you usually have to muster courage —it does not come easily to most of us who feel ourselves to be on the margins—and you feel tired out of proportion for voicing resistance, even if you are also exhilarated because you didn't let yourself be oppressed. Some of my courage comes from the fact that I am a tenured full professor reaching sixty: if I cannot speak now, when can I? I also indicate through body language and tone of voice that I expect to be listened to and heard; I have been known to ask an obviously dismissive listener: "Do you understand what I'm saying?" Or, "You appear to disagree with me; why is that?" In other words, by taking myself seriously, I get the courage to make others do so. My confidence has come with time and experience, the knowledge that you can probably say more than you think without untoward consequences. Usually, the worst that happens is that you're ignored. Often, nothing more serious occurs, and the fears you may have prove illusory. You may even find cohorts you didn't know you had. I remember taking a deep breath once and speaking against the tide of discussion. When I met no opposition—only others changing the subject—I decided to try another time and speak from the same position phrased differently. Still no response. After the meeting, many who had been silent gathered around me and told me that they thought I was "right on," that they basically agreed with me. I responded that if that was the case, then they would have to speak too, that I couldn't change things by myself. I urged that we each think about different directions we might take when the same issues were raised again, as they undoubtedly would be; that we try to find better strategies for dealing with the issues with which we were concerned. At subsequent meetings, I heard my words echoed by others. But even if you find yourself ignored or criticized, maintaining your integrity and standing up for yourself, others you care about, and the work that you value is worth the cost. And I've found that strength builds upon itself.

Sometimes it is more effective to speak to others privately. On several occasions, I have arranged to have lunch with a colleague to discuss antifeminism in my department. I would probably engage in such a discussion only if I thought a colleague was amenable to persuasion, was not consciously and unalterably prejudiced against feminist work. In such efforts, I have sometimes met with success; at other times, with failure. One of my successes concerns the selection of Scholars of the College, in the College of Liberal Arts at the University of Minnesota, a prestigious award that carries a $3,000 research stipend for each of three years. One year, when my department had to choose between three scholars, two men and a woman who did feminist work, it chose one of the men. Of the three, the woman scholar had the most distinguished record, yet she received only three votes—all from women. The other thirty-five votes went to male candidates, some of the women in our department voting for one or the other of them. On this occasion, no candidate or his or her friends lobbied for votes. I thought it was telling that *only* women voted for the feminist scholar, even though she had the strongest record, but that both women and men voted for the men. I made a point of exploring the significance of this vote with one of my male colleagues whom I consider a friend. He had not even noticed the striking discrepancy between the number of votes for each of the men and the mere three votes for the woman faculty member. Calling his attention to this difference, I explained to him that only women voted for the woman candidate. Because I had spoken to others about the nomination, I knew who the three of us who had voted for her were. I said that, given the records of the various candidates, I could only conclude that antifeminism was involved in the fact that *no* men voted for the woman candidate. Not only was she a woman competing with men, but also she was a feminist scholar, developing feminist theory and methods of inquiry in her research and taking a feminist perspective in the several areas in which she specialized. My colleague saw the cogency of this argument and agreed with my interpretation of events, which he would not have recognized on his own.

On this occasion, I decided not to let the matter rest there, but went to see the dean responsible for the selection of Scholars of the College. She agreed that women might often be disadvantaged in such departmental nominations and began to allow large departments, such as ours, to put forward two candidates. As soon as that change occurred, the feminist scholar was one of those nominated. The college selection committee chose her over our department's other candidate because she had the more impressive record. In this case, it also seems clear that the college committee had distance from the candidates and was free of the feelings of competition that existed within the department, which undoubtedly had contributed to defeating the feminist candidate at that level.

Several years before, under the auspices of a different dean, I, as Chair of Women's Studies, had nominated for Scholar of the College a faculty member widely recognized for feminist research and teaching. She did not receive the award, although a less-accomplished male scholar, whose record I knew well, did. When I was having a conversation with the Dean about Women's Studies' goals for the following year, I raised a question about our nomination for Scholar of the College. I asked whether the award was intended for mid-level career scholars or more accomplished ones. When he said that it was intended for the latter, I brought up the comparative records of the two scholars I knew and the fact that the one I had nominated did not receive the award. He looked perplexed and said that he had merely accepted the selection committee's recommendation. He added that the scholar I had nominated had exactly the qualifications that were desired and that, by all means, Women's Studies should nominate her again. I did, and she was selected. The committee may have chosen her on its own, or the Dean may have reviewed the selections to be sure they were not discriminatory. In any case, our conversation had made him aware that he needed to pay attention; I had, in effect, put him on notice. In both of these cases, individual intercession mattered. In one instance, it not only changed the outcome for one feminist scholar, but also changed the process so that other women might benefit in the future. By approaching the two deans about what I perceived as problems of equity for feminist scholars, I was indicating that they were ultimately accountable for the decisions that were made. We often have opportunities to remind administrators or others of their accountability, and in many instances, they will be willing and even eager to use their power well.

But speaking does not always bring success. On another occasion, I heard that the men in my department were angry because, through a legal settlement, women were allowed to make cases for equity raises in salary. Funds had been set aside by Central Administration through legal agreement to bring women's salaries up to men's. If women in the English Department had not applied for some of it, it would have been given to others who did. The money was for this purpose and no other, so it could not have been used for other things. A number of us had made such cases and received raises. The effect of our receipt of these increases in salary meant not only more money for us, but also more money in our departmental budget. Since funds for merit raises come to departments as a percentage of a department's total budget, a greater amount of money would now be available to English for merit raises each year. Such additional monies would go to the most meritorious, which in a particular year might or might not go to any of us who had received equity raises. In other words, we brought in money to the department and, potentially, to everyone in it. Still, I had learned, the men were generally aggrieved.

I decided to explain this situation to some of my friendly male colleagues since I thought they might be angry because they didn't fully understand the implications of the equity increases. The first friend, I shall call him Allen, listened but then began to complain about the state of his own salary and the failure of many chairs to win increases for the department as a whole. He felt that everyone's salaries were too low, and it seemed unfair for the women to get theirs raised. I repeated the facts that the department stood to gain from our raises and that if we had not made efforts to get the awarded money, it would simply have gone to other units. I told him, further, that the university had not been amenable to reasonable arguments for raising the salaries of the Humanities faculty and that the only way it would be so moved was through pressure—through lawsuits, the organization of unions, or other means. I said that I thought that the system was unfair, but that the women's failure to take advantage of the university's offer would in no way change the system, nor would it benefit the men. On the contrary, taking advantage of the moment to argue for a more equable salary would, ultimately, have benefits for the men in our department. Since this friend is reasonable and a person of goodwill, I expected him to see the point. Perhaps he did, but what he said was: "I hear what you're saying, but it's easier to be angry at individuals than at the impersonal institution, which doesn't provide a specific target." I replied, "But you must give up this anger at the women in the department: it is unfair, and it leads nowhere." I don't know whether this conversation gained anything for me or the other women; though Allen and I remain friendly colleagues, he has never said anything to me about our exchange to indicate that he began to see things differently.

Yet even when speaking does not achieve my aims, I feel stronger for having tried, for having spoken on my own behalf. In her essay in this volume, Greta Gaard attests to the power that comes from speaking, even in the peculiarly beleaguered environment in which lesbians often find themselves—oppressed as feminists *and* as lesbians: "Publishing stories about their harassment, speaking on the topic of heterosexism and homophobia, and coming out to colleagues and to students all seem effective strategies in various contexts." Gaard goes on to point out: "Whenever it is perceived safe by the individual lesbian herself, coming out in the classroom is ... an expedient method for challenging stereotypes and presuppositions" (136–37).

Alliances

These examples illustrate that individual resolve and action can help curb antifeminism and may, in the long term, make a difference. But relying only on yourself is usually slow and stressful. Allying with even one other colleague has advantages. When I first came to the University of Minnesota, I had the good fortune to find another feminist faculty member in my department; later there were two of us; and now, a number of others. Just having one made a difference, and when there were three of us, we planned curricula together, founded the Feminist Studies in Literature subfield, shared ideas for research, and read each other's papers. We strategized about difficult political moments and often did together what it would have been hard or impossible to do alone. Hard or impossible because it would have required too much courage since there was always the risk of some real loss. Hard or impossible because we needed the pressure of more than one to move a recalcitrant chair or committee—one of us could have been ignored, more were harder to dismiss. Hard or impossible because what was often wanted required, quite simply, too much work. We often needed each other to assure ourselves that we weren't crazy when others tried to convince us we were. I remember a faculty meeting when a distinguished male professor responded to one of us by implying that she held the notions she maintained about a particular matter only because she had been traumatized by her pretenure years, and that she had a "paranoid" view of the college. Though the consequences she predicted would follow from an administrative decision did so in only one or two years, the male professor never apologized, nor even admitted he had been wrong. At the time, the three of us had to assure ourselves that we were not the irrational ones here. His fear of facing conflict with those in authority provoked him into denial and an excessively defensive position. At best, he was naïve about university politics. He aimed his sights on a feminist colleague because it was easier to disagree with her than to change his own thinking.

Graduate students are especially vulnerable when they are alone on the receiving end of antifeminist attacks. It is important for them to seek the support of their peers and, if possible, to organize a graduate students' organization, so that its officers can express concerns of the group. As a faculty member, I often counsel students as to ways they can best deal with a situation in which they or their work is regarded with antifeminist prejudice. Most often, they can negotiate their own difficulties, but occasionally I intercede by talking to someone on their behalf or going with them to see an administrator. My mere offer to accompany them often gives them the courage to do it alone; knowing that someone validates their point of view and stands behind them can be enormously encouraging.

If you are the only feminist scholar in an academic department, you should look for colleagues in other units. It probably doesn't matter whether the unit is similar to yours, but it may be easier if you are in English to seek a feminist in another language department, so that the work each of you does will be more accessible to the other than if you were in, say, one of the sciences. But finally, it is important to join with other feminist colleagues in the academy, no matter whether they are in a discipline close to yours or not. As both a tenured and untenured faculty member, I have helped others with promotion and tenure cases. I have often given advice about dealing with a difficult chair or administrator. You can nearly always find those who can provide emotional support and much-needed practical help.

Though as a faculty member, I have most often called upon other faculty members for help, I have also benefited from the assistance of graduate students and members of the academic support staff. Though professional boundaries require tact and not burdening those over whom you have some authority with confidences or the quarrels you have with others, I am often made aware that those around you know when you are subject to antifeminist prejudices and that they try to help you. Graduate students, for example, go out of their way to thank me, to tell me how much they enjoy a class, and the like. Members of the academic support staff may offer various kinds of assistance. They may tell me that the department offers certain kinds of privileges if I have been left out of the loop or give me special help when I look particularly harried.

Though you can accomplish a great deal through informal alliances, formal associations may be more effective and necessary in situations where oppression is extreme. Such associations make it less necessary to go out on a limb as an individual, where you may be more vulnerable and less powerful. Many universities and colleges have graduate students' organizations, which may be enlisted on the side of feminists, since in many fields there are substantial groups of women and feminist scholars at the graduate level. Greta Gaard suggests that gays and lesbians may need to create a "'Lesbian Avengers of the Academy' association" to bring "support and activism from around the country" to persons experiencing harassment. Gaard cites an "antihomophobia hotline," created by Lynda Hart, a faculty member at the University of Pennsylvania. Hart describes the hotline as "a network of academics in all fields who are concerned about the rights of lesbian, gay, bisexual, transgendered and otherwise queer people in the academy." (137).

Institutional Change

However useful and successful individual and small alliances and actions are, we need to press ourselves to think institutionally. But how do we move from activism as individuals or in a small group to affect a department, a college, or the university as a whole?

The easiest way to begin is from positions of leadership, on departmental, college, or university committees or in administrative positions. If you are on your department's promotion and tenure committee, for example, you might go an extra step to review promotion and tenure policy documents, as Annette Kolodny suggests (24–25). Committee service at all levels offers many opportunities to affect policies that hamper feminist faculty members or their work. Most importantly, we ourselves need to be willing to assume administrative positions and to see that women and members of underrepresented groups are brought into such positions. As some of my examples illustrate, change is often most effectively made through a sympathetic administrator. Yet many shy away from administrative positions. Such reluctance is understandable. Certainly, administration is often incompatible with scholarly temperament. At this moment in the history of the United States, economic restraints and a political and social climate often unfavorable to academia make administration more difficult than it has been in the past. Yet most of us are capable of serving in various administrative capacities, and each of us needs to consider taking a turn. We need to think not *whether* it will be possible for us to serve, but *when* and how we can best do that. Not all of us have the skill or desire to be a college or university president. But all of us can assume active membership on important committees, chair committees, or take responsibility for writing policies.

It is, furthermore, important to support administrators who are sympathetic to feminist scholars and feminist inquiry. Annette Kolodny has outlined some of the ways such administrators are vulnerable and the need to be sensitive to their political situations (25–27). A colleague told me that she had not considered becoming a candidate for the administrative position she now holds, but that many had approached her and asked her to allow her nomination to stand. More importantly, she said, they offered their active, practical support, promising that if she were selected for the position, they would help her draft policies and serve on or chair necessary committees under her purview. She continues to have well-wishers; colleagues who thank her for her contributions; and those who telephone, send e-mail messages, and write to offer advice or assistance in difficult situations.

Several advantages accrue in having administrative support for feminist faculty members and graduate students and their work. First, administrative support confers legitimacy, which may be lacking without it. I once said to a dean who expressed admiration for the curriculum Feminist Studies in Literature had developed in the English department at the University of

Minnesota that it would mean a lot if he would say that publicly and to the chair of my department. He seemed surprised that his word could mean so much; I told him to remember that he "occupied the space he occupied." Second, administrative support can save us time and energy. The creation of formal alliances that must contend with indifferent or even hostile administrators takes an enormous amount of effort. I have speculated sometimes that one administrative weapon used consciously against feminists is simply foot-dragging. This strategy forces us to look after ourselves, to see where we need support, and to frame it for ourselves. Such administrators assure that feminist ideas always fall on barren ground, so their flourishing will be slower and less than it might have been. It's wonderful to have a dean or department head say, for example, "A mentoring group for untenured women is a great idea; I'll get going on it right away." Or even, "It's a great idea; go for it, let me or my staff know how we can help." To hear instead, "I don't really understand the purpose a mentoring group for untenured women would serve," or "I suppose you can organize such a group if anyone is interested in it" means that the administrator doesn't understand or doesn't care. This leaves all of the organizing up to those who usually have no staff support and relatively little power. Finally, supportive administrators can provide necessary resources, such as staff help and funds, which are often required in order to make a difference.

Universities and colleges typically have structures in place that are helpful to feminist scholars in networking with others on the campus, or in providing programs that can serve them. These include women's studies programs, women's centers, crisis and sexual violence centers, affirmative action and equal opportunity offices. Yet structures specifically designed to change the climate in which intellectual hostilities against women and minorities flourish are still needed. Let me describe such a structure at the University of Minnesota—its history and the way that it works.[2]

Minnesota Plan II, under the leadership of the all-University Commission on Women, was founded in 1988, following an important, though difficult, history in which the university had operated under the *Rajender Consent Decree*, a legal mandate intended to address discriminatory practices. In 1973, Shyamala Rajender, who had taught on annual appointments in the Chemistry Department for a number of years, brought a suit against the university, claiming discrimination on the basis of sex and national origin, when she applied for and failed to obtain a tenure-track position that became available in the Chemistry department. Though several university committees had recommended that Rajender be given the position, successive university presidents had rejected their recommendations. Rajender's lawsuit followed, eventually becoming a class-action suit involving other complainants. After seven years of negotiations, the parties agreed on a settlement out of court in 1980. It provided that the university would operate under the *Rajender Consent Decree* until 1989; and the period was ultimately extended until 1991. This wide-ranging decree:

> set affirmative action goals and timetables for hiring women, mandated specific hiring practices for all university units, and set forth several provisions to address problems in the chemistry department. Under the decree, any woman in the class may file an individual claim against the university if she believes she has been harmed by discrimination. People may also file petitions to change policies they believe discriminate against women generally. Probably the most significant of these was a petition on pay equity. Through a salary settlement reached in fall 1989, all women covered under the decree will receive permanent increases to their base salaries. (Spector, 191–192)

The decree made differences in hiring and promotion and salary inequities for women, but tensions resulted. In some areas, the climate for women may have actually worsened, as resentments forced underground smoldered and erupted in striking forms.

In the summer of 1987, resentments exploded in the Chemistry department. When Shyamala Rajender failed to receive a tenure-track appointment in Chemistry, no woman had been tenured in Chemistry in some sixty years. The consent decree stipulated that two of the next five hires in Chemistry had to be women. One day one of the women hired under this decree, and later tenured, came into her office to find a pile of feces on her desk. A group of senior women faculty members, mainly from the sciences, met with the Provost and Vice President for Academic Affairs to demand that he act. One of his actions, among a number, was to create a Special Assistant to the Vice President and to the Director of Equal Opportunity and Affirmative Action to look into the women's situation at the University of Minnesota. Janet Spector, a professor in Anthropology, who had chaired Women's Studies, was nominated and appointed. She had been on numerous university and college committees, serving two terms on the University Senate's Subcommittee on Equal Employment Opportunities for Women (EEOWC), the special committee mandated by the Rajender Consent Decree.

In her work, the Special Assistant was:

to assess the situation of academic women, particularly seeking out the viewpoint of women themselves; develop plans to improve and enhance the situations of women at the university and generate support for them among faculty, staff, and administrators; and co-ordinate the implementation of new or revised policies, program, and administrative arrangements developed within this planning framework. The Special Assistant was also expected to consult with colleges and units about improving work environments for women. (Spector, 194)

Spector began by reviewing literature that she found especially helpful, including "The New Agenda of Women for Higher Education," publications of the Project on the Status and Education of Women, and reports from other campuses, particularly the University of California system, Pennsylvania State, Arizona, and Wisconsin. And she interviewed 160 women, "a cross-section of faculty members, administrators, and academic professional staff members from various parts of the university" (195).

Though Spector did not find a unified "women's position," she identified themes that are not surprising in light of the essays in this volume. She concluded:

Regardless of their positions, women tend to feel overworked, undervalued, and peripheral in their departments or units. When women are far outnumbered by men in their units, they often feel isolated, highly visible, and over-scrutinized. Women in fields like nursing and home economics often feel good about their local environments but undervalued within the larger university culture. Some women feel they are not taken seriously by their male colleagues, or that they are sought out as experts on women's issues but little else.

There are persistent problems of "hidden" workloads for women, such as unacknowledged conflicts and tensions between family and career responsibilities and demands for committee service, student advising, and other institutionally undervalued activities. Many mentioned the issue of differential perceptions of men and women in professional reviews and assessments. For example, men who do substantial committee service are rewarded as good "team players"; women with a similar record are accused of avoiding research. Average female teachers are sometimes judged more harshly than their average male counterparts, who are not expected to do well in that arena. Finally, I heard persistent reports of low-level stress triggered by unprofessional behavior by colleagues, such as sexual joking and other trivializing or inappropriate remarks. Many women feel peripheral to the life of the institution. (195–196)

In response to what Spector learned, she created Minnesota Plan II, named to suggest a continuum between it and an earlier plan, initiated in

1959 and partially funded by the Carnegie Corporation. This earlier plan established a program for continuing education for women and a women's resource and counseling center. Minnesota Plan II, according to its recent *Guide to Improving the Campus Climate for Women,* "provides a comprehensive agenda for improving campus environments for women at the University of Minnesota." Through this plan:

> the University intends to strengthen its capacity to recruit, retain, and recognize the accomplishments of academic women; to enrich the content of courses and the climate of classrooms; to challenge prevailing norms, values, and attitudes that demean or devalue women; and to hold faculty, staff, and administrators more accountable for creating and maintaining healthy and productive work environments for all members of the University community. (2)

Leadership for the plan is an all-university Commission on Women, which considers "issues that cut across units" and Unit Planning Groups at the college level (Spector, 197).

Obviously, the University of Minnesota has invested resources to improve the climate for women through the Special Assistant's position, which has been regularized as Assistant Provost in the Office of the Senior Vice President for Academic Affairs. Quarterly commission meetings, which combine workshops and social elements, with a provided dinner, have been important in enhancing relationships among women from all parts of the university. The support of various central administrators and their willingness to help implement projects within it have been significant.

The impetus for a Special Director and the series of activities that resulted in Minnesota Plan II was a humiliating event followed by pressure from a powerful group of women faculty members exerted in response to that event. Yet this kind of effort to improve the climate for women, which should almost inevitably result in the improvement of the climate for all faculty members, might come from other sources.[3] It does require administrative cooperation.

Where We Are Now and What We Can Do About It

As the authors in this volume continually refer to the current backlash against feminists and others in the academy, I am reminded of the fragility of our gains. While describing Minnesota Plan II, which has accomplished a great deal in improving the academic climate at the University of Minnesota as a whole, but particularly as it affects women, I fear the threat of its erosion. Only last year, when I, as an administrator, went to see the Vice President for Research and Dean of the Graduate School, the Vice President and Provost for Arts, Sciences, and Engineering, or the Vice President for Student Affairs, I saw women with feminist consciousnesses. This year, if I go to the offices of those same administrators, they will all be men, and all but one of them white. Only a short time ago, the University's General Counsel and the Assistant to the President were, respectively, a black and a white woman with a keen awareness of women's issues; now those positions are filled by white men. While these men now in power may not discriminate against women, few of them understand or are interested in feminist inquiry or theory, issues affecting women, or even the climate for women at the University. Asked about the attrition of women administrators from the University of Minnesota, the President could only muster a lame defense: they couldn't have left if he hadn't hired them in the first place. I am dismayed to see women, claiming to be feminists, turning against other women and women's contributions to the movement that gave them the power of their positions and their voices.

But in the face of the backlash against us, I remember that the backlash itself is a result of the gains we have made. Those gains are real, and we need to remember to keep occupying the space we occupy. As Ferguson, Katrak, and Miner point out in their essay above, in the thirty years since the second-wave feminist movement began, there has been progress in the "educational and cultural life of the U.S.: the varied impacts of feminist thought inside and outside the academy, the establishment of women's studies and ethnic studies programs in academic institutions, and social welfare programs" (48). Remembering that feminism in the academy is linked with the activism of the civil rights struggle that began outside it, we must be prepared, as Ferguson, et al., urge:

> to take on new battles as attacks on feminism trade roles with hostility to ethnic studies, affirmative action, and multicultural education.... We must make a concerted effort to name antifeminist harassment as such. This will combat the obfuscation of various discriminations under the problematic evocations of political correctness. Our tasks of naming, discussion, and analysis will bring us to possibilities of working towards a more just and humane society. (59–60)

As scholars and teachers, now in many different fields, we have opportunities in our courses and in our research and writing to explore the issues raised in this volume. As Annette Kolodny points out, "The academy still remains the single institution in the United States that at least *claims* to protect access to unimpeded intellectual inquiry—for everyone in the society and on behalf of the society as a whole." She argues that "the indispensable requirement for combatting antifeminist intellectual harassment is the creative, energetic, ever-expanding persistence of feminist inquiry itself." She explains that "the impact of our work—the persuasiveness of our critical scrutiny, the compelling evidence produced by our research, and the disturbing questions that linger in the student's mind long after our classes are over—all these contribute to changing people's beliefs and perceptions, altering forever their categories of analysis and understanding" (28). She has suggested that conferences on the issues raised in this volume would be appropriate in an academic setting and would provide occasions for further analysis.

We should keep in mind, as an editor assured Ginsberg and Lennox, that there is an audience for feminist publications and that "editors are scrambling to find good feminist work." In a publishers' market, "feminist scholarship is a lively and vital field" (169). They warn against taking antifeminist intellectual harassment personally; the "worst of all possible responses," they argue is what others have defined as "the common practice of self-censorship" (190). In this view, they agree with Kolodny, who comments that "the moment we abandon our research, our pursuit of better interpretations, our thoughtful reappraisal of all received truths, our epistemological insistence on asking how we know what we think we know, in that moment antifeminist intellectual harassment will have prevailed" (28).

Because I have wanted to focus on transformation of the academic climate, which is often experienced as noxious, I have not discussed the routes of formal grievances. All universities have grievance processes that should be considered when antifeminist intellectual harassment is extreme or is coupled with sexual harassment, violence, or discriminatory practices. The specter of prohibitions against such behavior and appropriate grievance or legal procedures to deal with them often inhibits those who would transgress. Certainly, when the University of Minnesota was under the *Rajender Consent Decree*, women had a certain power and the possibility of redress that they lost once the decree had expired. But grievance and litigation are costly in time and stress; often their success is short-lived and applies only to a single individual. Such procedures are important, and, at times, we may be forced to use them as the only alternative. Yet what we need to work for is a change in thinking that will produce a change in behavior, which will make the need for grievance rare.

A prelude to cultural change is communication among those of us who would make it happen. We need to articulate our aims and join with each other to act on our own behalf. We need to continue the practice of consciousness-raising that we learned in the sixties. In looking particularly at the intersection of ageism and sexism, Mary Carpenter suggests the kinds of conversations that must go on in the academy across generations, especially among women. The current wave of new books by women in their thirties who wish to dissociate from feminism argue that there are silences between us that need to be broken. Dale Bauer and Katherine Rhoades describe, as well, the ways in which our students misperceive us and our aims as teachers. Patricia Williams believes that change will occur and that the current backlash will be defused only when we begin to "learn each other's history": this conversation "will require finding our own words and translating the symbols of each other's suffering" (93).

What is required of us now will not be easy. Williams describes the process by which we will learn each other's history:

> This conversation, whether on campuses or in Congress, will require some very hard work, lots of angry participants, and a high threshold for the noise of much wailing and gnashing of teeth. It will necessitate recognition of a fluid view of identity and community, in which the boundaries, phases, and fragments of our lives are always multiply intersecting, constantly shifting, in flux. (93).

And it will perhaps require changing shapes, giving up the calm that many of us have looked for in academic life. As Mary Carpenter advocates, "Far from promoting a vanilla maternity—a sacred obligation to pass on our mothers' texts and be good-enough mothers to our daughters—feminists should promote pregnant hags, menopausal and postmenopausal feminist academics who persist ... in a prolific, horrific, semiotic, and political performance that continues way beyond the usual limits of a foreseeable 'prime'" (160). Quoting the Lesbian Avengers, Greta Gaard recognizes the need to organize and fight back, "'Think about it. Being nice isn't going to get you anywhere.' Being organized, however, might save your job" (137).

What comes to mind as I think about the future is the well-known World War II Rosie the Riveter poster of a determined woman, her hair bound up in a scarf, her muscular arm raised in a clenched fist, and the words, "We Can Do It!" And Angela Davis's comment: "What I'm interested in is communities that are not static, that can change, that can respond to new historical needs. So I think it's a very exciting moment."[4]

Notes

1. I am indebted to Emilie Buchwald, Pamela Fletcher, and Martha Roth, the editors of *Transforming a Rape Culture,* for making me think in terms of transformation rather than remedy or mere strategies for survival.

2. For the history and description of the Minnesota Plan II, I am in large part indebted to Spector. The *Women's Studies Quarterly* special issue on "Curricular and Institutional Change," in which her article appears, is a valuable resource.

3. "The Campus Climate Revisited: Chilly for Women Faculty, Administrators, and Graduate Students," a report of the Project on the Status and Education of Women, is an excellent resource for describing ways of transforming the academic climate.

4. As quoted in Smith, 33.

Works Cited and Consulted

Buchwald, Emilie, Pamela Fletcher, and Martha Roth, eds. *Transforming a Rape Culture.* Minneapolis, MN: Milkweed Editions, 1993.

Commission on Women. *Guide to Improving the Campus Climate for Women.* Minneapolis, MN: University of Minnesota, 1993.

Lorde, Audre. *The Cancer Journals.* San Francisco: Aunt Lute Books, 1980.

Project on the Status and Education of Women. "The Campus Climate Revisited: Chilly for Women Faculty, Administrators, and Graduate Students." Washington, DC: Association of American Colleges, 1986.

Smith, Anna Deavere. *Fires in the Mirror: Crown Heights, Brooklyn and Other Identities.* New York: Anchor, 1993.

Spector, Janet. "The Minnesota Plan II: A Project to Improve the University Environment for Women Faculty, Administrators, and Academic Professional Staff." *Women's Studies Quarterly* 18, 1–2 (1990): 189–203.

Contributors

Dale Bauer is Professor of English and Women's Studies at the University of Wisconsin–Madison, where she also serves as Director of the Women's Studies Research Center. She has published books on Bakhtin/feminism and Edith Wharton/social politics, and essays on feminist theory and pedagogy. Her most recent work deals with the rise of social engineering and social control as influences upon modern American fiction.

Mary Wilson Carpenter is Associate Professor and Queen's National Scholar at Queen's University, Canada, where she teaches nineteenth-century British literature, gender theory, and women's studies courses. She has published articles in *Literature and History*, *PMLA*, *Genders*, *diacritics*, and *Victorian Poetry*, essays on nineteenth-century British women writers, and a book, *George Eliot and the Landscape of Time*.

VèVè Clark is Associate Professor of African and Caribbean Literatures and Cultures in the African American Studies Department at the University of California, Berkeley. She is coeditor of *The Legend of Maya Deren* and *Revising the Word and the World*. Professor Clark has published numerous articles on the Caribbean novel and theater, African American dance, and feminist pedagogy.

Moira Ferguson is James E. Ryan Chair in English and Women's Literature at the University of Nebraska–Lincoln. Her recent publications include *Subject to Others: British Women Writers and Colonial Slavery 1678–1834; Colonial and Gender Relations from Mary Wollstonecraft to Jamaica Kincaid;* and *Jamaica Kincaid: Where the Land Meets the Body.*

Greta Gaard is Associate Professor of Composition and Women's Studies at the University of Minnesota–Duluth. She has served for six years on the MLA Committee on the Status of Women in the Profession, first as the Gay and Lesbian Caucus Liaison and later as a full member, cochair, and chair of the committee. Her research in developing ecofeminist theory is seen in her edited anthology, *Ecofeminism: Women, Animals, Nature* (Temple, 1993), and in other essays in *Signs, Environmental Ethics, Feminist Teacher, Alternatives,*

The Ecologist, Z Papers, and others. Currently she is at work on her next book, *Ecological Politics: Ecofeminism and the Greens,* to be published by Temple University Press.

Shirley Nelson Garner is Professor and Chair of English at the University of Minnesota, Twin Cities. She has written articles on Shakespeare and women writers and is a coeditor of *The (M)other Tongue: Essays in Feminist Psychoanalytic Interpretation* and *Interpreting Women's Lives: Personal Narratives and Feminist Theory.* She is a founder of *Hurricane Alice: A Feminist Quarterly* and is on its editorial board.

Elaine Ginsberg is Professor of English at West Virginia University, where she teaches courses in American Literature, Critical Theory, and Women's Studies. Her most recent project is an edited collection of essays on "passing." From 1991 to 1994 she was a member of the MLA Committee on the Status of Women in the Profession.

Margaret Higonnet is Professor of English and Comparative Literature at the University of Connecticut. She has published on the topics of German Romantic theory, women's literature, children's literature, suicide, and World War I. Most recently she has edited *The Sense of Sex: Feminist Perspectives on Hardy*; *Reconfigured Spheres*; and *Borderwork: Feminist Engagements with Comparative Literature.*

Ketu H. Katrak, Professor of English at the University of Massachusetts–Amherst, specializes in postcolonial literatures in English from Africa, India, and the Caribbean, with an emphasis on Third-World women writers. Katrak is the author of *Wole Soyinka and Modern Tragedy: A Study of Dramatic Theory and Practice* and coeditor of "Desh-Videsh: South Asian Expatriate Writing and Art," a Special Issue of *The Massachusetts Review*, 29, 4 (Winter 1988–1989). She has published essays on Third-World literature and culture in *Nationalisms and Sexualities, The Journal of Asian Culture, Modern Fiction Studies,* and *College Literature,* among others. Katrak has also published poems in *Kavi* (India), *Arc* (Canada), and *The Penguin Anthology of Contemporary Indian Women Poets.*

Annette Kolodny is a Professor in the interdisciplinary Program in Comparative Cultural and Literary Studies at the University of Arizona. In 1993 she completed a five-year term as Dean of the College of Humanities at the University of Arizona. She is best known for her studies of the cultural mythology of the American frontiers, *The Lay of the Land* and *The Land before Her,* and for her many essays on feminist literary theory, including "Dancing through the Minefield." Mining her experience in academic administration, she is now writing a book on the future of higher education in the twenty-first century, with special attention to the situation of women.

Sara Lennox is Professor of Germanic Languages and Literatures and Director of the Social Thought and Political Economy Program at the University of Massachusetts–Amherst. She is the editor of *Auf der Suche nach den Gärten unserer Mütter: Feministische Kulturkritik aus Amerika* and coeditor of *Nietzsche Heute: Die Rezeption seines Werkes nach 1968*. She has published articles on various twentieth-century German and Austrian authors, women's writing in East and West Germany, and feminist pedagogy, literary theory, and the feminist movement in Germany and the U.S. She is currently writing a book on the Austrian writer Ingeborg Bachmann.

Valerie Miner is the author of six novels: *A Walking Fire, All Good Women, Winter's Edge, Murder in the English Department, Movement,* and *Blood Sisters*. She has also published *Trespassing and Other Stories* and *Rumors from the Cauldron: Selected Essays, Reviews and Reportage*. Currently she is Professor of English at the University of Minnesota. She served on the MLA Commission on the Status of Women in the Profession from 1987 to 1991.

Katherine Rhoades is a doctoral candidate in the Department of Educational Policy Studies at the University of Wisconsin–Madison. Her dissertation, "Women's Studies Students and the Politics of Empowerment," is a qualitative study of a diverse group of women's-studies students at a large, public university in the Midwest. Rhoades is interested in the intersections between the politics of education, feminist theories, and qualitative research methodologies. She has written about Hmong refugee students in two U.S. high schools and about the meanings of collaboration in feminist research.

Patricia Williams, Professor of Law at Columbia University, is author of *The Alchemy of Race and Rights* and *The Rooster's Egg*, of which her essay here is a portion. She is a contributing editor of *The Nation*. She also serves on the board of the National Organization for Women's Legal Defense and Education Fund, the Board of Scholars of *Ms.* Magazine, the board of the Center for Constitutional Rights, and the Board of Governors of the Society of American Law Teachers.

Index

Index

Index